AF572414

TACKLE TALK

ALSO BY THE AUTHORS

The Complete Book of Weakfishing
The Complete Book Of Striped Bass Fishing

TACKLE TALK

By Henry Lyman and Frank Woolner

South Brunswick and New York: A. S. BARNES AND COMPANY
London: THOMAS YOSELOFF LTD

Library of Congress Catalogue Card Number: 70-124209

A. S. Barnes and Co., Inc.
Cranbury, New Jersey 08512

Thomas Yoseloff Ltd
108 New Bond Street
London W1Y OQX, England

ISBN 0-498-07640-7
Printed in the United States of America

CONTENTS

FOREWORD

A HOST OF GOOD PEOPLE ARE RESPONSIBLE FOR THE MATERIAL contained in this book, and some of them will never guess that they have contributed keystone bits of intelligence to bolster the expertise of marine angling. Since it has been our good fortune to cast lines into many of the world's salt waters and to trade shop talk with multitudes of anglers, it is only fair to assume that we have absorbed a smattering of knowledge about sport fishing in the sea.

As publisher and editor, respectively, of *Salt Water Sportsman Magazine,* the only truly marine sport fishing journal in the world, we have studied the subtleties of oceanic angling for a great many years. Sometimes it seems to us that the time span started a few hours after the last dinosaur expired on earth. We have fished together and worked together; we have known and we have enjoyed the company of the greatest marine anglers in our time. It would be easy to drop names, but we resist the temptation because thousands of everyday fishermen, from Oxford dons to reticent natives on South American jungle coasts have added bits and pieces of information which we hereby pass along—with thanks to all of the pioneers.

Practically all the material in this book has, at one time or another, been printed under our bylines in *Salt Water Sportsman,* much of it in "Tackle Talk," a venerable column which has caught and held the fancy of marine anglers for more than thirty years. Our object—initially and today—is an honest discussion of basic angling, advanced techniques, tools of the trade, new developments, and theory of importance to men who go down to the sea for fish and fun. This is a how-to book, not a blood-and-thunder tale of high adventure.

Indeed, since the very essence of life is change, we strive to maintain an open mind. Evolution plays its magic in angling, as elsewhere; therefore each separate chapter in this book has been rewritten and updated so that it applies to now, rather than back-when. The material is tailored to the 70's.

Obviously, our book is a collaboration: therefore each of the chapters owes its origin to one or the other of us, but each has been corrected, added to, and smoothed by the party of the second part. The secret of successful collaboration lies in an ability to accept criticism and correction from one's partner, to argue and to reach a decision, to rewrite one another's most treasured passages until such time as rhetoric submits to fact. Before any one piece is completed we growl, bicker, and sometimes doubt one another. In the end we agree, and wonder why we argued in the first place.

It is our hope that the work is better as a result. Certainly two observers who are dedicated to the same sport should be able to detail facts more precisely than any single individual. We are fortunate in that we can work together, and we have no axes to grind—other than accuracy in the presentation of information about the tools and the how-to of successful marine sport fishing.

Hal Lyman
Frank Woolner
Boston, Massachusetts.

TACKLE TALK

1

SURFMAN'S CHOICE

JUST TO SET THE RECORD STRAIGHT, WE ARE NOT GOING TO FOOL around with semantics. *Webster's Third New International Dictionary* defines surf casting as "The technique or act of casting artificial or natural baits into the open ocean or in a bay where waves break on a beach."

You will note that *Webster's* definition is lean and factual, with no reference to tackle required. You may also note, in checking credits, that Hal Lyman—co-author of this book—is listed as a consultant. If that's a sticky wicket, make the most of it!

We labor the point for good reason. Away back in the days when marine angling was in its infancy, all surf casting was done with long, heavy cane or split bamboo rods, big squidding reels and linen line. Object was to heave a baited hook and large sinker, or a block tin squid, as far as possible from the beach. This was commendable at the time—and remains commendable under certain circumstances. The big sticks are still with us.

Fortunately, so far as anglers are concerned, it is not always necessary to cast a country mile, nor to use big baits and lures. Indeed there are multitudinous occasions when just the opposite is true. Traditionally, the image of the classic surf caster remains a rugged character armed with a Herculean rod and plagued by tremendous breakers. Actually, today's sportsman uses a wide variety of weapons to cast "artificial or natural baits into the open ocean or in a bay where waves break on the beach."

This, of course, accounts for the rather stunned expression on the face of a qualified marine angler or dealer when a beginner asks: "What kind of an outfit should I buy for surf casting?"

For perfectly obvious reasons there is no single answer. What kind of surf casting? What kind of fish—and where? How about your personal qualifications?

Advanced anglers often make recommendations without taking cognizance of the fact that a beginner starts from zero. It's easy to extol the virtues of a high surf conventional outfit, but we tend to forget that the squidding reel requires an educated thumb. In addition, the big outfit—in many areas—may be too much artillery. We hate to admit it, but the conventional high surf combination has become extremely specialized.

Spinning is easier, hence it is ideal for the beginner who wants to catch fish right from the outset. Granted, there are occasions when your traditional squidder—if he is a master of his tackle—will cause spincasters to eat their hearts out. Similarly, when surf-running game fish are gobbling small lures, the man with the big outfit may be frustrated.

Semipros boast a variety of weapons: they go into action with everything from seagoing fly rods on up through one-handed spinning to heavy spinning and, finally, the high surf conventional outfit. Each combination insures sport and bragging-size catches when the time is right.

Beginners understandably flinch at the expense involved in purchasing three or four separate outfits. Later, they'll be more than happy to invest in variety—but the initial desire is an all-purpose rig. There is no such thing, of course, yet there are tools that offer a simple, almost foolproof introduction to surf casting. All of these—and our friends in the high surf fraternity will hate us—revolve around the spinning reel.

If there is any near-thing all-purpose surf casting outfit, it would have to be a tubular fiberglass spinning rod measuring about nine feet from tiptop to butt cap (a two-handed stick calibrated to cast lures in the 1½ to 3 ounce weight range), together with an open-faced reel which incorporates a smooth drag and is filled with 15 to 20 pound test round nylon monofilament line.

Such an outfit will play merry hell with a great variety of surf fish. The line test suggested here is relatively heavy, but a beginner should use line somewhat stouter than that chosen by an advanced angler. The name of the game is success, not frustration caused by parted gear. Scale down and get delicate after you've learned the basics.

Now spinning tackle is graduated from ultra-light on up to formidable (and very specialized) surf heavers. Each rig is ideally chosen under certain circumstances. You can have a ball with the ultra-light outfit when mackerel and summer blues are running close to the beach. Indeed, if you've learned your trade, such gossamer rigs will take surprisingly big fish.

We are very fond of a one-handed spinning outfit which is calibrated to cast anything from 1/4 to 1 1/2 ounce lures on lines testing 8 to 10 pounds. Often, when striped bass and bluefish are within the limited casting range of this rig—say 100 feet—it is deadlier than anything on the coast. Basically a small-fish combination, such an outfit can demolish heavyweights. Striped bass of better than 50 pounds have been landed by anglers so equipped. Hundreds of great lures, ranging all the way from metal squids through plugs and soft plastic tempters, are available to the light spincaster.

Or, you can go the other way and beef up spinning tackle to a point where it challenges the high surf addict's production rod. Now a man requires a 10 to 14 foot stick calibrated to handle big lures and hefty bait-sinker combinations. The reel must be bucket-sized and filled with 20 pound test mono, plus a shock leader.

Actually, whether you choose spinning—which is easiest and therefore a best choice for the beginner—or conventional revolving spool tackle, very light or very heavy will prove to be specialized. The work-horse outfit will be a happy compromise, a rig that will toss standard 1 1/2 to 3 ounce lures, or bait-sinker combinations of approximately the same weight. Note that you can heave slightly heavier baits because they are lobbed rather than snap-cast.

Traditionally, the conventional squidding reel and long rod—a stick measuring 9 1/2 to 11 feet—together with 36 pound test braided line or something a bit lighter in nylon monofilament, say 25 to 30 pound test, is a surfman's primary weapon. Such a rig will cast lures ranging from 2 to 4 ounces with ease, and it will insure distance. Properly balanced and employing a lure of proper weight and air characteristics, this combination should command all water within 100 yards of the caster.

Revolving spool's popularity is declining, for no other reason than a lack of skill on the part of anglers. Beginners find spinning easy, so they shrug off the advantages of revolving spool—which requires a greater measure of expertise. It used to be a simple matter for the inland plug caster to progress to conventional surf casting because he owned a trained thumb and had only to master the business of working with both hands. Nowadays, plug casting has become a poor relation—thanks to the ease of spinning. It is, nonetheless, a highly profitable method and one that takes fish for thousands of advanced anglers.

With revolving spool, either the light plug casting or heavy surf casting rigs, you get an ultimate in power, accuracy, and control of fighting fish. The single handicap is a necessity to master a revolving spool reel during the cast. This takes time, but no magic is involved. Once an angler learns to coordinate, to lay line smoothly with his left thumb, and to feather the bell of the spool with his right thumb during a cast, this outfit pays its freight. There is none of the line twist so commonly associated with spinning (unless you employ a lure that revolves in the water), no delicate mechanisms to foul up at an inopportune time. Finally, the revolving spool reel insures better balance than the spinning winch.

As elsewhere in the field of sport fishing tackle, you can go light or very heavy. Surf casters can employ fresh-water bait casting tackle for short-range work, although comparably light spinning seems more effective on an overall basis. Exceptions would include the working of bucktail jigs on night tides, where the bait casting reel's slower retrieve and general feel is an advantage. Bait casting is most efficient where accuracy and control are factors—such as spot-casting to pockets in weeds or mangroves and the subsequent maneuvering of fish out of such pockets. This, of course, seldom is a necessity in true surf casting.

For all around heavy work, the 10½ to 11 foot surf rod is best chosen, and it should be a stick calibrated to handle lures weighing 2 to 4 ounces with ease. Choose a wide-spooled squidding reel and either nylon braided line in the 36 pound test bracket, or round nylon monofilament from 25 to 30 pound test. There is a difference in handling, hence some enthusiasts use braid at night (when they can't see to dig out backlashes) and mono during the day—for longer casts.

On Cape Cod and at Hatteras, a select group of specialists use very heavy surf rods. These are "heavers" or "production" sticks, depending on local nomenclature. They measure 10½ to 11 feet in length and are at their best in heaving lures or baits in the 3 to 5 ounce bracket. These big rods are extremely specialized, and are usually employed with squidding reels and 45 pound test line. Much lighter lines are employed with a long shock leader to absorb the tremendous stresses of the cast.

This combination is solely dedicated to the long cast. It is an offshoot of the tournament surf casting stick developed by Virginia's highly successful tidewater anglers and its only office is to place a lure or bait away out there. The rod is a mankiller but it is effective. It is one of the finest distance-casting instruments ever developed, and it is one of the worst fish-fighting tools in this weary world. Don't go to this if you're a beginner; like ultra-light, it is a weapon for the highly proficient. Earn your wings on trainers before you fly fighters!

Whether you choose spinning or conventional for your first surf rod, be advised that the one-piece stick is most efficient. On the scene of action you'll find that every ounce counts and that it is profitable to position a reel exactly where it is most comfortable. Fixed reel seats are fine, but sometimes they don't match your arm length. A simple cork-taped rod butt may not look as voluptuous as the glittering, metal reel-seated model, but it may prove more practical.

On the other hand, some of us are cramped for space and we must have long rods that break down for storage and transportation. The take-down rod is a second choice on the seafront, but there is little margin of difference. A surf stick that is built in two pieces, butt and tip, is no great horror—although ferrules can be troublesome. The trend is toward fitted glass-to-glass ferrules, with no metal involved. These seem to be strong and impervious to corrosion. Obviously they are great traveling sticks, where breakdown is necessary to provide easy storage.

Twenty years ago mention of a fly rod as a surf-casting weapon would have been laughed to scorn. Today's aficionados are not so hidebound, and the long wand has proved itself quite capable under those proverbial certain conditions. A fly rod can be very deadly when game fish are walloping small bait close to shore. Popping bugs and streamer flies can rack up fish in the wash, where a plug or jig would be impossible to work.

You'll want a heavy stick, something calibrated to a number 10 or 11 forward taper line. For most uses the floating line will be most effective, but there is room for the sinker as well. Reels which incorporate smooth drags are nice but not always necessary. Any big, well-made single-action reel should suffice.

You will need lots of backing, say 150 to 200 yards of 20 to 25 pound test Dacron braid. Nail-knot a short hank—say 20 inches—of 30 pound test nylon monofilament to the end of the fly line, and then attach a tapered leader to this with a blood knot. The leader should be at least nine feet long and slimmed down to 12 pound test—or 15, if you're no adventurer. Let the experts go fine. As a beginner, you want to catch a fish. Generally speaking, marine gamesters are anything but leader-shy.

You can use any combination for surf casting, because fish take all sizes of baits and they feed all the way from the suds to the outer bars. You'll like featherweight rigs for close-in casting and small to medium-sized gamesters, but you'll need big rigs to reach away out there. It's your ball game, and you'd best decide what you want to do. Better check your skills before you decide.

Nobody can offer pertinent advice without a knowledge of your particular requirements and expertise. However, the local tackle shop's proprietor, if he is a smart character who has done it all, can recommend an adequate outfit. Favor shops frequented by experts, unless you know exactly what you want, and take the advice of the bewhiskered regulars you'll meet there.

One other thing. Lean toward name-brand tackle. There's a lot of junk on the market, but little of it is peddled by the old, established firms. The American tackle maker may offer an occasional dog, but most of his gear will be time-tested and excellent. Look to the well-known manufacturers and (unless you are an expert) beware of earth-shaking guarantees. In fishing, there are no miracles.

2

MARINE FISHING REELS

WHEN THE LATE WILLIAM BOSCHEN DEVELOPED THE FIRST INternal drag system on a free-spool reel at the turn of the century, he changed the whole concept of angling in marine waters. The reel, instead of being merely a storage device for holding line and controlled only by thumb pressure, became an integral part of the tackle used to subdue larger species of game fish.

About 20 years later, Holden Illingworth in England developed another revolutionary design in the fishing-reel world with the invention of the stationary spool, or spinning, reel. However, this device, perfected in the early 1920's, did not receive wide acceptance in America until after World War II when monofilament line became commonly available. Since then, the growth of spinning as an angling method has become phenomenal.

Forty years ago, the salt water sport fisherman had little choice among reels offered for ocean use. Today, this choice is almost overwhelming, with the result that even some experienced anglers have doubts as to what type, style, and size of reel to choose. Let us consider some of the factors.

The so-called conventional salt water reel, which is not as conventional as it used to be, is the free-spool type—that is, the spool upon which the line is wound revolves around its own axis. By turning the reel handle once, the spool is made to turn more than once through a system of gears. These gears may be disengaged by a lever or other device so that the spool revolves freely when casting or when letting out line. The drag is simply an adjustable braking system against which the fish must pull line from the spool. The reel handle does not turn backward when the clutch is engaged, thus saving the angler's knuckles from a beating.

So much for the basic free-spool facts. Questions then arise as to choice of reel size, retrieve ratio; wide, narrow, lightweight or heavy metal spools, and level winding devices.

Sizes of trolling reels in general are designated by the numeral system of 1/0, 2/0, 3/0, and so on, with the larger reels bearing the higher numbers. Today a 16/0 is the biggest reel in standard production models available. Unfortunately all manufacturers do not agree on what the size numbers mean. For example, a 4/0 made by one company holds approximately 450 yards of 30 pound test Dacron, while that of another holds almost 575 yards. However, reel makers indicate in their catalogs the capacities of various spools and the angler can be guided by these.

Obviously, selection of any reel must be made to match the rod, line, lure and—most important—the fish anticipated. A 12/0 heavy trolling reel is not suited to a surf casting rod. We have always felt that the lightest *practical* reel for the quarry expected is the best choice. If an angler wants to try for 500 pound fish on 15 pound test line, that is his right. However, for such stunt fishing, he will need a reel having far more line capacity than is normally associated with such light line.

Obviously also, it is impossible to call the hits accurately when you are after game fish. Every now and then some finny behemoth will strike when least expected and the results join others in the one-that-got-away category. That is simply a chance every fisherman must be willing to take.

As a very rough guide to selecting a trolling reel, the table below may be helpful for those in doubt. More skillful anglers of course will be able to subdue larger fish with lighter reels and lines than those used by neophytes. Line test is indicated in pounds, approximate capacity is in yards, and the fish weight is an extremely rough figure in pounds indicating the size range of catches that may be handled comfortably without excessive danger of line breakage.

Reel Size	Line Test	Capacity	Fish Weight
1/0	12	250	25
2/0	20	300	35
3/0	25	300	50
4/0	30	450	80
6/0	50	500	120
9/0	80	500	200
12/0	130	600	500
16/0	130	1000	800

Every reel size available in the market is not included because of the variations among manufacturers already mentioned. Line tests are those more commonly used in practical fishing. Reel capacities of course will vary with the type of line—monofilament, braided nylon, Dacron, and linen.

Retrieve ratio varies greatly even among trolling reels. One big-game model, for example, has a device for changing the ratio of spool to handle from 2:1 to 1:1 when the angler wishes to pump a monster out of the depths. As a general rule, the larger the reel, the lower the retrieve ratio. This saves wear and tear not only on the gear mechanism but also on the fisherman.

When fighting a swift and active gladiator like the sailfish, it is often necessary to pick up line rapidly. For this reason, many manufacturers have developed lighter reels with retrieve ratios of 3:1 or even higher. Casters have felt the need for even faster retrieve to make a lure move rapidly through the water, and reels with a 4:1 ratio at the moment appear to boast the top speed limit. If the demand for higher ratios increases, chances are good that engineers will meet it. In making a choice, the angler should balance the need to get line in rapidly against the size of the fish expected. A low retrieve ratio is almost mandatory when the quarry is large.

Reel spool widths for regular trolling are fairly standard among all manufacturers. Design is such that line capacity, weight of the whole reel, and balance for ease of handling are consistent. The caster, however, created a new demand. As line leaves a narrow spool and the diameter of the line mass is reduced, the spool turns more and more rapidly—with the result that chances of backlash are multiplied. Particularly in larger, free-spool casting reels for high surf use, this problem became acute.

Not being stupid, manufacturers set to work and designed wide spool models that filled the bill. Although revolutionary speed—which has no connection with politics—increases slightly, it is within the bounds of control on these wide spool reels. If casting is the primary use for a reel, select the wide spool models.

A specialized reel for trolling came into being with the development of wire, lead core, and even some monofilament lines. Because it is difficult to lay such lines evenly with the human thumb on the retrieve, narrow spools were developed. These cut down total reel weight while still adapting themselves to the lines used.

Spool material also varies. A heavy metal spool, needed for

taking the strain of battling big game, is not suited to casting a light lure. Plastics, special metals, and even combinations of the two materials are now available for almost every possible fishing contingency. It should be noted in particular that reel selection for use with monofilament lines should be made carefully. A spool not designed for mono may shatter when playing a fish.

Although the experienced caster may consider a level-wind device a nuisance on a casting reel, many newcomers to the sport experience difficulty in laying line smoothly on the retrieve. While a great many experts employ the level-wind device in small casting (bait casting) reels, major problems lie in the delicate mechanism involved. Although the loss of distance in casting is minimal, grains of sand have a way of lodging in the worm gears of level-wind surf casting reels. Several devices that lay the line evenly on the retrieve, but which are not engaged on the cast, have been invented. Unfortunately, none of these is foolproof, so those who wish to become topnotch surf casters with a free-spool reel must develop an educated thumb.

No matter what type of reel for marine angling is selected, a smooth drag is an advantage. If a spool binds when the drag heats up, or if it grabs suddenly at any time, fish will be lost. Although strains on such braking mechanisms are greatest in the big game field, even a small-bait casting model can cause grief if the drag is faulty. Often the angler himself is to blame when he lubricates a drag excessively. As the old saying goes, when all else fails, read the manufacturer's instructions.

Although not widely used, there is a type of braking mechanism, built into the reel handle rather than into the gear complex, known as a cub drag. For reasons which we have always found obscure, it is considered by some to be more sporting than the conventional drag. The angler must hang onto the reel handle in order to have the cub drag take effect. Since he is usually hanging onto that handle anyway when fighting a fish, the sportsmanship involved seems questionable.

When choosing between a free-spool reel and a spinning reel, one primary fact should always be kept in mind: *The spinning reel is designed basically for casting comparatively light lures.*

Certainly a spinning reel may be used for other types of fishing and, within reasonable limits, will work well enough. However, if the fisherman plans to spend the greater part of his time trolling or still-fishing, he would be well advised to select a free-spool model.

There are two major advantages of spinning reels. First, an absolute newcomer to casting can master the technique with a spinning reel actually in minutes. While lacking the expertise of a veteran, this tyro can immediately place a lure where it will reach fish. There is no need for agonizing hours of practice and firsthand experience in picking out backlashes. Unquestionably the stationary spool reel has created more enthusiastic anglers in recent times than any other development in angling history.

The second major advantage of the spinning reel is that it will handle light, almost invisible line and enable the fisherman to present tiny lures to his quarry. Devotees of the free-spool reel will point out that the skilled caster can also present equally light lures. True enough, perhaps. However, the skill required comes only with months or even years of practice. The *average* fisherman can be in business with a spinning reel far more quickly.

We do not intend to belabor the arguments concerning distance casting and the tossing of heavy lures. Suffice it to say that a spinning reel is a wise choice for the average angler who wishes to cast lures, natural or artificial, ranging in weights from fractions of an ounce up to approximately three ounces. Heavier lures can be cast with the use of a spinning reel, but remember our original mention of *practical* fishing.

This wide range of lure weights covers a multitude of reel sizes. If the various manufacturers of free-spool models cannot agree upon the exact meaning of numerical designations, they still must be considered the height of conformity when compared with those who make spinning reels. Each company has a completely different system of size numbering, if it has any apparent system at all.

Total reel weight and the line capacity of its spool will give a basic indication of size. Fortunately, the makers tend to go into considerable detail on all specifications of their spinning reels, and many match the reels up with balancing rods and lures. This makes choice by the angler much simpler.

Because the stationary spool reel is basically a light casting outfit, as noted, latitude in choice of monofilament line for use with the reel is not nearly as wide as in the case of free-spool types. For example, although a 6/0 conventional reel is best matched with 50 pound test line, it can handle 30 or 80 pound also. A spinning reel designed for best use with 8 pound mono might handle 6 or 10 pound, but it would function poorly if filled with 4 or 15 pound test. In brief, the selector of a spinning reel should be much more fussy concerning the exact breaking strain of the line he plans to use than his conventional counterpart.

Tabular presentation of reel sizes, line test and capacity, together with expected fish weight, is almost impossible when spinning reels are being considered. There are too many variables, such as rod length and stiffness, lure weight, length of cast required, and basic angling conditions. In our opinion, the minimum practical line test for day-to-day marine spinning is 6 pound, while the maximum is 20 pound test. Except when you are after very small fish, the reel spool should hold at least 200 yards of the line selected, and often 300.

Choice of manual pick-up, full bail or pick-up arm models is largely a matter of individual preference. If displays in the average tackle store are any criteria, it seems evident that the full bail is most popular in the American salt water market. It should be noted that many spinning reels can be converted to manual if the angler does not wish to depend on flawless functioning of the bail spring—a bit of mechanism which is, indeed, prone to break at the most inopportune moment.

As is true with free-spool models, retrieve speed ratios vary widely. Since the spinning reel is primarily a casting tool, ratios tend to be higher than the conventional types. The fastest that has come to our attention is 6:1.

Latest newcomer to the marine scene is the spin-casting reel. Mounted on top of the rod like a free-spool type, it uses the basic principle of the spinning reel with a pick-up device revolving inside a housing around a stationary spool. Because of this housing, such reels are often called closed-face spinning reels. Salt has been the great enemy of these, not only because of its corrosive powers—common to any reel used on the marine scene—but because the salt tends to cake inside the housing.

This problem evidently has been whipped in some of the more recent models designed for light tackle work. Whether it will be licked also in larger models designed for the high surf remains to be seen.

No matter what reel may be selected, it pays to choose quality. It also pays to choose models that are designed basically for salt-water use. Even careful washing in fresh water after a visit to the sea will not save a model designed for the lakes and streams of America. The extra cost of marine reels more than pays off in trouble-free fishing.

3
SOFT LINES

CHOOSING A LINE IN THE EARLY DAYS OF SALT-WATER ANGLING WAS a comparatively easy task. If you were a sinker bouncer who used a handline, the choice was tarred, twisted cotton. If you were one of the elite, who boasted a rod and reel, twisted linen took top billing. The few who challenged ocean inhabitants with fly and bait casting outfits had to settle for braided silk which, however coated and "enameled," rotted and became weak in a very short time.

The tarred cotton handline is still with us. Although some big game anglers stick with twisted linen, now known generically as Cuttyhunk, it is rapidly vanishing from the sport fishing scene. Even in fresh water, silk braid today is a rarity and simply is not used on the ocean front. Man-made synthetic fibers have taken over everywhere. The only exception is wire line, which, by stretching a point, might be considered to be a man-made synthetic of sorts.

Before choosing a line for fishing, it is well to understand at least the basics of modern manufacturing methods and the qualities of the materials commonly used. The chemical formulas involved are a bit above the layman's head and even the allegedly popular descriptions become confusing. For example, nylon is the generic term for a long-chain synthetic polymeric amide, which has recurring amide groups as a part of the main polymer chain. This is nice to know, of course, but is of very little help in catching a fish. The fact that the synthetics are made from resins derived from air, water, coal and petroleum is more easily understood.

Once the mixture has been prepared by chemists who know what they are doing, it is heated to high temperature and the gooey mass resulting is then forced by great pressure through small holes in a metal plate. The gossamer strands come out in much the same manner as toothpaste comes out of a tube. These are stretched, while hot, then cooled and perhaps stretched again, depending upon the wishes of the manufacturer. The strands are then ready for processing into fishing line, either as monofilament or as line braided together from many small-diameter monofilaments. Coloring can be added to the original mixture or applied to the filaments in the cooling process.

The above description necessarily is oversimplified. Quality control varies greatly in such things as uniformity in diameter of the individual strands, elimination of bubbles in the extrusion process, and exact temperatures used when cooling in order to obtain the same stiffness in all batches of the same line. In making cheap lines, some of the refinements in basic manufacture of the filaments themselves are bypassed.

Nylon was one of the first synthetics to be used to any extent in the manufacture of fishing lines. Depending upon the formula used for the basic resin, this material may stretch before breaking from 15 to about 30 percent of its length when dry, and from 20 to about 35 percent when wet. Overcoming this stretch factor in the raw material was a major problem in the early days, but modern nylon lines now tend toward the lower end of the percentage figures cited. It should be made clear that some stretch is desirable in any line as a safety factor while playing a fish.

Nylon lines lose some of their strength—usually less than 10 per cent—when wet. In time they will deteriorate if exposed to strong sunlight. In actual fishing practice, this deterioration is not a factor to cause much worry because the line on the top of the spool, which is regularly exposed, will be cut back due to normal wear and tear long before sunlight can do excessive damage. It should be considered, however, when storing nylon. A dark drawer is preferable to an open shelf if storage is for long periods.

Although nylon absorbs far less water than the old linen line, it actually will take on as much as 12 per cent of its own weight when wetted. Braided lines, due to their many-filamented structure, obviously will take on more water than monofilaments. This actually is an advantage to the caster using a free-spool reel. If no water were present, heat generated by the reel spool whirling against the thumb would be extremely uncomfortable.

Dacron, which followed nylon on the fishing scene, varies a negligible amount from nylon as far as breaking strength is concerned, wet or dry. It absorbs practically no water and therefore is a hot line, in the true sense of the word, for casting. Given the same diameter of filaments, it is slightly weaker than nylon. However, it stretches only about 10 per cent and has a high resistance to deterioration from sunlight. Dacron braid therefore has become popular as a trolling line in both small- and big-game fishing circles.

The most recent contribution from line-makers is a braid manufactured under a new formula from extremely fine-diameter filaments, which results in a product called Micron that is stronger for its size than nylon or Dacron equivalents. Stretch factor appears to be somewhere between its two predecessors and water absorption qualities are roughly equivalent to those of braided nylon. It can therefore be used for both trolling and casting. As is true of all line materials, this one will be better evaluated after a few seasons of use on the angling front. At first acquaintance, we are impressed: there is no tendency to groove the left thumb nor burn the right.

As the name implies, braided lines are woven together by machines which are very similar to those used in the textile industry. Although many of the first braids were made around a core of line itself—a hangover from the manufacturing of buggy whips, incidentally—most today are hollow braided. The finished product has no central material in it other than air. Thanks to a variety of ingenious machines and treatment processes, these lines can be made oval or round in cross-section, stiff or limp, tough or soft, smooth or rough, buoyant or sinking. In the case of fly lines, they are even made to taper or to surround other materials. Colors may be varied widely, even in a single length of line, to indicate how much has been let off the reel.

Recently, in a sort of turn-back-the-clock operation, fine nylon and other braids have been used with success by spin-casters. Perhaps improvements in braids have banished early faults which made them a poor choice in fixed-spool fishing. It is obvious that braid, no matter of what material, is extremely versatile.

Monofilament, made from a single strand, is not quite as versatile, although manufacturers offer a wide selection of mono with different qualities. For the angler using spinning tackle, monofilament nylon is superior to any other material for general use. More difficult to handle than braid when using a free-spool reel, this material, particularly in the lighter tests, has also become popular with conventional casters. It is also seen more and more frequently on trolling reels. Even though stretch presents difficulties when you are going after heavyweights, and though mono is not as easy to spool on the reel as braid, its low visibility and low water resistance have contributed to its use by many trollers, bottom and drift fishermen.

Monofilament has one great advantage over other types of line: it is comparatively low in cost. Anglers with slender pocketbooks often are willing to overlook some of its shortcomings for this reason alone.

Various qualities must be examined when selecting the proper line for a particular type of fishing. Strength for diameter desired ranks high as one of these qualities. To the layman, it might seem that a single strand must necessarily be stronger in any given diameter than multiple strands braided together to the same dimensions. Such is not always the case. The resins used in the raw materials from which the lines are made, the extruding techniques, and the braiding methods cause considerable variation.

Included in strength must be the breaking point of any line after a knot has been tied in it. Using any of the approved jam knots of today, knot strength of nylon and Dacron are roughly comparable. Mono connections are not as strong, particularly after continued use—for the single filament tends to cut into itself.

Fishermen, line manufacturers, and even record-keepers base their ideas of line strength on the number of pounds of steady pull it takes to part the line after it has been firmly secured to a solid object. This undoubtedly is the only practical, measurable, and uniform method of classification. However, what might be termed shock strength must also be considered. When a fish strikes, leaps, or changes course suddenly during the battle, there is an abrupt strain put on the line—and this strain is far in excess of that resulting from a straight run. Similarly, in casting, the sudden strain comes at the start of the cast, which is why many anglers utilize a length of forward trace, or shock line, much heavier than that which fills their reels.

Obviously, elimination of all elasticity in any type of line will result in chances of something having to give under strain. In the case of wire, the angler must be particularly alert in order to avoid breakage, for this material has practically no built-in stretch. Those who fish with wire regularly claim, with some justification, that outlawing it for world-record catches by the International Game Fishing Association is unrealistic because of this. Their angling alertness must be exceptionally keen.

Too much stretch in other line materials will mean that sufficient power cannot be transmitted to the hook to set it, or that casting distance is reduced. The energy needed for the job is used up by the elasticity of the line. Choice therefore is a compromise. As a general rule, more elasticity can be used to advantage with hard-hitting species, such as wahoo and the acrobatic billfishes. A line with less stretch is desirable if the fish must be kept under close control, as when angling around obstructions. If the quarry has a hard mouth, elasticity is best held to a minimum so that the hook can be set effectively.

Note particularly that lines with considerable stretch, such as monofilaments, should be employed on reels designed for their use. That's because synthetics are cursed with a thing called "memory," a tendency to elongate and become finer in diameter under pressure and to return to their original diameter after the strain has been relieved. This is particularly true of nylon, whether mono or braid, and it is the reason why some reels "explode" or break into small pieces when a tightly packed line relaxes after the battle and resumes its original diameter. After playing a fish for a long time on either mono or nylon braid, it is advisable to strip line off the reel spool and allow it to return to its basic diameter back in the wake where it can cause no harm. Remember that diameter decreases under tension, but builds back when strains are relaxed.

Wherever spin-fishermen gather, conversation eventually turns to the limpness of one monofilament line as opposed to another. All other factors being equal, such limpness usually is considered to be an advantage on a spinning reel. This is true within reasonable limits. The extent of those limits may best be illustrated by filling a spinning reel spool with soft cotton thread and then trying to cast with it. The tangles of loops and knots that whirl off the reel spool are incredible to behold. The compromise is to use line that does not behave like cotton thread, yet does not act like a coiled spring when spooled. Those using mono on a free-spool casting reel are not as enchanted with the value of extreme limpness and, in general, seek a stiffer line than the spin-fishermen.

Braids are limper than their equivalent monofilaments. However, they can be braided tightly to make a hard line, or more loosely to make a soft one. The former type tends to be more resistant to any abrasion; the latter, a trifle easier to handle on the reel spool. Tougher lines obviously should be chosen if fishing is done primarily in areas where obstructions are common. Charter skippers lean toward these lines also, for their tackle may take a beating from inexperienced hands.

As a general rule, the tougher lines are not finished as smoothly on their surface as the softer ones. Except in casting, this presents no problem. The caster, however, may wear a livid groove in his left thumb when level-lining on the retrieve. In addition, even though friction may be increased only slightly by the rough-surfaced line, casting distance is diminished.

Anglers trying to reach greater depths when trolling, and those fishing bottom baits in strong tidal currents, are concerned with the water resistance offered by the line used. The rougher the line's surface and the larger its diameter, the more resistance. Monofilament, despite the fact that its diameter in any given pound test is larger than equivalent braids, meets the task best.

In really trying to plumb the depths, wire is the obvious answer —and more on this later. We now deal with the soft lines available to marine anglers.

These, in recent years, must include the modern salt water fly line. The forward taper type is most popular among fishermen in the briny. Such lines should be matched to the rods even more closely than elsewhere among the many combinations. In fly casting there is a vital relationship between the rod and the weight and type of line used.

Buoyancy, or lack of it, plays an important part in the selection of flylines. A floating line is easily picked up off the water at the start of a cast and, obviously, will present the lure on or near the water's surface. A sinking line must be stripped in almost to the angler's feet before pick-up, to avoid excessive strain on the rod tip. Also obviously, the sinking line will present a lure below the surface.

On the market today are countless varieties of these two extremes. A floating line of braided nylon may have a sinking head of Dacron. Combinations of the two materials, special finishes and variations in braiding techniques produce results that differ considerably in specific gravity. Choice depends upon the type of fishing done, the tackle used, weather conditions most frequently encountered and, finally, the skill of the angler.

One thing is unique about fly line as compared to other types: no one worries about its breaking strain. Unless the line is worn to a frazzle or deeply cut on some obstruction, it will be far stronger than the light leader used.

To consider choice of line color is to open up a Pandora's box of optical argument worthy of an article in itself. (And we'll do this later.) Basically, the idea is to make line invisible to the fish, yet visible to the fisherman so that he can see just what is going on during presentation of the lure and during the fight.

Discussion swirls primarily around just what is visible to the fish. For example, a few years ago many anglers and line manufacturers were convinced that red and shades of red disappeared more quickly in the depths than any other color. A red line therefore seemed ideal for deep water work. Success with such line was not startling and the reason may be explained by the fact that researchers recently have learned that such shades do *not* truly disappear. White lines against the sky may be invisible to fish below them, but perhaps blue lines would be better in fine weather and dark lines better when it is overcast. A mottled mono might turn the trick when it is overcast-bright or partly cloudy. The arguments go on.

Fundamentally, a line that does not contrast sharply with its air and water surroundings can be considered a good basic choice. However, until scientists working in the field of color perception in fish can state definitely just what finny creatures can and cannot see, accurate selection falls in the realm of fascinating theory.

At any rate, it pays to buy lines that are of good quality and that are backed by the reputations of reliable manufacturers. Bargain string may or may not be satisfactory when used to tie up packages. It has no place on the reel of a dedicated angler.

4
METAL LINES

PERHAPS RIGHTLY, ALTHOUGH WE CANNOT AGREE, THE AUGUST International Game Fish Association does not recognize catches made on wire line. Once, in the days when "wire" meant a cable of such flexible strength that no battler had a chance to escape after a hook had been set, this ban might have been logical. Nowadays, light tackle *can* mean wire, as well as midget reels, gossamer leaders, and buggy-whip rods.

Most of us delight in taking game fish on the surface. We thrill to that jarring top-water strike, usually accompanied by a bombburst of white spray. Braids, nylon monofilament, and coated fly lines are well suited to this operation, and we wouldn't have it otherwise. Few *prefer* to take fish in the depths.

Unfortunately, those who fish marine waters cannot change the nature of the beast they seek. Some species naturally feed close to the bottom and others seek lower levels as midsummer heat raises surface temperatures. In order to succeed it becomes necessary to troll a bait or lure away down in the strike zone. A man becomes somewhat ridiculous when he persists in ignoring the obvious.

Modern metal lines are manufactured in a wide variety of diameters and tests. You can go light or heavy, as circumstances seem to demand. You can give a fish all manner of odds, after it has been hooked—and still manage to hook it in the first place. This is important, for any angling expedition is a dry run unless you are able to make contact with game fish.

The need for wire line is universal and not tied to any one seaboard. There are occasions when metal, and only metal, will take a lure or bait to the depths frequented by Caribbean wahoo. Southern king mackerel often swarm well below the operational range of light lines. Northern striped bass, especially in the summer months, hug the offshore reefs and will not rise to take a surface lure. Bluefish often feed deep. Even the great game fish may be enticed by a tempter presented right over the bottom—although few big-game anglers have experimented with wire line.

If this is not enough, wire can mean the difference between success and failure in very shallow water where a bait must be presented on the bottom at a considerable distance from a trolling boat. Deny this if you will, but note that wire-liners have proved their point beyond any shadow of doubt.

In the salt chuck of today there are three basic metal lines: these are single-strand wire, twisted wire, and lead-cored nylon. All are effective and none is all-purpose. Braided or twisted wire is least popular because most of the early types had an annoying habit of coiling like a spring after a few hard battles.

Lead-core is favored by some charter skippers because it is easiest for a novice patron to handle. Twisted or braided wire shares this credit. Both types mold to the reel spool and resist the wild fluffing of single-strand wire when a fisherman's thumb is poorly educated.

Lead-cored nylon lines generally are marked in "colors," each hue indicating a certain yardage. Thus an angler can tell by the color exactly how much line he is dragging astern. (Skippers usually mark single-strand with plastic tape, wire wraps, or even beads of solder, but exact range-finding is difficult for any other than the advanced craftsman.)

We are not suggesting that lead-core is an amateur's line—far from it! Because of its larger diameter and greater resistance to water, lead-core sinks less rapidly than single-strand wire. It is, therefore, tremendously successful in areas where game fish are found at mid-levels rather than right on the bottom, and where the strike zone does not require deep penetration.

Lead-cored line is just that—a thin core of soft lead within a sleeve of braided nylon. The heavy metal, which serves to take the line down, has no appreciable strength—therefore its covering supplies all of the muscle. This is fine, so long as there is no prolonged contact with a rough sandy, rocky, or shelly bottom which will fray and destroy the nylon sleeve.

So far as light tackle is concerned, there is no argument. Granting that each material approaches meat-fishing levels when you insist upon overpowering tests and diameters, single-strand must be chosen for truly light work. Much finer filaments, commensurate with pound-test ratings, are available in this material.

But—single-strand wire, whether one of the relatively soft types or the somewhat hardier and springier stainless steel, is frankly difficult to handle. A clumsy or ham-handed fisherman will achieve some of the most obstinate tangles in this watery world. There is little margin for error, yet this is the price one pays for performance.

In streaming such a line, it is necessary to maintain light pressure on the reel's spool to prevent any overrun. Backlashes are more serious than those incurred in fishing with braid or mono, for they usually lead to kinks—which can mean crystallization and weakening of the metal. With wire you'll be smooth, or you'll be sorry.

The trick lies in light pressure on the spool as line pays out. Never give this thoroughbred its head, for you'll wind up with trouble if you do. With practice, single-strand can be streamed at high speed—but it does take practice. Don't try to jump the gun unless you like to fight long odds.

Once mastered, wire is a mighty versatile line. You can go from very light tests on up to big stuff for huge fish in raging offshore rips. A 15 to 20 pound test wire line is surprisingly fine in diameter. Acrobatic game fish hooked on these weights will zoom into the air with all of the disregard they show toward ordinary nylon monofilaments or braids. An angler will note two unusual fringe benefits.

First, and most obvious, is the fact that he will hook game fish in the depths when surface trolling proves unproductive. Second, the battler who tackles a lure attached to wire will feel twice as strong, because wire has a minimum of stretch. You will be tied to that fish as with a bar of iron, and the sensation is likely to be a happy one.

Single-strand wire slices down, and it does so quickly. You will be able to troll less yardage than you would with lead-core or with a line of neutral buoyancy which is dragged into the depths by sinkers or planers. Moreover, aside from kinks, this line is relatively immune to abrasion or other abuse: it is both tough and strong.

The abrasion factor is important when you are trolling a considerable length of wire in shoal water. If this sounds like a contradiction in terms, be assured that it is not. In some areas it is necessary to drag as much as 100 yards of wire in depths ranging from five to fifteen feet in order to interest game fish. Granted, most of the wire is on the bottom—where it is subject to the not-so-gentle attention of sand, rocks, and shells—but this is necessary, since the fish will not be inclined to bite for a certain length of time after a boat's passage—say 100 yards of time measured in slow trolling. If 100 yards of line is trolled, it will take x-number of minutes before the lure is presented. By that time, fish spooked by the cruising boat will have sagged back into their chosen feeding area and will be more likely to strike.

This is the big secret of wire trolling for striped bass in shoal water. The long line, a full 300 feet, and sometimes as much as 600 feet, allows the fish time to recover their composure after the passage of a boat. They circle back into preferred feeding grounds, and that's when the baited hook or lure comes wriggling along.

Wire is a frustrating material, until you learn its secrets. In some areas the fish-killers find that it is possible to use no more than 100 feet of the stuff spliced to adequate backing. In this case all of the wire is streamed and the braid is left to take the punishment meted out by jigging or trolling. When conditions permit, this is wise.

That's because all of the single-strand wires are subject to crystallization. If you jig a wire against a stationary rod tip long enough, the sharp angle of the wire against the tiptop will set up a process of crystallization and the wire will ultimately break at point of contact. Often, when this happens, the angler will curse the line maker—and ignore his own error in flexing the metal at a single point until such time as its molecules rebel.

Wherever possible, for this reason, stream all wire and then use backing to absorb the punishment of jigging. This is most easily accomplished when a certain length of deep-going line is decided upon: it is less practical when depth or differences in technique require more or less length of line.

In the event that one must work a lure at a depth which does not utilize all of the wire, protect your interests by a rather continuous change in line length. Jig a half-dozen times, and then drop back a foot. Repeat the process. Now reel in two feet. Try to avoid the systematic flexing of any portion of wire over a period of time. To do so may be disastrous.

Modern single-strand wires are flexible, but they still present much resistance to guides, especially when the line is bent at a

45-degree angle from the tiptop. Roller guides are supreme in this work: they will insure greater sport and less parted gear. A roller tiptop is a minimum investment. Without such a tiptop, a wire-line fisherman labors under a major disadvantage. He will groove his rings and he will find it very difficult to pump up a fish which has taken position in the depths right underneath his boat. Rollers are good insurance for any fishing technique other than casting and they are just about a necessity in wire-line trolling.

There is an unfortunate tendency among fishermen to buy the finest of wire, and then to neglect backing. Many feel that any old, discarded braid will do for this office, and little cognizance is taken of test ratings. Common logic indicates that backing is a major component of the combination. Usually, if you are streaming all of the wire on a reel's spool, the first hectic minutes of a fight with a big fish will see much backing disappear into the wide blue yonder.

Dacron braid probably rates highest as wire line backing. The material is tough and boasts a minimum of elasticity. Nylon braid can be used, although it is less practical. Some favor nylon monofilament, although this is the worst possible backing because of its elasticity and spool-busting memory.

Backing should be of slightly higher test than the lead-off wire, because it will be subjected to ever-increasing pressure as line is stripped off against a drag. Light backing, or that which is frayed or otherwise damaged, may mean the loss of a fish—plus an entire hank of valuable metal line. A good rule of thumb here, as in most tackle combinations, is a calculated beefing up of gear from a light leader to a slightly heavier line and a still heavier length of backing. Each component should be job-rated and free of weakening blemishes, frays, or kinks.

A key-loop knot is probably the best connection between wire and backing. (It can be used at the business end, too, but a lot of specialists prefer a swivel to join wire and leader.) You can use a small swivel to join line and backing: some do, but it is a lumpy arrangement and serves no good purpose. Better learn to tie the key-loop.

Leaders in wire-line fishing naturally depend upon the fish sought. Those who seek striped bass may find nylon monofilament quite adequate. The dredger who desires bluefish can gamble with mono, but he is better advised to use a short trace of wire at the bitter end of the mono to guard against the chopper's formidable dental armament. Often wire can be threaded through a bottom-bumping lure, in which case no leader is required. It is wise to note, however, that the action of the lure may subsequently crystallize the metal at the point where it enters the lure's lead head. Wire is a line, not—in this case—a leader. An angler is always wise to choose terminal tackle best suited to his technique and his quarry.

One rig, used by inland trollers who seek landlocked salmon and lake trout, has been employed with good results on the bluefishing grounds. A hank of monofilament measuring 100 feet is attached to the end of a light wire line. To the end of this mono trace, a small, dull-colored swivel connects a short length of much lighter test mono with, if necessary, a foot or so of wire ahead of the lure.

In theory, the long monofilament leader does two things: it has almost neutral buoyancy, so it does not slap a trolled lure right against the bottom. Light mono also insures less weight to inhibit the action of a lure. The tippet—if that final few feet of lighter test mono can be so designated—prevents loss of much line in the event of bottom fouling. Of course, a foot or so of wire, tipping the tippet, is insurance against the cutting teeth of bluefish.

Finally, after a fish strikes and the deep-going wire has been retrieved, the quarry is played on that final 100 feet of light mono. The combination is effective and, believe it or not, can be highly satisfactory when employed with a powerful fly rod, a single-action reel—and maybe a silent prayer. (Salt water fly-rodders please note: fish taken on this rig should not be accepted as records in the feather merchant's world.)

In spite of IGFA's current rejection of wire as a "sporting" method, we feel that the intelligent representatives of that unique organization will someday reverse their stand. Modern wire lines are a far cry from the old cables.

Meanwhile, wire and lead-cored lines are great connections to game fish. They're sporting, and they're productive. If you can't claim a record you can, at the very least, catch a lot of fish and have a lot of fun!

5 BACKING

NO BLOOD-AND-THUNDER FISHING STORY IS QUITE COMPLETE WITHout one anecdote about the "monster" that runs off every yard of line and goes deep into the backing. This happens, to be sure, but rarely so often on the fishing grounds as in the magazines. It is axiomatic that a lost fish is always a lunker.

Perhaps, at this point, it would be well to define the word. "Backing" means reserve line which is knotted or spliced to the primary fishing line as insurance when a game fish makes extraordinarily long runs. There are other reasons for employment, these to be examined as we go along.

Initially, though—and with two important exceptions—it should be noted that marine game fish seldom strip off enough running line to expose the backing, if any is used. The exceptions, of course, refer to fly casting and wire-line trolling. In each of these cases the primary line is relatively short, and backing becomes an absolute necessity: in effect, it *becomes* the running line.

So, if you want to be sticky about it, there are just two good reasons for backing. One is the employment of a short primary line; another is the necessity for a cushioning material which also serves as reserve in the event of a long run. We have purposely written "good," instead of "valid" reasons. Backing can be profitably employed as a filler. Let's examine its blue-chip credits.

A salt water fly line rarely measures better than 35 yards. A crack fisherman easily lays out 70 foot casts, and may even grunt and groan his way to the 100 foot mark. After the strike, a fish has only to peel off something less than, say, 15 yards and he's into the backing. Some marine gamesters are known to streak away for 100 or more yards before they can be turned. Obviously, the salt water fly line must be backed, and to the tune of 100 or 200 yards.

Wire-line trollers wisely use just enough metal to get their lures down to payoff depths. Depending on wire-line test, areas and species sought, this length may vary from 100 feet to 100 yards. All additional yardage is synthetic braid. There are a couple of reasons why such backing makes good sense.

First, of course, there is a necessity for just so much wire to get lures down into the strike zone. Second, wire is tough on guides, be they roller or ring. Rings quickly develop grooves, and —while rollers themselves survive—bridges tend to be scored by the harsh metal when anglers cant rods in jigging.

To combat this attrition, one simply streams all of the wire, plus two or three feet of backing. Thereafter, the angler can troll or jig with nothing but a soft braid caressing the guides. Perhaps more important, if you are willing to kiss off rod guide wear, the constant jigging of wire which is strung through a tiptop can cause that wire to crystallize and part easily.

In this age of atoms and plastics, monofilament line is used for practically everything. Mono is a modern miracle, and yet it has flaws: one of these is that curious property experts call "memory," discussed in Chapter 3.

Compared to wire and the modern soft braids, mono is quite elastic. When you are playing fish it stretches—and remains stretched for a short period after it has been reeled back on the spool. Then, sometimes within seconds, the stuff "remembers" that it has been stretched—and expands to its original diameter.

The "memory" of nylon monofilament has wrecked a great many reels, and it will destroy more of them in the foreseeable future. While some conventional reel spools have been built to withstand this pressure, others have not. The angler's best insurance is a cushion of braid in the form of backing.

Therefore, casters who use mono on revolving spool reels, and particularly on those reels which are designed for casting rather than trolling, may load the dice in their own favor by insisting that the underlying 25 per cent of the spool's capacity is braided backing. The reserve will cushion memory-plagued mono, and will also curb the odd fish that peels off an inordinate amount of running line.

The problem is rarely encountered with a spinning reel, for these spools have been designed to absorb the pressure of tightly packed monofilament. While many spin-fishermen like a small amount of backing, there is no real need for it.

Spinning enthusiasts often use backing which, for want of a

better word, should be called "filler." The practice is a poor one if you anticipate record-sized fish, but it minimizes the cost of replacement lines and may work well enough if you don't hang something big enough to visit far horizons.

Briefly, instead of filling a reel spool with, say, 200 yards of new line, the angler decides that no fish he hooks is likely to peel off more than 100. Accordingly, instead of buying a 200 yard replacement spool, he purchases half that much—and uses half of the old line as backing.

There is merit in the technique where narrow-spooled spinning reels are concerned. Some of these, in spite of industry propaganda to the effect that there is no line friction in spinning, get mighty cranky when the line level goes down more than midway in the spool. This is a case for filler, pure and simple, yet it also indicates the need for adequate width as well as depth in a threadline spool.

Such fillers are also used by bait and surf casting addicts where smaller fish are sought, casting distance is minimal, and gamesters are unlikely to run off much yardage. However, the practice is a calculated risk. Any knot detracts from the strength of the line, and the fish that "goes into the backing" is the one you want more than anything else in this pop-eyed world. Why gamble to save a pittance?

Too many otherwise bright fishermen seem to think that backing is less important than the primary line. Just the opposite is true. Good backing is insurance when all of the chips are down. Backing should never be a hank of ancient line: it should be brand new, securely knotted or spliced to the running line. After all, this may be the critical point where you turn a record-breaker or lose everything.

In the final analysis, type and test rating, together with necessary length, are most important. Dacron braid makes an ideal backing because it has little stretch and is fine in diameter for its pound test rating. Braided nylon is second on the totem pole, second because it possesses a degree more of elasticity than Dacron. Old-fashioned linen, or Cuttyhunk, is third. Linen is tough and far from elastic, yet it is subject to rot and it uses more space than braided Dacron.

Nylon monofilament is the worst possible backing, unless it is used as "filler" on a narrow-spooled spinning reel. On any other reel it is a poor choice and may, thanks to the memory quotient mentioned previously, contribute to the sudden destruction of the reel.

Pound test rating and length must be determined by job requirements. In fly casting, for example, you may want as much backing as possible—and tests will vary with the fish sought and the angling conditions.

In Florida flats fishing for bonefish, most of the backing is likely to be in the air, so a relatively light test can be used. However, few marine feather merchants go below 18 pound test for backing, and the norm would probably be 20. For big tarpon, experts like Stu Apte are likely to choose 28 pound test Dacron.

Similarly, a northern striped bass fisherman prefers 20 to 27 pound test because he is stuck into new problems. Here the gamester can go deep and he can drag the running line (backing) across some mighty rough and barnacle-encrusted boulders. The fish is unlikely to race for 100 yards, but it is very apt to dive and make trouble within 30 to 50 yards.

Now an angler may be wise to employ the heaviest backing, commensurate with required yardage, that he can pack on his single-action reel. Obviously 27 pound test will take more punishment than 18, yet there'll be less of it. You should have at least 150 yards of braid behind the fly line, and preferably 200. Some big, ocean-going fly reels feature even greater capacity. Make it the best available. Reserve line is just as important as that which sets the hook, and perhaps a shade more important.

It is this reserve line, or backing, which most often absorbs the first powerful runs of a game fish. By that token backing must be flawless and securely knotted or spliced to the line. There must be enough of it to counter every determined run. This means a full spool, regardless of fly line length or the length of a shot of wire. Three things should be kept in mind at all times, and two of them are vitally important.

First, and this is particularly applicable in fly casting, one must understand that the leader tippet is the weakest link in the line chain. At least, it should be! However, a 15 pound test length of backing might well part before a 12 pound test tippet—*if a game fish were towing the entire fly line, plus a considerable amount of backing*. In fact, were you to stream enough line, the resistance created would soon part the backing without any fish to aid.

Fortunately for fly fishermen, unless they are the adventurous type who toy with black marlin and other high-velocity pelagic gamesters, fish commonly taken on the long wand do not rip off 200 yards of line in a sustained burst of speed.

This does happen to wire-liners, however, and the wire-line angler should be sure that his backing is stout enough to absorb the tremendous stresses developed by such a maneuver. Usually, backing employed on any trolling reel should be as heavy, if not heavier, than the primary line. This, if you hanker for light tackle IGFA records, poses another problem.

Although wire line is not accepted by the International Game Fish Association in any record claim, the use of backing *is* recognized—and carefully qualified, as follows:

"*Backing:* If two lines of different test strength, *spliced or tied together* are used in taking a fish, that catch shall be classified under the heavier of the two lines and a sample of both lines must be submitted."

The joint between any primary line and backing must be secure, and the knot or splice will vary with the various materials. In some cases no two anglers will agree. Careful splicing is uniformly recommended where equal, or nearly equal, diameters of braid are concerned. A blood knot will also suffice, but it is not as foolproof as splicing.

On the other hand, if monofilament is joined to monofilament of approximately the same test, there is no better connection than the blood knot. Make at least five turns with each end of line. Draw up slowly and moisten as the knot is tightened. Finally, trim off the ends. The blood knot, incidentally, is effective also where light braids—too light to be joined with a splice—must be connected.

For lines with major differences in diameter, such as a light Dacron braid joined to a fly line, the nail knot or the key loop may be used. Many fly casters prefer spliced loops. Nail knots and the key loop are also recommended when line and backing are of different basic materials. The key loop is favored for joining wire and braid, although some deep trollers like to connect heavy wire and braid by tying a short loop into the soft line, then tying a single becket bend into this loop with the end of the wire. The bend is drawn tight with pliers and the connection is completed by "marrying" the tag end of wire—twisting it back into the main part. Care should be taken to insure against kinks, and the bitter end of the wire should be broken off to guard against a finger-cutting edge.

Backing, as such, too often is taken for granted. The average salt water sportsman sometimes thinks of it as a necessary evil, a filler or an anchor. It is, actually, reserve line—and line that may prove critical in a knock-down, drag-out battle with a record-sized fish. Accord it every bit as much concern as the primary line.

6
THE HUMBLE HOOK

FISHERMEN ARE A PECULIAR BREED. IT ALWAYS AMAZES US TO SEE an angler, who has spent thousands of dollars on a boat, tackle and equipment, fussing over the cost of the cheapest part of his outfit—the hook. Such false economy usually ends with the loss of a fish so that the thousands of dollars' investment is sacrificed for a few pennies.

Knowledge of hooks, their differences, and the reasons for these differences is vital in angling. Unfortunately there is no single hook that is ideal for all fishing; therefore choice at best is a compromise. The species sought and the tackle used to catch it both have bearing upon the final choice, but basic understanding of hook construction is helpful in making the selection.

Today, almost without exception, salt water fishhooks are made of steel or some similar alloy. Small hooks are manufactured by drawing wire to the required diameter, bending and cutting the wire by various mechanical means into the shape desired, and then tempering the finished product. The quality and temper of the metal naturally determines the reliability of the hook and, as with any item of fishing tackle, you pay more for good products than for shoddy ones.

In manufacturing larger hooks, a process known as forging is often used. A forged hook is not just bent into shape and then tempered. After the bend has been made, the hook wire is hammered along part of the shank and all of the bend so that it is flat on two sides. Then the tempering follows. This gives added strength where it is needed to prevent the bend from straightening under stress.

Because of the corrosive action of salt water, a fresh water fishhook is almost worthless to the marine angler. Cheap ocean hooks are blued, but this type of finish does not stand up well, with the result that rust will soon destroy the metal. Japanned hooks—hooks coated with a black lacquer—are used primarily in the making of salmon flies and will stand up briefly in salt water. A similar lacquer gives what is called a bronzed finish and this finish also soon succumbs to the corrosive action of the sea.

To battle corrosive action, various metals are used to plate salt water hooks. Gold and silver work well in fresh water, but the plating is so thin that rust will soon break through when used in the briny unless great care is exercised after each use. Along certain sections of the southern Pacific coast, cadmium and nickel-plated hooks are popular, and they stand up well. By far the greatest proportion of marine hooks, however, are tinned. Although the plating wears off eventually, this type holds the number one spot.

Finally, there are hooks made from various noncorrosive alloys that do not rust at all. Stainless steel will be the hook material of the future, but that metal has yet to surmount all problems. Early stainless steel hooks tended to be brittle, so that eyes and points often fractured at the most unhandy moments. Nowadays, this type of barb is challenging the old high carbon steel article.

Several nickel alloys have been marketed. While they resist corrosion, all are softer than steel and their points are apt to blunt upon contact with a hard surface. Moreover, to insure the required strength, most of the soft alloy hooks are made of rather heavy wire, a fault in itself.

Naturally the size of a hook will have a considerable effect upon its basic strength and upon the type of fish it may catch. A newcomer to the marine scene may become confused by the numbering of hook sizes, but the system is simple enough once it is understood. The smallest hook in common use—and rather uncommon in ocean fishing—is a number 20. From that size, hooks become progressively one-sixteenth of an inch longer as the size number *decreases*. This measurement does not include the eye. Thus, a number 7 will be one-sixteenth of an inch longer than a number 8. For reasons best known to a hook maker in Redditch, England, who established the size system, when size number 3 is reached, figures change. A number 2 hook is one-eighth of an inch longer than a number 3, a number 1 is one-eighth of an inch longer than a number 2, and so on. It should be noted that some manufacturers do not stick to this system 100 per cent, but it is the basic method of measuring hook sizes.

What happens to this numbering system when size number 1 is

reached? Simple enough: the size numbers are designated by a following zero and *increase* as the size numbers increase. Thus a 2/0 is one-eighth of an inch longer than a 1/0, a 3/0 is one-eighth of an inch longer than a 2/0, and so on, up to size number 5/0. At that point the increase in length is stepped up by half-inch jumps with the result that a 6/0 is a half-inch longer than a 5/0. Unfortunately, use of this basic system in this country is a bit confused because some manufacturers do not change to the half-inch jump at all while others change as the fancy suits them. Suffice it to say that the higher the number with a zero following it, the larger the hook itself.

In addition to the actual size of the hook, the diameter of the wire from which it is made is important. Here again manufacturers do not agree on standards for designating wire sizes. In general, there is light wire, heavy wire, and then sizes of wire indicated by the letter X. Thus an XX heavy or strong hook will be made of wire greater in diameter than an X heavy or strong; an XXX heavy will be even stouter, and so on, up to a total of six X's.

Qualities of the various weights of wire should always be kept in mind when selecting hooks. Light wire hooks, all other things being equal, penetrate a fish's mouth more readily, but also wear through, or buttonhole, quickly. Light wire also, of course, bends easily. However, when fragile natural baits are used, these light hooks are more practical because they do not tear the bait to pieces and, if the bait is a live one, their lightness allows freedom of movement.

Heavy wire hooks, on the other hand, are stronger, do not spring when they strike something hard, such as a tarpon's bony jaw, and do not bend under the impact of toothed species. Although they do not penetrate as readily, they are apt to hold more securely once they have penetrated.

Driving a hook home on the strike so that the barb is firmly embedded in the fish's jaw is a problem that has given rise to many different styles of hook. Add to this problem the necessity for having a hook hold after it has penetrated and the lads on the drafting boards begin to mutter to themselves. Throw in the facts that fish may take a lure in a rush, in gentle nibbles or in some manner between these two extremes; that the quarry may come from head on, from the side, from below or from the rear; that it may leap and shake its head after being hooked, or fight a long underwater battle; that the mouth structure may be hard, soft, or in between, and it is easy to see why no single hook can be considered ideal for all types of fishing.

Referring to any diagram of a typical hook, the following facts should be noted when making a selection. A short barb, spear, or bite means that the hook will penetrate more easily, but also that it will be thrown more easily. A short gap—known also as throat—in a hook may limit its effectiveness on the strike; in addition, it will not drive deeply into a fish. However, a wide gap, although it takes a bigger "bite" into the flesh, allows more play in the hook itself and tends to wear a spot through the flesh—known as buttonholing. This permits the hook to work free unless constant pressure is kept on it. If the hook bend is large and generally circular in arc, it takes more power to set the hook since the pull of the line is not parallel to the spear. Once embedded in the fish's mouth, however, chances of a fish throwing such a hook are reduced.

Variation in the length of shank has several results. A short-shanked hook will be swallowed more deeply by a game fish and also may be hidden more readily in a natural bait so that the quarry will not feel it if mouthing the bait. This means often that the entire hook will be well inside the fish's mouth or even down in the gullet—a mixed blessing. Although such hooking will hold, a toothed gamester will be able to chomp happily on the leader, and a specimen with a small mouth will pose a problem in hook recovery once the fish has been beached or boated. Use of a long-shanked hook prevents the leader from being chomped and makes unhooking an easy task. However, the shank itself may alarm a nibbler so that it never takes the hook at all. Again, the choice is a compromise.

Hook shanks may be bent in many ways, such as those with a hump in the middle, used for securing a piece of cork or plastic when making small floating lures. When cut so that there are jagged projections, the term "sliced" is used. The purpose of slicing is to keep a natural bait, such as a salmon egg, from slipping off the hook itself. Cutting a series of small ridges gives what is called a marked shank. This is done when tying snelled hooks so that the snelling material will not slip after being wound on with thread.

There are various types of hook eyes that are commonly used by salt water anglers. The most common is the simple ringed eye in which the hook wire is bent in a circle perpendicular to the plane of the hook itself. A modification of this is the open-eye hook. Here, the eye is not entirely closed and the temper of the metal is comparatively soft. Such hooks, often trebles, are used for quick replacements on lures when the originals have become damaged. Closure can be made easily with a pair of pliers.

Turned-down eyes and turned-up eyes—known as TDE and TUE, respectively, by hook manufacturers—are more commonly found in fresh water hooks, but also have their place on the marine scene. For example, when using a snelled hook, it will allow the snell to lie evenly along the shank without a bend at the eye itself.

A brazed eye, found mainly in big-game hooks, means simply that the eye is welded, brazed, or soldered where it meets the shank after the eye bend has been completed. This insures added strength and prevents opening the eye under heavy strain. Also found primarily among big-game hooks is the needle eye in which the tip end of the shank is drilled and not bent at all. The advantage of such an eye is that it may be strung through a natural bait easily without fouling.

Traveling to the other end of the hook for a moment, it should be noted that there are different types of points as well as different types of eyes. The cheaper hooks usually have spear points, rounded on all sides. A hollow point is not hollow at all: it is ground on the inside of the barb to make it sharper to start with and more easily sharpened after use. When ground on the outside edges of the barb also, a diamond point is formed. In cross section, the tip of such a point is in the classic diamond shape—hence the name. Finally, there is the turned-in point, which continues the bend of the hook right through spear, barb, and point. All these modifications aim at one thing—sharpness, with resulting ease of penetration. A fisherman can help the manufacturer toward this goal by touching up the points with a small hone or file.

A final item in hook structure should be mentioned. Some hooks are bent slightly sidewise at the spot between the shank and the start of the bend. In other words, the hook point is offset at an angle to the plane of the shank. If bent to the right, viewed from the top of the hook with the eye toward you, such a hook is called kirbed. If bent to the left, it is called reversed. The purpose of such kirbing or reversing is so that the hook will not slide out of the fish's mouth without hitting flesh. Such hooks have their advantages, but it should be noted that they tend to spin when trolled or cast and also that they require slightly more force to set than do conventional straight models.

Technically, penetration of the hook depends to a large extent upon the balance of the hook itself. If a hook is suspended from its point and allowed to hang freely, the theory is that penetration will improve in direct ratio as the spear becomes more nearly parallel to the pull of the line. This theory may be sound enough from the engineering point of view, but in practice it should be qualified. For example, a hook with a very short shank hung in this manner will swing so that it is almost at right angles to the direction of line pull. Another long-shanked hook with exactly the same bend and of the same size will hang almost parallel. Under actual fishing conditions, the short-shanked hook will penetrate as well as, or even better, than its long-shanked equivalent.

When it comes to holding power, we agree with the engineers within reasonable limits. Hang a hook on a nail, let it swing a little and wait until it comes to rest. Note whether or not the spear is parallel to the direction of line pull. The more nearly parallel it is, all other factors being equal, the better the holding power and the less chance that the hook will back out during the fish's battle.

In selecting a hook, there are certain points to make to distinguish the good product from the bad. First examine the eye. There should be no appreciable gap between eye and shank and no roughness whether or not the eye is brazed. Plating throughout the hook should be even and not lumpy. Note the barb and point to see that both are sharp and not bent or distorted in any way. In some cheap hooks the barb is cut so deeply that it and the point will break off with little strain. Test the hook by putting the point into a piece of wood and pulling smartly on the eye. The metal should not bend or snap.

Hooks should be selected with all of the many variables in mind. Besides, they should be balanced to the tackle used. It is impossible to set a 12/0 hook with a light spinning rig using 4 pound test line. A huge tuna outfit terminating in a number 6 light wire hook is equally foolish. These are outrageous examples, but the logic remains valid.

Two facts concerning hooks are open to no dispute. First, a sharp hook is better than a dull one. Second, the small amount spent on hooks should be spent well. It pays many times over to purchase well-made products rather than second-rate, cheap ones.

7
SINKERS

EONS AGO, WHEN SOME COASTAL CAVEMAN FIGURED THAT THERE were more fish on or near the bottom than at the surface, he tied a rock to his primitive line—and filled the larder. Cleverly shaped stones, fashioned for this very purpose, have been discovered among the artifacts of ancient Inca and pre-Inca civilizations in South America.

Ever since those prehistoric times, anglers have been using sinkers of one sort or another for the same basic purpose. Designs have become more sophisticated over the centuries, yet the fundamental idea of carrying a lure or bait down to the feeding level of the fish has not changed.

Today, with a few exceptions which will be mentioned in due course, sinkers are made of lead. This metal is ideally suited to the purpose, for it boasts high density, is comparatively cheap, is soft and easily melted so that it can be readily bent or molded, and it withstands the corrosive action of salt water. In this area of angling, for a wonder, man-made synthetics have not taken over.

When it comes to choosing the proper sinker for a given angling situation, several variables must be considered. First, obviously, is the depth at which the hook must be presented. Next, there is the tackle and the method of fishing. Finally, there is the water itself, the degree of current flow or tidal action, the bottom characteristics of the ocean floor. Two basic shapes are most often employed: these are the sharp-edged pyramid and the rounded dipsey. The egg sinker enjoys third place as an all-around type. Scaling sinkers, diamond shapes, plows, and many others are locally important. They have been designed for specific tasks and, although useful, are not important on a coastal scale.

According to all laws of logic, the heavier a sinker is, the deeper it will go. When it comes to marine angling, some of the laws of logic have been repealed, and this is one of them. When bottom-fishing from a boat, pier, or bridge in waters where there is no considerable current, a two-ounce sinker will plumb just as great a depth as a six-ounce weight, other factors being equal. If the fisherman uses a heavy line of nylon braid and a comparatively buoyant bait, such as a whole mullet, the six-ounce weight actually may not take the offering down as well as a two-ounce sinker fished on fine monofilament with a piece of clam for bait. Here, as elsewhere, fine balance is important.

Since a complete absence of current is rare in marine waters, the ideal solution is to use as light a sinker as is practical and efficient, for several reasons: first, a heavy sinker exerts undue stress on terminal tackle and, if the weight is to held off bottom, on the arms of the angler. Also, the heavier the weight, the harder it is to feel a slight nibble. Once a fish has been hooked, a ponderous sinker gives the quarry an advantage—leverage enables it to get rid of the hook either by a direct pull or by entangling the weight in some obstruction. Finally, even if in open water, the fish will not wage as spirited a battle when weighted down with excess lead as when unencumbered.

Naturally, fairly heavy tackle is required when bottom-fishing far offshore in a big ground swell or strong current. On the red snapper grounds of the Gulf of Mexico, for example, a whispy spinning rod, six-pound test monofilament and a one-ounce sinker would be something less than ideal. The sinker should be of sufficient weight and shape to get down quickly and to hold bottom once it gets there. The rod and reel combination must be suited to the purpose.

Such deep-down angling often is termed still-fishing, although practically nothing in the angler-tackle-water combination actually remains motionless. Sinkers most commonly selected for this work are the dipsey and bank types. The former, which is round in cross-section, will not foul on broken bottom as easily as the latter, which is hexagonal in cross-section. However, the bank holds better on sandy or muddy bottoms.

Cone and pyramid sinkers, although more commonly used by those who cast from the beach, are also good for offshore bottom-fishing when holding power is desired. For maximum digging-in qualities, the eye on such sinkers should be at the broad end of the cone or pyramid rather than at its apex. In some models of this type there are eyes at both ends, and these eyes are split so that more "sections" of sinker may be added as required.

Among the many specialized still-fishing sinkers, one of the most common, particularly along the northeast coast, is the drail. This is shaped something like a kidney with a short neck. Hanging at an angle to the line, its advantage is a measure of sensitivity: a nibble may be felt more readily than one transmitted through a straight-hanging weight.

Where the ocean floor is particularly rugged, it may be wise to attach any sinker to the line via a bit of thread or other material that features a much lower breaking strain than the line itself. By so doing, the lead can be broken off while line, leader, and hook are salvaged. Those who are economically minded sometimes use small bags of sand in lieu of sinkers, so the loss doesn't matter.

While there is little question that trollers should avoid shiny or colored sinkers—because the fish may strike them instead of the following lure—such is not necessarily true when still-fishing. The sinker itself may be decorated to act as an added attractor. For many bottom-feeding species, we have found that red or yellow waterproof enamels applied to the weight itself may attract fish. Flounders, for example, seem to take baits with greater abandon when a sinker is brilliantly colored. Further, the success of the old-time chrome-plated mackerel and codfish jigs, which are really nothing other than sinkers armed with hooks, indicates that flash has its charms.

Sinkers may be used as attractors in other ways. Some years ago an ingenious hollow sinker appeared on the market. Chum could be stuffed into the thing and, as this seeped out, it drew fish to the general vicinity of the baited hook. Whether this device is still available, we do not know, but many bottom fishermen employ the same basic principle by dipping their sinkers into a container of cod-liver oil before use.

If it is necessary to cast in order to place a bait in the desired spot when bottom-fishing, some other variables are involved. Obviously, the sinker must be heavy enough to draw line off the reel on the cast itself. In addition, the hook must be held in the place desired after it has submerged. Surf and pier fishermen are often plagued by ocean currents running parallel to the beach. Such currents, acting on line, sinker and bait, tend to roll terminal tackle along the ocean floor until it becomes a tangled mess. To some degree, air resistance characteristics of the sinker must be considered if the cast is to be a long one.

Surfmen who use bait find the pyramid sinker most practical. If the eye is on the broad base of this type, it will hold well on soft bottom; if at the apex, it will hold on broken bottom, yet will not foul excessively. The pier caster can get away with bank or dipsey types, since his angle of pull is greater from the horizontal, and rolling is not so much a problem.

Increasing the weight of a casting sinker also increases its holding power. However, there comes a time when the weight is too great for the rod used. It is then that specialized sinkers for such fishing come into their own. The multiple coin and pyramid, mentioned earlier, are two of these—unfortunately not always available in seaside tackle shops. Their multisurfaced exteriors present additional friction in soft sand or mud. The plow sinker, which looks a little like a truncated slingshot handle, works exceptionally well in heavy currents and on soft bottom. This type we have seen only on the Pacific coast and it deserves wider recognition elsewhere.

No discussion of casting sinkers would be complete without mention of the fish-finder rig. These are offered in a variety of shapes and types—and a simple snap swivel will serve the purpose in a pinch. The sinker is attached to the lower end of the fish-finder and the line passes through an eye, loop, or sleeve at the upper end. A swivel at the end of the leader prevents the fish-finder from riding down to the hook on the cast. When the sinker hits bottom and digs in, its weight is taken off the line and leader so that an angler may feel the slightest touch on the bait. Slack may then be granted without disturbing the sinker, so that channel bass—and other species that tend to mouth the bait before gobbling it—will not become alarmed. Fish-finders, incidentally, may be used very successfully by any still-fisherman, but are ideal for surfmen.

A modification of the fish-finder idea is the so-called egg sinker, an oblong spheroid with a hole drilled through its center. Although more widely used for trolling than casting, it serves the same purpose as the fish-finder in bottom-fishing. The egg sinker is well adapted to light tackle use and is more streamlined than the pyramid, dipsey, or plow. Unfortunately, it rolls over a smooth bottom like a marble and, even on rough bottom, tends to throw loops into the line. It is widely used in the tropics, but its efficiency is questionable.

Trolling sinkers are generally more streamlined than those used for still-fishing. Water resistance is a thing to be avoided and, in addition, a sinker that is not streamlined is apt to have a bubble form at its trailing edge. This bubble often will attract a fish, with the result that a strike will sever the line. Trolling sinkers should be attached between line and leader, not directly ahead of the bait or lure. The exception is when a sinker is entirely hidden in the bait itself or is incorporated in the lure, as is the case with bucktail-type jigs.

Egg sinkers, as noted, are often used for trolling. They are reasonably well streamlined and, if the hole through the center is almost exactly the same diameter as the line, are fairly effective in keeping weeds and other debris clear of leader and lure. However, the torpedo, which has a ring at each end, is easier to snap on and off. Variations on the torpedo are legion: some have built-in snaps and swivels, others feature split rings so that no knotting is required to secure them to the line. Shapes vary slightly, giving rise to such terms as cigar sinkers, bullet sinkers, and so on.

Changing the placement of the eye on a torpedo will change its trolling characteristics. If the leading eye is secured to the top of the lead, about a third of the way back from the nose, the sinker tends to dive more steeply. By flattening this same type on the upper leading edge, it will act as a plane and dig even deeper. However, if high speeds are attempted with such a sinker, it tends to turn on its side or back and porpoise to the surface, thus ruining its effectiveness. Note that this type of sinker should not be confused with the many deep-planing devices which are especially designed to take a lure down via hydrostatic effects.

One thing should always be kept in mind when using trolling sinkers: the speed of the boat has a tremendous effect upon the depth at which they will ride. A light lead at slow speed will carry the hook down much farther than a heavy weight moving rapidly. Minor variations in depth, when passing over a known hole, may be effected by dipping the rod tip smartly. This has the same effect as the sudden slowing of the boat. Allowing line to run off the reel does the same thing but is not recommended. If a fish hits at this crucial point, the result may be catastrophic! Tangles and backlashes result when a fish strikes on free spool.

Keeled sinkers, used in conjunction with swivels, can be very useful if the lure or bait spins when moved through the water. If caught without a keeled sinker, bending a slim, torpedo type into a slight arc will serve as an improvisation.

For light tackle trollers, the coin or heart sinker makes an excellent keel. Used a great deal in fresh water, these sinkers have never become very popular in the briny. Thy are made from flat sheets of lead and shaped as their names imply. A score, or groove, is cut through the sheet's center. The lead is then simply folded over the line and squeezed into place.

Various other clamp-on sinkers are available. Most common

among light tackle buffs is the split shot, which is available in a wide variety of weights. Torpedo-shaped leads, scored through the center, with small metal flaps on each end, may be used if more heft is desired. In using any of these, care should be exercised to insure that the line or leader is not damaged. Lead, even though a soft metal, can still cut synthetic fibers. For this reason, some patent clinch-on sinkers are fitted with rubber linings.

Some years ago, when spinning first became popular in this country, the so-called "floating sinker" achieved some fame. This device, a seeming contradiction in terms, is a small plastic bubble weighted so subtly that it actually has neutral buoyancy when immersed in water. Its purpose is to add weight to a very light lure, for the purpose of casting. We mention it only because, if someone speaks of a "floating sinker," it does not mean that he is a qualified candidate for the funny farm.

Another specialized sinker is the Pacific cannonball—one of the few angling weights made of iron rather than lead. Used when slow-trolling for salmon, the sinker is disposable. It is attached to a release device so that, when the fish strikes, the sinker drops off the line and the angler fights his quarry without any impediment. It's a good and logical gimmick, even if it costs something like 35 cents per strike.

This is just one of many efforts to rig sinkers so that they free themselves from the line on the strike. In deep trolling for big game, one most commonly illustrated in angling literature is the so-called "underwater outrigger." Here, a heavy sinker is lowered on a separate line placed fairly well forward in a sport fishing craft. This weight is then attached to the angler's line by a clothespin clip or a thread that will part when a fish hits. Theoretically, the sinker is then hauled in at leisure.

On paper, this appears simple and effective. In actual practice, it is anything but! Lowering the separate sinker and the lure or bait at exactly the same speed is a trick in itself. Once lowered, particularly in a choppy sea, the sinker has a nasty way of drawing the angler's line into the propeller. When, as, and if a strike results, getting the sinker back on deck during the resulting confusion—without fouling propeller or line—is not as easy as it sounds. Without question the rig works, but it does not work as well as might be expected.

A plentiful variety of basic sinkers should be included in every angler's tackle box. We always toss in a small square of sheet lead: this can be cut into any shape and size, wrapped around anything that needs to be sunk and, in brief, is most versatile. Lead wire is handy, particularly if weight needs to be added to a lure or to the body of a natural bait. Wrapping the wire around the hook shank, prior to rigging the bait itself, is simple and effective. Such fine strips of lead can also take a plug to desired depths when conditions warrant.

Study sinkers. They're important on those occasions when you get right down to it!

8

LEADERS

LEADERSHIP IS A QUALITY SOUGHT BY LARGE CORPORATIONS AND similar outfits when selecting people to fill executive jobs. The old story goes that one tycoon asked an assistant to comb the ranks of his staff for a young man who had more leadership capabilities than the tycoon himself and, if he were found, to fire him immediately!

On the fishing front, we once heard—and only once—the term used in a different way. An old boat skipper had a young mate who was most adept at rigging terminal tackle of all sorts.

"That young feller," said the ancient, "has a real talent for leader-ship."

The term is not a bad one, since there are those who seem to be able to select and rig leaders of all kinds with a knack lacking among us common mortals. Any angler, however, can improve his skill along these lines by analyzing just what he expects the leader to do in assisting him to catch a fish.

All leaders do not serve the same purpose by any means. A wire or twisted cable wire, for example, is used primarily to give added strength against a fish's teeth or abrasion, while light monofilament is selected primarily for its qualities of invisibility, light weight, and flexibility. Between these extremes are all sorts of variables which must be taken into account when making a choice.

When marine sport fishing was in its infancy, carbon steel wire —plain, galvanized, or tinned—was the standard leader material after twisted copper wire had been found to be a poor substitute. This type of single-strand metal was given the general name of "piano wire." It is no longer commonly found on the angling scene for one simple reason—it rusts out after comparatively little use.

However, piano wire is still one of the strongest materials for its diameter known: therefore, when visibility of the leader is a problem, particularly in big game fishing, and breaking strain is important as well, it is the choice of some offshore men. In the lighter gauges, carbon steel rates about 5 per cent stronger than its equivalent in stainless, but more than 20 per cent stronger when the 200 pound breaking test is reached.

With the advent of stainless steel, the rusting problem was cured and leaders from this material are most popular in the single-strand metal group today. Strength is measured by gauge, which ranges from number 2—.011 inches in diameter and a breaking test of about 27 pounds, to number 16—0.37 inches in diameter and a breaking test of about 320 pounds. Monel and similar alloys are more flexible than regular stainless steel, but rarely are used for leader material because of relatively large diameter per pound of test.

Advantages of stainless wire are many. It costs comparatively little so that a leader made from this steel may be discarded without much loss. Leaders can be cut in almost any length from a coil. Such coils are usually packaged in 25-foot lengths or may be purchased in 1000-foot spools. The wire can be twisted quickly around a hook or swivel and will stand a tremendous amount of abrasion from any source. Three or more twists should be finished off with the wire wrapped closely. Do not cut the end off after the wrapping process has been completed: break it off by working the loose end backward and forward. The wire will break close to the main part of the leader and will leave no sharp cutting edge.

Stiffness of single-strand wire is an advantage in some circumstances. For natural baits, in particular, often it is desirable to have the hook held rigidly in position so that it does not wobble or so that the bait does not flip back on itself when trolled. In using a strip bait, stainless may be bent into a handy safety-pin shape to hold the strip in place on the hook. It may also be used as a spreader to hold the hook away from the line when bottom-fishing.

This same stiffness produces one of the major disadvantages of all single-strand wire—kinking. Toss a loop into this material, pull it tight with a jerk—and it is then possible to snap even the strongest leader with only a few pounds of pressure. Billfish can wrap their snouts around a wire and do the job all too successfully. There is only one good solution to kinked wire problems—get rid of that particular piece of wire as rapidly as possible!

For those who must use wire because of the quarry they seek, manufacturers began to experiment with various types of twisted and braided metal made up of several strands of fine-diameter material. Early efforts left a good deal to be desired, even though the kinking bugaboo was overcome. Today, braided wire is a rarity, but excellent twisted wire of small diameter and high breaking strain is now on the market at prices only slightly higher than the single-strand. Most such cable is heat-treated to give it a bronze finish that cuts down visibility.

Because of improvements in manufacturing techniques and in the basic materials used, differences in leader diameter between cable and single-strand stainless are only approximately 10 per cent, with the cable the larger of the two. When dealing with thousandths of an inch, the average angler or fish will have difficulty telling one from the other as far as bulk is concerned. When flexibility is a primary consideration, therefore, cable is the choice.

Commercially prepared leaders made of this material often are soldered, for it is difficult to twist or wrap many strands so that they hold securely. The home workshop buff who wants to try his hand at this method should clean the area to be soldered with a 50 per cent solution of muriatic acid, then do the soldering. Pure zinc is more effective for such work than commercial solder, but no matter what is used, the whole process is a nuisance and cannot be done handily afloat or on the beach.

To overcome this disadvantage, the metal sleeve, crimped onto the leader in the desired place with specially designed tools, the prime weapon of which is an instrument that looks like a long-handled pliers, has been developed. The soft metal sleeves come in sizes to fit all types of cable wire. The important thing to remember when using the sleeves is that their inside diameter must be sufficient to accommodate two thicknesses of the leader used.

Because tiny, sharp ends of cable can cause severe cuts when boating a fish by grasping the leader, we always use sleeves that hold *three* thicknesses. First the sleeve is passed over the standing part of the cable. The end is then tucked through to form the required loop. Next we tuck the ragged end back into the sleeve and snug up the wire tightly. This results in no ragged end protruding after the sleeve is crimped into place.

Particularly in big game fishing, cable wire loops are often made by using a series of simple overhand knots around the standing part of the leader. This gives added strength at the hook eye while still permitting the hook to swing freely. One thing to remember when using such a knot—and we still forget it after many years—is that the sleeve or sleeves should be slid over the leader before making the loop.

Versatility of cable wire was improved even more when nylon

entered the fishing-tackle picture. By coating fine cable with this material, it was made possible to knot it in much the same manner as monofilament itself. This type of leader has many of the advantages of mono, yet still will withstand the teeth of such predators as barracuda and bluefish. Lightweight metal sleeves may be used to form loops if desired.

One difficulty when tying knots in nylon-covered cable is that a kink is apt to develop just in front of the knot when it is snugged up. This is particularly true when using the lighter tests. We have found that a simple figure-of-eight knot is the answer. There is no kinking, and we have yet to see such a connecting method pull out.

Monofilament nylon has become more and more popular as a leader material over the years, even in big game circles. The very heavy tests are crimped and care must be taken to have a sleeve sufficiently large so that the mono is not damaged when force is applied with the crimping pliers. The subject of knots to use on such leaders is a study in itself. Suffice it to say that mono tends to slip, so simple hitches or jam knots may pull out after much use. Touching the bitter end of the material with a lighted match or cigarette ember will help to prevent this, for the intense heat causes a little knob to form as the nylon melts.

A single strand of nylon obviously is the least visible of all leaders. Also, mono may be obtained in all variations of stiffness or limpness, in a wide variety of weights and colors, and even in tapered form for the fly fisherman. A short section on the end of a wire or cable leader is great insurance against bill-wrapping. Similarly, the surf caster prefers monofilament leaders on such inshore sluggers as channel bass and stripers. Wire, otherwise acceptable, tends to kink and spiral when a surf fish rolls and slaps as it is planed ashore on a wave. Mono is more pliable.

Only when it comes to excessive wear and tear from sharp objects does a monofilament leader fall down badly. Barnacles and oyster shells, a quick snap by a shark, a sudden taut contact with jagged rock, coral, or other similar underwater hazard will sever nylon in a matter of seconds.

In some cases this very quality may be put to good use. For example, a surf fisherman using bait may be plagued by sharks. If he selects wire or cable leaders, he may spend hours battling some toothed monster that he has no desire to catch. By using mono, the shark will soon cut through the nylon and escape with only the extreme terminal tackle sacrificed, and the angler can then return to his fishing for more gentle species.

So much for the materials from which leaders may be made.

Next comes one of the most common questions asked by newcomers to the ocean scene: How long should a leader be? Obviously much depends upon the methods of angling being used, and the circumstances.

Looking first at the offshore group, International Game Fish Association rules state that a leader must be no more than 30 feet long when using line over 50 pound test, and no more than 15 feet long when using line under that breaking strength. In actual practice, a 30 foot leader is a rarity. To bring a fish alongside with 30 feet of wire slicing through the air at a high rate of speed is not only difficult but dangerous. A general rule of thumb for any trolling in the big game classification is to select a leader that is a foot or two longer than the largest fish expected. Choice therefore depends upon the optimism of the angler!

When trolling for smaller game, many stick with the IGFA 15-foot limit. In our opinion, unless there are special conditions, such as exceptional clarity of water, a leader of this length is excessive. Again, as a general rule of thumb, we prefer a leader double the length of the largest fish anticipated. However, in trolling, it should not be less than three feet, even for the smallest of gamesters.

The obvious exception is when trolling or casting with monofilament under conditions where no leader of any sort may be needed. If the quarry does not have savage teeth and if obstructions are at a minimum, often the hook or lure may be tied directly to the line.

Casting presents different problems from those found in trolling. If, using stainless wire, it is impossible to connect it to the line in such a manner that it will pass freely through the rod guides, length is limited to whatever the caster can handle between the rod tip and the hook. If wire is required in greater length, due to particular conditions, nylon-covered cable will serve for longer leaders. This can be tied into the line fairly smoothly with a key loop knot so that the wire extends from the reel spool up through the guides and thus to the hook at the outset of the cast. (The key loop knot can be used to connect single-strand or standard cable too.)

When using nylon-covered cable for long leaders used in casting, check them frequently. Heat and friction caused by the cast may wear the covering off the cable, and the exposed metal will then file through a guide's ring in quick order—if the leader does not break first.

Shock lines of heavy monofilament have come into wide use both by those using spinning reels and those using free spool mills. Line may be spliced or tied into the leader material so that the connection actually is under a couple of turns around the reel spool itself. This means that the leader, serving a second purpose as a shock line, may be twice the length of the rod. Where such lengthy traces are used with a conventional surf casting outfit, an angler must learn to guide the connecting knot close to the spool's bell, so that—during the cast—he will not gouge a livid groove in his right thumb.

Fly fishermen fall into a special category. The leader used by any feather merchant serves two purposes: first, it disguises the connection between the lure and the comparatively heavy line; second, it must be of sufficient length, taper, and proper stiffness to cause the fly to flip out and over at the end of the cast. A heavy shock tippet, used when the quarry is large and has abrasive jaws, may be added, and in some cases there is need for a very short length of light wire to defeat toothy gamesters. There is no ideal, all-around length for a marine fly leader. Choice depends upon rod, line, ability of the caster—and the wariness of the fish sought. Probably 9 to 14 feet, from butt to tippet end, is near average.

Usually it is wise to utilize a short length of heavy mono as a butt for the leader itself. This short length is attached to the end of the fly line via a seized loop or a nail knot. The leader is then tied in via a blood knot. If a very short length of heavy mono—say 80 to 100 pounds test—is necessary to defeat big tarpon or billfish, this 12 inch hank should be attached with a Stu Apte improved blood knot. A key loop is best for a short wire tippet. For most marine fly casting, a relatively short monofilament leader, say 9 feet, is adequate, and there is little need to taper to an extremely fine tippet. With few exceptions, oceanic game fish exhibit no leader-shyness.

It should be noted, incidentally, that only in fly-fishing circles are leaders still designated by a system of numbers and letters—and even the number system, originally established for Spanish silkworm gut, is nearly extinct. Formerly, nylon that tested 15 pounds was designated as 0/5, when about 13 pounds as 2/5—and so on, until 9/5, or 5 pound test, was reached. Lesser breaking strain then shifted to X for 4.3 pounds, 1 X for 3.5 pounds, and so to 5 X for 1.25 pounds. The X tippets are still so designated, although rarely used in salt water, but most mono is simply classified by its diameter and breaking strain. For all practical purposes, forget the X tests on the sea front.

In selecting leaders, the most common error is to choose material that is heavier than required for the fish sought. Heavy leaders, no matter of what material, are more visible, tend to kill the action of the lure or bait, and present greater water resistance than those of smaller diameter. Except in the case of fly fishing, the connecting link between line and hook normally is of far greater strength than the line itself. Unless exceptional wear and tear on the leader is expected, it is foolish to carry too far this difference in breaking strain.

Leaders can be constructed right on the scene of action, but a majority of anglers either buy them ready made—or rig a sufficient number to insure adequacy on a trip. Traces of varying length, weight, and material usurp little space in a tackle box—and they're there when you need them. Obviously, if a leader becomes frayed, twisted, kinked, or worn in any way, a smart fisherman discards it. The scant amount of time, trouble, and cost to replace them pays off in fish landed.

9
GOOD CONNECTIONS

WHOEVER FIRST PROPOUNDED THE IMMUTABLE LAW THAT A chain's strength depends on its weakest link must have been an angler who had just lost a big fish because of knot failure—either a clean break, or that little terminal curl which tells its own sad story.

Although hardly germane to this subject, we produce one classic bend with the greatest of ease; it is a wind loop cleverly whipped into a leader tippet while fly casting. Sometimes we are even able to create a fancy figure-eight. Both are easily and swiftly accomplished, although never purposely; they look like bona fide knots—and they promptly decrease a leader's pound test by something like 50 per cent.

That's the trouble with knots. Some of the easiest to tie are also easiest to break. If you happen to be excited and therefore all thumbs, it is quite human to err and to come up with a gold-plated failure. Inept fastenings lose as many fish as tight drags. Effective knots mark the skilled sport fisherman, while poor fastenings insure tales of the one that got away.

No black magic is involved in the creation of efficient knots. Indeed, while hundreds of intricate connections have been devised, a mere handful suffice for 90 per cent of marine angling. It is well to note that all knots are compromises: the trick lies in selecting that which is best suited to a particular requirement.

Quite as important is the exercise of care in tying a knot. It is hardly enough to insure that turns are correct by the numbers, for if these turns are not snugged up smoothly they may ride over one another and defeat the very purpose of the connection by stretching or cutting. Tie each knot slowly, and pay close attention to detail.

Probably the most important of all knots used by light-tackle anglers is the improved clinch. This one is preferred for connecting a monofilament line to a swivel, or to the lure itself. Properly tied, this fastening boasts nearly 100 per cent of the line's pound test.

The trick, here, is to make at least five turns around the standing line. Knot strength diminishes in exact ratio to the decrease of turns, up to that point. Skimp, and you cheat yourself.

Having made the required five turns, bring the bitter end of the line or leader back through the big loop as illustrated. Finally, snug the knot tight—but do not challenge the line's rated test in tightening. This is no major problem when relatively heavy mono is used, but stretching can weaken lighter strands. Snug it up, but don't play Tarzan.

This five-turn rule remains important when tying the improved blood knot, an excellent connection for lines or leaders of equal or slightly varying diameters. In tying, lap the ends of the strands, allowing adequate length for wraps. Spiral one end around the standing line of the other, *at least five turns*, and then bend the bitter end back over the wraps. Place this end between the strands, and pinch it in place with your fingers as the second strand is wrapped and returned in the same manner.

An improved blood knot should be snugged up smoothly and carefully. Some anglers like to moisten the coils with saliva as they are drawn tight. This provides lubrication which may aid in the construction of a perfect knot—and is a good tip in making any light-tackle connection. Clip ends flush, and the knot is completed.

When lines and leaders of considerably unequal diameters are to be joined, the Stu Apte improved blood knot is called for. In this case the line boasting smaller diameter is doubled to increase its bulk. The knot is similar to its predecessor, the improved blood knot, but is more difficult to tie. It is usually necessary to use one's fingernails to push the loops together as the fastening is snugged up.

Some knots masquerade under various aliases. The key loop knot, for example, is also known as the line-to-leader and the Albright special. It is effective in joining line to leader, or line to wire, with the connection insured by jamming rather than twisting and knotting. Like the Stu Apte improved blood knot, this connection is valuable when two lines of considerably different size or type are joined. Completed, it is small, neat, and strong—but does not rate as high in strength as the Stu Apte improved blood knot or the standard blood knot.

In fashioning an improved end loop, one of two chosen by anglers when a loop is desired at the very end of a line, the bitter end is doubled and the five-turn rule applied.

Initially, form a double strand, allowing enough length for the five wraps mentioned. Spiral the double end over the standing line, and bring it back through the terminal loop. Snug up smoothly, and clip trailing ends. Properly constructed, this knot should insure 90 to 95 percent of line test strength.

Because the perfection loop, favored by many anglers, does not incorporate five or more turns around the standing line, it tests out at only 70 to 80 percent of line test. Nonetheless, this fastening is popular, and is illustrated here. It is a neat, easily tied connection, but hardly adequate where extremely light end tackle is used.

Wherever a dropper must be incorporated into line or leader, the angler had best rely on an easily tied dropper loop knot. To execute this one, make a multiple overhand twist at the point desired; grasp the center of the large loop, as shown, and thrust it through the center of the twists. Use a finger or a pencil to keep this loop from pulling out, and then draw the wraps up tight.

Note that the size of the large loop will dictate the size and length of the dropper. Often in bottom-fishing, where stiff monofilament is used to keep a baited hook from tangling with the standing line or leader, this dropper may extend four to six inches at right angles to the leader.

Most important to a fly caster, but valuable whenever one of two lines to be joined is fabricated of a softer material than the other, is the nail knot. This, again, is a jamming devise which, properly snugged up, is highly efficient. The nail knot is generally used to fasten a monofilament leader butt to the terminal end of a fly line, but it may also be used to attach backing to such a line.

Called the "nail knot" because it is more easily constructed with the aid of a tapering steel shaft, such as an ordinary nail, than without any tool, the connection's efficiency depends on five or more turns, followed by painstaking care in snugging up the wraps. The nail is slowly withdrawn as turns are tightened, thus preventing one wrap from riding over another. Upon completion, ends of mono and fly line are snipped off to insure a small, streamlined connection.

Marine fly-rodders are divided in their affections for the nail knot and the spliced loop as a connection. Even the writers of this book disagree. Lyman relies on spliced loops, while Woolner prefers nail knots.

The spliced loop takes more time to tie, and some say that it offers more resistance than a nail knot in sliding through the guides. It is a strong, workmanlike and stable connection. Moreover, it facilitates rapid changes in leaders or backing. To create this loop you remove the enamel coating at two spots on the end of a fly line, as shown; wrap the fibers to connect a loop, and complete by winding with fine silk or nylon thread which is then coated with spar varnish. Liquid rubber can be employed as a final coating—and is also used over the nail knot to ease passage through the guides.

On the offshore grounds a host of rather complicated knots are used. One of the easiest to tie, and also one of the most efficient, is the Bimini twist, also called the Bimini roll—and also called the 100 percent knot. In practice, two men usually combine to tie this one, although a single angler can turn the trick easily if he uses some sort of post to hold the initial loop.

The line is wrapped or spiraled at least 20 times, and then snugged up to the head of the loop, so that twists are neatly aligned, but not crossed. The bitter end is then half-hitched around first one side, and then the other side of the loop—and is finally half-hitched around the entire base of the loop. The resulting connection is stable and neat, surprisingly tough and much used by offshore anglers.

Sometimes basic fishing calls for specialized knots. It is quite possible to tie a single hook to a monofilament line or leader with the improved clinch which is so popular among light tackle anglers, but other connections have proved more effective in certain cases. Two of these are the return knot and the quick snell. They are roughly similar, but the first named is more efficient when extremely light monofilament is used.

In the return knot there are just two bends, with the line jammed securely. The connection is small and neat. Be sure that loops are pressed back over the eye of the hook in tying.

The quick snell lends itself to lines or leaders over, say, 10 pound test. Thread mono through the hook's eye and wrap it around the shank five times (that magic five again!) before bringing the bitter end back to pass between the mono and the hook's shank next to the eye. Draw up slowly, tighten, and you have an instant snell. Clip the end of the leader within one-eighth inch of the hook eye and you will fashion a bait-holder.

Advanced anglers pride themselves on knowledge of a variety of knots, many of which are intricate and difficult to tie. Knots and splices are a science in themselves and we recommend that the serious fisherman investigate each new departure and every time-tested fastening. Those described here are basic and dual-purpose; most of them are applicable where single-strand monofilament or braided lines are used. They are the connections we cannot do without.

Until that happy day when advanced technology makes it possible to fuse line and leader, or leader and lure, with the flick of an electronic gadget, we are going to need knots. We'd better learn how to tie them.

10

THE BUCKTAIL JIG

IF SOME IRASCIBLE SEA GOD HAD THE ABILITY—AND THE WHIM—to limit each angler to a single lure, which would you choose? We'd have to vote for a simple killer which is variously called a bugeye, doodlebug, bullhead, or bucktail.

No other artificial lure is so deserving of praise; none is so deadly on so many different sport and game fish. Yet, for some unfathomable reason, a majority of salt water anglers believe that the bucktail is specialized and limited in the scope of its effectiveness. Few recognize the lure's tremendous versatility.

Bucktail fanciers smile at this education gap and enjoy a measure of unholy glee when some newspaper or magazine prints a picture of a jig with the hook riding *down*. This particular lure happens to count among its blessings the fact that it proceeds through the water with hook point up.

If this were the jig's sole virtue, we would not discuss it here, for many fine artificials *do* swim barb down, occasionally snag bottom—and catch lots of game fish.

Gentlemen who manufacture nylon or feather-dressed lead-headed lures may object to the generic word "bucktail." We use it, because the word seems to have become part of the nautical language. A great many anglers of our acquaintance go so far as to discourse on "feather bucktails," or "nylon bucktails." Some are brave enough to mention "rubber worm bucktails." So be it.

More important than a name is the fact that this simple, indeed ancient, lure is one that the salt water angler can't do without. Bucktails are potent throughout the world and they will take a vast number of game species under a variety of fishing conditions.

The lead-headed jig is manufactured in a bewildering assortment of shapes, weights, and sizes. Most popular are the bullet-headed and the lima bean types, but there is definite need for such variations as the horizontally flattened shallow water jig, and for keeled types that go deep in heavy currents.

Similarly, no single dressing is all-purpose. Natural bucktail (deer tail) features breathing action in the water, and it tapers to a fine point. Feathers guarantee a slithery, come-hither motion when the lure is retrieved. Nylon fibers glisten and, depending on the way they are attached to the jig, offer varying degrees of action in the water.

You will find that certain game fish, when they are selective, generally hit one of the three basic dressings—yet there are days when marabou (an extremely soft and fluffy feather), Mylar strips, soft plastic skirts, worms, or other "rubber" dressings lead the hit parade.

So far as durability is concerned, nylon fiber takes all honors. The synthetic material is tough and its shine is a definite asset. Most nylon-dressed lures appear unnatural to the angler because the dressing is squared or cut to equal length. There's no taper from head to tail. (Whether this also appears unnatural to game fish is a moot point. Certainly the blocky jigs catch fish, and the latest nylon bucktails—with tapering fibers—seem no more effective.)

Bucktail and feathers can be tied so that they taper nicely in the water. Both possess fine breathing action. Major handicap is the destructibility of the natural dressing. Sharp-toothed game fish soon shred deer hair and the various feathers.

Among other dressings of particular note are: marabou, polar bear hair, Mylar, and a new cornucopia of rubber or soft plastic eel tails, worms, and skirts.

Marabou, originally harvested from an African stork, but often surreptitiously plucked from a white domestic turkey, is so remarkably flexible that the slightest water motion gives it writhing action. Its major fault is its delicacy. Even soft-mouthed fish will soon tear all the marabou dressing off a jig. In salt water the material is most often used on bonefish skimmers.

Polar bear hair is more durable than bucktail and it boasts a fine luster. Natural polar bear hair is creamy to light yellow in color, rarely pure white, and the stuff is expensive.

Mylar, one of the space-age developments, is a plastic film coated with metal. It is very durable and is generally used in fine strips which are mixed in with other types of dressing. Bucktails dressed entirely with Mylar have been effective, particularly in deep jigging.

Rubber and soft plastic fibers, often prepared as "skirts" for lures, may be very effective. Some of them tend to dry out and stiffen after a period in the tackle box, and it is never wise to store such plastic products with hard or painted lures. The chemicals in the plastics leach out and will act like paint remover.

Very recently "rubber worm bucktails" have conquered the seaboard. Here, a soft plastic worm or eel tail is employed instead of the usual hair or feather dressing. Success of the artificial is such that it has become a standard.

While several tackle manufacturers produce a variety of jig types, these are not always available along the entire seaboard. Freight charges on baits that are predominantly lead discourage wide distribution. Therefore many of the better artificials are locally molded, and anglers often make their own.

In all fairness, it should be stated that several manufacturers have produced jigs so successful that they are in demand everywhere. Needless to say, these models are also copied everywhere.

Since bucktails are effective in shallow or deep water, with or without current, when cast, trolled or jigged—and on night or day tides—it follows that variations in size, weight, type, and color are necessary.

Ultra-light spinning tackle is ideally chosen for the tiny ⅛ to ¼ ounce jigs. These, together with slightly heavier bucktails, up to perhaps one-half ounce, are popular on tropical bonefish flats.

At the other extreme, anglers who jig for huge cod, groupers, amberjack, or similar deep-feeding brutes want bucktails in the 3 to 4 ounce class—or heavier. Actually, anything bulkier than 3 ounces is difficult to find in the average sporting goods shop. These heavyweights are featured by dealers close to the fishing grounds, such as in Miami, Florida, where a surprising number of enthusiasts jig the deep reefs for a multitude of great gamesters.

Skimmer types, those which are horizontally flattened to resist the force of gravity, are best suited to extremely shallow water. Bullet-headed and keeled types plummet into the depths. The lima bean shape offers a maximum of action when retrieved.

On a coastal basis, all-white or all-yellow bucktails probably outnumber the sum total of those painted and dressed in other colors. However, there is a need for jigs of many hues. Red and white is often deadly. Blue and white sometimes hits the jackpot. We've seen pink jigs deadly on occasion, and have seen days when brown, black, or combinations of brown and white, or black and white were killers.

Bucktails can be effective just as they come from the maker; however, anglers often feel that the lure is too heavily dressed, or that it is incomplete without the addition of a pork rind strip or a piece of squid—the latter most often used in trolling.

Skipping sweeteners for the moment, it is true that a majority of factory-made jigs are too heavily dressed, and that some are improved by snipping away a third of the hair or feathers. Those who manufacture bucktails are aware of this failing, but they are also aware of the fact that beginners buy a lion's share of their production—and the beginner thinks he is being short-changed if his lure is not very heavily dressed. Therefore—a lure to catch fish, but also a lure to catch fishermen!

Pork rinds—and they are available in several colors—are attached to the hook, so that they stream naturally. Besides lifelike action of the rind, this trailer adds length to the lure. You create an artificial that *looks* like a big bait but is light enough to cast with sporting tackle.

When fish get persnickety and scorn the pork rind casually attached to the barb, try anchoring it higher on the hook shank, so that it will stream more naturally from the very center of the dressing. To do this, first thread the rind on to the hook shank, and then employ a small rubber band to act as a buffer on the shank *below* the pork strip.

Trailer hooks and pork rind with small hooks attached are used to foil short-strikers. In the former, simply attach an additional hook to that which is built into the jig, eye to barb. The trailer-hook pork rind is packaged ready to use and is favored in many areas.

While such a strip often proves effective, it seems to us that the addition of trailing hooks slows rind action and may sometimes diminish the fish-taking capability of the bait. Trailer-hooked rigs tend to foul on the cast; they pick up more sea lettuce and grass than the single-hooked lure, and they can be a nuisance.

Trollers often swear by a strip of squid on a bucktail's hook, and light-tackle addicts who cast for a variety of small game in the tropics are similarly convinced that a bit of fresh shrimp will sweeten the lure just enough to draw strikes from cautious feeders. Undoubtedly the squid strip boasts some action, and the niblet of shrimp provides taste and scent.

Day or night, bucktails trolled behind large and small boats catch fish. Used with high-riding lines of nylon monofilament or braid, the lead-headed lures tempt speedy, near-surface predators.

Bumped along the bottom, they'll snatch the deep-feeders. Worked at intermediate depths with wire line, another group of game species falls like tenpins.

The angler who trolls a bucktail at constant speed, without rod action, will catch *some* game fish—but the man who "fishes" the jig will always account for more trophies. Occasionally it is sufficient to drag a bucktail through the edges of a feeding school of stripers, blues, or mackerel to insure strikes. However, jigging the lures so that they dart, dive, and flutter through the water is the most productive technique.

Veterans on the offshore grounds can jig a trolled bait for hours, yet remain as fresh as the proverbial daisy. The beginner often finds this hard work, until he learns the easy rhythm that keeps a bucktail darting and diving in the wake.

You can jig from a fighting chair, simply by raising and lowering the rod tip at regular intervals. Better still, stand at the rail, point your rod tip toward the water, and then find the pace and rhythm best suited to you—and to the fish.

Bucktails are effective lures for deep-jigging, a technique that will interest a surprising number of sport and game fish. Here, the trick is to permit the lure to plummet rapidly into the depths, so that no appreciable belly of line streams in the current, and then keep the tempter darting and twisting just above the bottom.

Usually, it is wise to employ the heaviest practical lure. Drop it all the way to the bottom; then retrieve a few turns of line until the bait is suspended just over the ground, and proceed to jig. In the Northeast, cod, pollock, bluefish—even tautog—will grab a deep-jigged bucktail. Pacific lingcod and rockfish are quite as eager, and the tropical enthusiast will find a whole host of game fish, from groupers to amberjack and various mackerels, on the prod.

Often the deep-jigging expert will locate the feeding level of game fish by dropping his lure all the way to the bottom, and then retrieving it in a series of jigs. The method is particularly effective on bluefish and pollock when they are rushing bait at intermediate depths. As the lure comes by, on its way to the surface, they latch on.

Surf casters, bait casters, and spin-fishermen all make use of the bucktail. They do so on all American coasts and to tempt most of the nation's game species. When the first spring thaw hits the New England states, casters find that cod have moved inshore—and will gobble a bucktail worked slowly over a sand or clay bottom.

At the same time—and throughout the year—Florida's light-tackle addicts bag a grand roster of battlers on jigs worked close to the surface. The lead-headed tempter is a cosmopolitan favorite, and for good reason.

Tropical anglers often use the "Florida whip" in retrieving a bucktail lure. Sports who seek game fish in other areas may not call it the Florida whip, but their angling technique is similar. Basically, the "whip" is a fast, snapping retrieve. The lure is brought along at high speed and is regularly bounced forward by periodic whipping of the rod. Depending on the species sought and on the temperature of the water, experts increase or decrease the speed of retrieve.

Generally, predators will rush a fast-moving bait. Even the seatrout, or southern spotted weakfish, can be goaded into walloping a rapidly darting and diving bucktail. Snook, tarpon, redfish, bluefish, and a host of other trophy gamesters go for this plebeian hunk of lead and hair.

If fast-moving surface fighters aren't present, or if they happen to be bottom-grubbing, it often pays to work a bucktail right down on the coral or eel grass. Pompano want tiny jigs that hop along, leaving puffs of sand behind them. Snook find it hard to resist the slowly worked jig, and bottom bouncing often succeeds with northern stripers.

Where gamesters are lying in a tidal current, waiting for food to be swept down to them, try casting up and across the flow, making the retrieve prescribe a long arc. This is standard practice among northern striped bass fishermen on both coasts, and it works on many other game species. Always vary speeds to suit the occasion and the species sought. At night, with few exceptions, retrieves should be slowed to a minimum.

Bucktails lend themselves to the creation of several combination lures. For trolling, a swimming plug and a jig—the jig ahead and the plug astern, with separate leaders attached to a three-way swivel—often load fish boxes. Anglers in some areas, notably in the Chesapeake Bay area, have always scored with "Christmas tree" spreaders which employ three, four, or more jigs. (This is the original of the famed "umbrella" and coathanger rigs that have become so popular among northern deep trollers in recent years. The umbrella and coathanger, however, usually employ tube lures instead of bucktails.)

Then there's the bucktail and surface splasher combination that so often has proved itself on seatrout, pollock, redfish, and striped bass. An outgrowth of the old southern popping cork and shrimp rig, this one makes use of a hardwood dowel as a casting weight and splasher, with a small bucktail streamed behind it. The commotion draws gamesters, and the bucktail takes them.

A few anglers prefer to use an armed plug in lieu of the hookless splasher. They remove the terminal barb on the plug, and thus have a dual-purpose combination. Doubles are not uncommon, but the fully armed rig is difficult to cast without fouling.

Bucktails require a good deal of maintenance, for paint tends to chip, and feathers, bucktail, or nylon tends to soak up every particle of rust. Kept clean and dry—try to do it when fishing is fast—the lures will last for years. Worked hard and neglected, they require periodic repair.

Don't worry about the glass eyes that get knocked out of lead-headed beauties: usually these are more important to the fisherman than to the fish. *Do* touch up paint finishes, and *do* replace dressing that has become ragged or stained.

First, remove the old bucktail, feathers, nylon or what-have-you with a sharp knife. Dip the lead head in the paint of your chosen color. Lacquer will do, but the new epoxy paints take a greater amount of punishment in stride.

Length and amount of dressing used is a matter of preference. We prefer sparse dressing, but admit that fish sometimes go for the fluffy jig. At any rate, nylon rod winding thread makes a good fastener for the dressing. Use a whip finish to hold the fastening securely, and then anoint the winding with a fast-drying waterproof cement.

Since the rebuilding of bucktail jigs is a chore at best, we postpone the evil day by drying jigs as rapidly as possibile after each day on the coast. Every now and then, of course, a bucket of brine sloshes into our small boat—and finds its unerring way to an open tackle box full of large and small bucktail jigs!

When that happens, we choke down high blood pressure and see that every lure is washed in fresh water and dried before the salt has a chance to produce rust. Delay this maintenance for as little as 24 hours, and you'll delight the tackle manufacturers by replacing an entire boxful of jigs!

11

PLUGS AND SQUIDS

DURING A CERTAIN SLICE OF TIME BETWEEN THE GAY NINETIES AND World War II a host of surf casters along the North Atlantic coast became self-appointed purists. They scorned natural bait and used a series of metal lures which were known as block tin squids.

This trend was so very pronounced that a man who employed metal soon earned the title of "squidder," and he considered himself a cut above contemporaries, just as the early day fly angler looked down on inland water companions who tempted trout with worms or hardware.

Immediately after World War II, thousands of fresh water anglers descended upon the sea, and those who had cut their milk teeth on inland black bass were entranced with the possibilities of the wooden plug. Within a matter of years, these new messiahs were patronizing the traditional squidder and maintaining that the only sporting way to take a fish was—via a plug!

Purists are rather ridiculous people: they may attain a high degree of skill in the use of that artificial which they deem solely acceptable, yet these specialists cannot compete on even terms with anglers who have mastered all the various techniques. Fortunately, purism is a vanishing sophistry, conquered by intelligence.

Of course this does not mean that any advanced angler must favor all angling methods equally. Some still prefer the clean, accurate presentation of a metal jig. Others would rather take one game fish on a surface plug than a host of scrappers on deep-fished lures. A majority uses each tempter where it is best employed. In any event, the squid came first.

Initially, the drail: it was a plebeian lump of shiny metal, roughly fish-shaped so that it would wobble as it was dragged shoreward. The old heave-and-haul handliners whirled this creation about their heads and sent it far out over the waves. Then, hand over hand, they dragged it shoreward—and caught many a game fish in so doing.

The squidder was a new breed, for he used rod and line—usually the Calcutta cane or custom split bamboo mounting a reel filled with twisted linen Cuttyhunk line. Since it became possible to cast a lure close to 100 yards, and to retrieve the tempter at speeds exceeding those managed by the handliner, new jigs were designed. Some of the early squids were classics, and they remain effective to this day.

Initially, all were called "block tin," because the metal lures of those days were cast from that reasonably malleable, glowing metal. Even today, we wonder whether there is not something very important in the gleam of tin. With the exception of custom jigs, it is long gone. If you do not make your own, forget it—for pure tin is expensive, far beyond the budgets of manufacturers who must produce lures at minimum cost.

In the heyday of the squidder, lures in dozens of shapes were important. There was the Ferron Jig, a high-riding beauty with a swinging hook; the bent sand eel in a variety of conformations; the wobbling spoon, the keeled jig, the diamond. All accomplished great slaughter—and their descendants are quite as effective. Often an old design, such as the Johnston Jig with its deep keel and free-swinging hook, makes modern lures hunt cover. There is ample room for all of the various types, and they'll come back as the years wheel.

Curiously, squidding declined in the 60's, and a very few metal jig types began to monopolize the waterfront. Chief among these was the elongated, knife-handle wobbler best exemplified by the Hopkins Jig. Acme's Kastmaster, a carbon copy of the old Eda Splune, came on strong. (We have hand-tooled facsimiles of this lure from South Africa and Australia.) Diamond jigs have remained important, and there are hosts of keeled jigs which serve as casting lures and deep-down offerings. Heavy casting spoons, patterned after Eppinger's famed Dardevle, are deadly. All of the many patterns continue to catch fish.

A metal squid—and it is difficult to separate a squid from a casting spoon—is a basic lure, usually relying on action and flash to tempt a strike. Many feature hooks dressed with feathers, hair, or synthetic materials, and some may be enhanced by adding pork rind as a sweetener. They are generally easy to cast and to manipulate. They will take almost any game fish that swims in the ocean, hence they should never be considered a surfman's tool alone.

The classic surf caster developed a definite technique with his tin squid. He cast it far over the breakers, but never haphazardly. The cast was made so that the squid knifed in just behind a curling wave—so that it would swim in the relatively calm water behind the white turbulence. Retrieve was initiated immediately—and this is quite as important where such a lure is used in tempting snook or other game fish in mangrove-bordered tropical waters. You drop it in and move it rapidly, for the tin squid simulates a frightened bait fish.

Sometimes, when game fish are feeding on or close to bottom, it is necessary to pause after the cast, to allow the squid to plummet into the depths. Then a slower, interrupted retrieve may pay off in strikes. An angler must second-guess his quarry and provide the action most nearly simulating that of forage species.

Almost always, the squid is a daytime lure: it is a flasher, resembling fleeing or wounded bait. There are exceptions, but these usually incorporate such additions as eelskins attached to the metal wobblers' extremities. Eelskin-squids can be very effective on night-feeding gamesters, and in this case the retrieve is slowed to a minimum. The squid becomes no more than a wobble plate and a casting weight for the attached eelskin.

Soft plastic eel tails may be used instead of the real McCoy, and these often prove effective. Such lures become small brothers of the soft plastic "rigged eel," best represented by the Alou Eel which, in turn, is an artificial copy of the old fresh eel and "whistle" combination. For those who came in late, the original "whistle" was a short length of copper plumber's tubing, shaped to impart action to an attached eel.

Plugs may be more versatile than all-metal and combination lures, if only because they are effective at all hours of the day and night. This is an American invention, generally credited to James Heddon, whose descendants still manage the firm he founded, but Heddon simply modernized a lure used by the Indians. Long before white men arrived on this continent, natives employed carrot-shaped lengths of pine or spruce, stained with vegetable dyes, to catch fish.

Without any doubt, the plug moved into salt water by a circuitous route, first employed by inland black bass fishermen and then essayed on snook, tarpon, seatrout, and a host of other semitropical gamesters in the tidewater of the deep South. As late as the beginning of World War II, plugs were curiosities on the striped bass fishing grounds of the Northeast. One of the first to succeed on famed Cape Cod Canal in Massachusetts was a musky-sized version of Creek Chub's Pikie Minnow. Surf casters used the lure as a surface splasher by the simple expedient of bending its wobble plate straight down. They called it the "blue plug," and it was a resounding success until new lures appeared late in the war years. In all fairness, Creek Chub's original Pikie Minnow remains one of the world's great marine fishing lures.

There are something like seven basic plug designs in existence; the rest are variations. Academic anglers and lure manufacturers may argue this evaluation, trumpeting the fact that hundreds of individual baits are marketed. They're right, but a careful check will show that all fall into certain types. The fact that each variation offers some special nuance of action does not place it apart. Add to the following general types, if you can.

1. *Surface swimmers.* These are lures which work right on or in the surface film and sometimes travel an inch or so below. They include a whole host of plugs fitted with wobble plates and designed to simulate wounded bait.

2. *Subsurface swimmers* are plugs designed to swim below the surface film. Depending on weight distribution and engineering, they may wriggle at levels anywhere from a foot or two to considerable depths below the surface.

3. *Darters* differ from subsurface swimmers only in erratic action. There are many variations.

4. *Poppers.* The family includes such standards as the ancient "broomstick" with its many modern look-alikes, the hollow-headed and cup-faced types. All splash or pop on the surface. Some, like the fine little Gibbs Pencil Popper, dart with inspired rod action.

5. *Surface commotion plugs* differ from the poppers in that they rely on propellers, fore and aft, or spoons (flap-tails) to stir up a rumpus.

6. *Surface sliders* stir little commotion other than that imparted by rod action. They are streamlined lures, without wobble plates, spinners, or other attention-getters. Examples are the Heddon Spook and the Pflueger Ballerina. Bob Pond's famed Reverse Atom, to date popular only in New England, is another example.

7. *Torpedo plugs,* like the surface sliders, must be given rod action to succeed. They are generally cigar-shaped, sometimes slab-sided, and are produced in floating, neutral buoyancy and sinking versions. The standard L&S Mirrolure is a highly successful example.

Nit-pickers may question the exclusion of such magnificent plugs as the Helin Flatfish and the Rapala or Rebel Finnish minnow types as representatives of separate categories. These are subsurface swimmers, tremendously successful variations—but variations nonetheless. Each of the basic categories boasts dozens of offshoots that have succeeded, and will succeed in the future.

Plugs are used to tempt a multitude of salt water game fish at all hours of the day and night, hence any discussion of proper use must be qualified. The tactics which trigger strikes from one species may fail with another. Similarly, there is a place for all the many sizes of lures, a fact that brings joy to the hearts of manufacturers. Bearing in mind the injunction that there are exceptions, the following is generally true.

All the various plugs catch fish by day, and many serve during the night hours. While there are notable exceptions, anglers usually feel that the poppers, surface commotion, and slider types best lend themselves to a rapid retrieve under the sun. That they will catch fish at night has been amply demonstrated, yet few expect them to fare as well as the other types between sunset and dawn.

Surface and subsurface swimmers, darters, and torpedo plugs are far better producers at night. Since the lures in these categories also tempt fish during daylight, they might well be regarded as all-purpose. Unfortunately for those with tidy, mathematical minds, the popper, surface commotion, and slider types can be most exciting lures when gamesters are inclined to take them. The average plugger counts no thrill so great as that moment when a pugnacious game fish explodes behind a surface popper, finally engulfing it in a bomb burst of flying spray.

Speed of retrieve depends on many factors, but primarily on the desires of the fish sought. Usually, but not always, a popper or surface-commotion lure is worked rapidly. Pop-and-reel becomes almost one word, and poppers used on such speed demons as the jack crevalle simply cannot be retrieved too rapidly. There are occasions where action should be slowed to a tantalizing pop and halt, followed by a slow crawl forward—terminated by another pop. For best results there is no better admonition than "Make it look alive!"

Swimmers, darters, and torpedo plugs seldom are worked as rapidly as the poppers, and retrieve must be tailored to the temper of particular game species. Almost always—again note our reluctance to be dogmatic—a plug's action must be slowed during the night hours: indeed, at times it pays to retrieve so slowly that the bait practically dreams alone. Many a great nighttime gamester has been hooked on a plug held almost stationary in the current. If occasionally challenged, it's a good rule of thumb to speed retrieve during the day and slow down at night.

Color schemes are very important, for a great many game fish seem to be highly selective in this regard. Even at night, there is evidence that warriors like the striped bass can differentiate between hues. If colleagues are scoring with a blue mullet finish, while your squid-red facsimile is doing nothing, better change. Curiously, specific finishes seem to enjoy success during short periods. Then, one tide later, the infuriating fish decide to switch their allegiance to another hue. Be prepared for this. Accept the fact that another color, or another size of any given plug may turn failure into success. It pays to experiment, and any plugger should be a thoroughgoing opportunist.

One of our universal failings, as anglers, is the fond belief that a swimming or darting plug need only be cast out there and reeled in. It stands to reason that built-in action is enough to tempt game fish—and we can only tell you that such reason is erroneous. Any lure, regardless of its design, must be worked to insure best results. Varying speeds of retrieve, pauses, sudden jerks which impart frantic action—all contribute to the effectiveness of a plug.

There are, in addition, tricks employed by the regulars on every seaboard. There is the addition of bucktail-dressed tail hooks, or weight via strip-lead wound around the hooks. There is the little matter of bending the pull-wire up or down to control the diving characteristics of the plug. Bend the pull-wire up and the plug will dive at a steeper angle: bend it down, and the lure will be more inclined to work on the surface. The angle of wobble plate entry can be changed, and the plug's action will be changed thereby.

All these minor alterations affect a lure's action, hence they must be taken into consideration. The mere addition of a bucktail-dressed hook will slow the wriggling action of a plug, and weight—unless it is placed right at the balance—will do the same. Sometimes a slowed action is favored when the bait is cast into strong tidal currents or rips. Well-educated anglers calculate such changes, and they catch more fish as a result. Duffers, seeking alibis, regard the regulars' success as luck.

Never hold your breath while you wait for Lady Luck to smile!

12

FLY IN THE SALT

IN VIEW OF THE FACT THAT ANGLERS HAVE BEEN USING LONG wands on marine waters for a couple of centuries, the present scarcity of traditional fly patterns is downright astonishing. By comparison with the bewildering multitudes of tempters designed for inland trout and Atlantic salmon angling, the oceanic list of accepted flies is a poverty area.

There is a better than fair chance that salt water sportsmen will contribute a great deal to this field during the 70's. Indeed, more innovations in marine fly design came out of the 1960's than were posted during a preceding century. Of course this surge of interest was created by a boom in marine fly casting—a boom that shows no immediate symptom of decline.

However, the very nature of marine fly casting may war against "pattern" as defined by inland purists. So far, instead of the precise matching and marrying of colors and dressings, the oceanic trend is toward type and design. There are exceptions to this rule, but they are very few.

Now, before you pause to write poison-pen letters, we freely acknowledge the existence of salt water flies tied to resemble specific bait species. There is, for example, the Pink Shrimp, undoubtedly approaching pattern. Hair and hackle have been combined to produce a host of pseudo-shrimp in various color schemes and sizes. They're effective, but when you come right down to it, they're types. The same designation applies to streamer flies tied to simulate specific baitfish: they're abundant, yet very few have achieved the status of pattern. Unlike inland classics, there is little insistence upon specific dressings.

Very likely we labor a point that should be obvious. Exact pattern may be unnecessary on salt water, because the marine game fish has less chance to examine a particular tidbit prior to striking. Therefore general color, size, action, and basic construction may be far more important than the precise marrying of exotic fur, feathers, tinsel, and hair. The recipe, in other words, is far removed from that used to concoct an inland tempter.

This is logical, if only because marine fishes generally feed on smaller fishes, crustaceans, and assorted sea creatures that bear little resemblance to the insects so avidly sought by inland gamesters. We suggest that the angler who is steeped in fresh water fly casting tradition errs when he seeks to impose this tradition upon salt water fly development.

Certainly there is little need for the dry fly in marine angling. Just as surely, some coastal anglers have taken oceanic fishes on dry flies—and there may be isolated cases where such artificials would pay off. Generally, though, the floating bug is most effective on the briny, and one should note that the salt water bug is a definite type.

Wet flies are not so decidedly alien, although those tied to resemble dead insects or nymphs are better presented in a trout or salmon stream than on the bounding main. Note that the inland classicist does not consider streamer patterns and shrimp imitations as true wet flies.

That leaves streamer flies and floating bugs. The two are superior salt water lures, and it is here that the innovators have progressed with type, if not with exact pattern. Let's examine the semantics of the thing.

You may, if you so desire, call the Brooks Blonde series pattern. They are bucktail streamer types, with hair tied fore and aft. This insures a longer fly and possibly one with more seductive action than the basic bucktail streamer. The true Blonde is tied with tinsel between two hanks of bucktail, although some prefer to use a body of chenille.

We hold that the very designation, "series," argues against definite pattern in the inland sense. There are a variety of colors, ranging from the pure white Platinum Blonde to yellow, black, red, and simple combinations. All are fine streamers for general salt water use. Perhaps each should be considered pattern, but only if tinsel, bucktail, and color scheme are maintained with accuracy.

Fact of the matter is that inventive marine anglers have paid little attention to precise color schemes and dressing. The Blonde often appears with chenille body, with imaginative combinations of colors, with polar bear, goat hair, or rooster hackle instead of the original bucktail. Nowadays, the avant garde fisherman often insists upon Mylar strips added to the basic dressing.

Type, again, is more important than exact pattern in the reversed-hackle breather fly which enjoyed great popularity in the tropics some years ago but which is now just another attractor in the kit of a feather merchant. This is a good type, incidentally, one that should retain its persuasive powers for many years.

We will always have with us the basic salt water streamer fly, which is constructed of feathers, hair, or synthetic strands and is, simply, a baitfish-sized attractor. The literature indicates a few classic patterns, such as the Gibbs Striper and Palmer-Diller, Bonbright, Bead Head, and Candlefish. Even here, dressings are vague and replete with variations. The Candlefish, for example, is built in a variety of colors, often utilizing a central streak of white. A great *series* of flies, but is any one of them pattern?

Some of the most successful streamers are simple one- or two-colored basic lures. All-white and all-yellow bucktails probably catch more fish than all other color schemes combined. This doesn't cancel out the effectiveness of other colors or color combinations, for all seem to produce in certain slots of time and space.

Size, shape, and general color all contribute to effectiveness. A five-inch streamer certainly does not tempt bonefish as well as a much smaller offering, but the man who seeks trophy striped bass or billfish actually wants a lure that is too bulky and wind-resistant to cast very far with a fly rod. Big fish often dote on big baits. Moreover, some gamesters want a fast-moving lure, and it is physically impossible to move a fly fast enough to interest all comers. (Unless you troll, of course, and that's not considered kosher by the true fly caster.)

Therefore, we see experiments in which flies are given the appearance of great size and bulk, but are relatively easy to cast. The Woolner Snake series is one of these: it uses a flexible Mylar piping body that extends far beyond the hook's point, plus long and sparse bucktail dressing. Arthur Fusco of Boston has developed a variation of this, which he calls the Tomahawk. Both flies cast well, create the appearance of size—but on the debit side they are pretty perishable. One big striper may mangle a Snake, and a bluefish will chew the thing to shreds.

George Cornish of New Jersey attacked the problem another way. He used a long-shanked hook, dressed the forward portion with chenille, and attached a long plume of marabou at the tail.

George's Blossom series, well wetted down, casts well, looks good, and has caught a lot of fish. Because marabou is quite delicate, the destruction factor is increased—but the fly is easy to construct and it draws strikes.

Cornish's long-shanked hook serves another purpose: it helps to defeat sharp-toothed fishes that would otherwise inhale the entire tempter and cut a nylon leader tippet. The same reasoning probably spurred development of flies that are supposed to resemble various needlefishes: the entire hook shank is bare, or closely wrapped and varnished, with the lure's dressing streaming aft, well beyond the barb.

Bernard "Lefty" Kreh of Florida is convinced that Mylar strips, which add glitter to a streamer fly, can mean the difference. Lefty's one of the world's great fly casters, and his Mylar flies are extremely popular around Miami and the Keys. There is no doubt that the dressing is effective, but—like every other dressing—it is no cure-all. Glitter should be used sparingly, interspersed with hair or feathers. Flash, not bulk, is the requirement.

Usually—and again there are exceptions—sparse dressing is preferable to full. The sparse fly casts better and offers more seductive action in the water. Sometimes it is necessary to add buoying hair or hackle when a fly is used in very shallow water. There, too, the artificial may often simulate a tiny crab or other crustacean, hence browns, yellows and blues are worked into the color scheme. Shades of pink have become increasingly popular in recent years.

In shallow water, light wire hooks, for obvious reasons, are favored over heavy barbs. You would think that weedless hooks, those fitted with fine piano-wire guards, would solve the problem of fouling, but this addition has made no great impression upon the oceanic angler. Wire guards can be effective on big flies, where end tackle is heavy enough to overpower the lure's bulk and where casts must be made close to, or into, shoreside brush. There's another solution: use bucktail or hackle as a weed guard.

Inverted dressing is no johnny-come-lately: it has been used for many years as a device to keep flies from fouling in grass or other aquatic vegetation. You simply tie the fly with dressing on the inside of the hook's shank so that it streams over the point of the barb. Keeled hooks are now readily available, but you can do a pretty good job with the standard straight-shank.

Like streamer flies and shrimp imitations, popping and skipping bugs are ideally suited to marine use—when they are tailored to the sea. In coastal waters an angler generally battles wind and requires a long cast to reach his chosen target. Therefore a salt water bug should boast good air characteristics. Squat versions, so popular for the taking of inland black bass, can be used, yet they have certain built-in disadvantages.

First off, inland bugs simulate—bugs! Or big night moths, frogs, even swimming mice. They are, for the most part, short-range weapons, so there is no appreciable handicap (indeed there is virtue) in a proliferation of hackle, rubber legs, and bucktail wings. All these additions offer resistance in the air, hence they do handicap the distance-conscious salt water man. *His* bug strives to copy a wounded baitfish on the surface, a skittering squid, shrimp, or other marine delicacy.

Think type, not rigid pattern, but do not assume that the marine bug lacks special virtues. Evolution has made it long in silhouette, streamlined, and relatively easy to cast. Up front, hackle is held to a minimum. Feather or bucktail dressing streams aft, adding an impression of length, plus wriggling action. The hook must be big to insure adequate bite, and the barb should be positioned well behind the solid body of the lure.

A salt water bug can be cupped or dish-faced to insure commotion during the retrieve, or bullet-headed for skipping action. The former is most often employed, but skipping types have a definite place. Fly rod enthusiasts who seek billfish and other species of big game often go to huge skip bugs. Most of these are difficult to cast, but effective ranges are short. Some offshore addicts cheat a little and allow the lure to stream back in the wake of a trolling boat. This is effective, but there is some question whether it should be considered fly casting.

While a big hook, comparatively speaking, is necessary to insure bite, the angler faces the difficulty of setting a heavy wire barb with a limber rod and a light leader tippet. Also, the setting of a hook is made more difficult with every foot of line out beyond, say, the 50 foot mark. Exceed that range and hook-setting problems will multiply.

It might be academically interesting to present a chart of exact hook sizes to use on each of the various marine game fishes, but any such list would have to be a maybe-and-or thing. There is a definite need for bugs (and flies) of all sizes. Unfortunately, even among the salt water battlers of a single species, such as snook or striped bass, the size range of fish sought will dictate the most profitable size of hook to use.

Joe Brooks, who probably knows more about marine fly-rodding than anyone else in the world, suggests Number 1 hooks for bonefish and "for snook in canals." That Number 1 undoubtedly suffices for bonefish, although the gray ghost will take lures armed with larger or smaller hooks. Small snook, together with small striped bass and a legion of other like-sized gamesters, can be racked up with the Number 1 barb. However—and we think Joe would agree—big snook and big stripers are best taken on hooks in the range of 1/0 to 3/0. We have noted that Joe prefers the latter when he is eyeballing trophy stripers, and we think he's right.

A man might not go far wrong if he toted streamers and popping bugs armed with hooks in the 1/0 to 3/0 range for general work, together with a few miniatures (Number 8 to Number 1) for shad, small snook, and other lightweights, plus occasional offshore feather-dusters sporting 6/0 singles of 2 X strength. These big streamers, skimmers, and poppers are used on amberjack and billfish.

Hook size and type must depend on the species sought and the tackle employed. It is imperative, however, that the lightest *practical* wire be employed in any barb which arms a fly, and that the point be razor-sharp. Finish should be rust-resistant, which means tin, cadmium plate, or stainless. We prefer tinned hooks, but this is a personal preference.

Popper bodies may be made of clipped bucktail, cork, balsa wood, or any of several flotation plastic materials—not necessarily in that order. Color schemes remain a moot point, with basic hues still most popular. Home mechanics and tackle manufacturers create lures in a wide variety and combination of colors, with fish-scale flanks and staring eyes, yet there is no overpowering evidence that the intricately painted bug is superior to the plain-Jane offering. All-white, all-yellow, and combinations of blue and white, green and white, or red and white are most prominently displayed in the tackle boxes of experts. Red sometimes pays off, and the all-black article can be very effective, particularly after dark. Occasionally one of the new fluorescent colors, such as "neon-red" or "blaze-orange," turns the trick. The choice is wide and an angler should keep in mind the fact that he intends to simulate the color of some specific marine bait species to tempt a specified game species.

It is true that salt water fly casting becomes more popular with each succeeding year, but it would be irresponsible to compare this method—in number of anglers involved—with spinning, trolling, surf and bait casting. Feather merchants remain a very small group of happy specialists, often handicapped by inland traditions which do not apply on the big, raucous ocean.

There'll be further advances, and we'll honor the inventors of new departures. With few exceptions, though, we suggest that the salt water fly and floating bug be categorized by type, rather than by the intricate pattern system of the inland purist.

13
MULTIPLE LURES

SOMETIME DURING THE MID-60'S A GROUP OF ENTERPRISING MONtauk charter skippers on Long Island, New York, began to employ multiple trolling rigs on striped bass and bluefish. The first of these weapons were called "coathangers" because of their general configuration. Later, as the rig evolved into a four-armed contraption, it became the "umbrella." With the latter, often armed with five to nine or more lures, hook-ups of two, three, or more fish at a time became commonplace.

By 1969, the umbrella's reputation as a meat-fishing instrument had spread along the entire East coast. Bob Andrews of Orleans, Massachusetts, caught precisely 83 pounds of striped bass the first time he lowered the thing over the side. Bob had a triple, each fish weighing better than 25 pounds.

As successive reports detailed the effectiveness of this new rig, sportsmen sounded an alarm. Individual anglers and many charter skippers demanded that the weapon be outlawed—by whom, was a bit uncertain. Just as the banning of a book in Boston in the old days would send readers scurrying to bookstores in other cities, this hue and cry quite naturally publicized this new killer, and every hungry rodsman on the North Atlantic seaboard hastened to acquire one. By the summer of 1969 an umbrella, complete with nine surgical tube lures, sold for as much as $35.00 and demand far exceeded supply. Prices came down early in 1970 as a host of lure-makers got into the act; still, a completely rigged umbrella remained an expensive package.

Physically, the tackle consists of a four-armed, stainless steel spreader, each arm radiating from a streamlined central sinker. Lures are attached to the end of each arm and one is streamed from the central weight itself. Often four additional lures are added, fixed to loops positioned midway on each arm—and there are greedy heroes who employ even more hooked tempters.

Obviously, in order to troll such a conglomeration of lead, steel wire, and darting lures as represented by the basic umbrella pattern, a fisherman must resort to heavy tackle and wire line in the 60 pound test class. Modifications on this basic rig, as will be noted in a moment, can change this picture. However, the multi-hooked umbrella downgrades sport, especially when two or more big fish are hooked at the same time. Commercial rod and line fishermen may be delighted, even though they find it necessary to handline a bulky collection of hooked fish. The sport involved is something else again.

This multi-hooked umbrella is not a pleasant thing to use. By its very nature, it is prone to tangle. Upon muscling two or three big bass or blues to boatside, the angler must dodge flying hooks while he attempts to subdue thrashing fish with gaff and club. Fully armed, this is a meat fisherman's gimmick—and it can be a dangerous one in unskilled or inept hands.

Initially, those who developed this rig used a variety of lures. These ranged from diamond jigs through bucktails, and even included a school of swimming plugs. After a few seasons of trial-and-error experimentation, greatest success seemed reserved for umbrellas armed with surgical tube lures in a wide selection of colors. Red is preferred by many, but every known hue has chalked up victories.

Apparently, the tremendous killing power of this rig is due to the fact that it simulates a school of bait. Therefore some pioneering sportsmen have produced umbrellas which create this illusion, but still qualify as sporting lures. These models feature lightweight umbrellas which can be used with much lighter tackle than that required for the original. A single armed lure streams from the central weight and is positioned well back from the darting teasers. These teasers lack hooks and serve only as window dressing, so the combination is capable of taking no more than one fish at a time.

The same principle of simulating a school of bait was developed to a fine art by Captain Otto Reut, now retired, who won his way to angling fame fishing off Sandy Hook, New Jersey. Otto would fish three or more rods over the transom and would position the rod tips so that all lures ran at the same depth, practically side by side. This system, which had its share of tangles of course, used the umbrella concept without its resulting cumbersome rig.

Practically all of the coathanger and umbrella rigs are most effective when they are trolled on wire line. They have been used with sporadic success when dragged on monofilament, but this is the exception to prove a rule. Metal line usually is required to take the package down into a gamester's strike zone and, perhaps, to cause it to troll evenly.

Outdoor writers generally seem to feel that the trolling spreader is something very new. It is not. In our *Complete Book of Striped Bass Fishing*, first printed in 1954, spreaders are described and a version of the coathanger is illustrated. We did not envision four-armed umbrellas at the time, but we noted that "as many as five hooks can be employed at once . . . doubles and triples may be caught. . . ."

The coathanger, then dubbed "deep trolling spreader rig," came out of the Chesapeake Bay and it was used long before some of this era's successful charter skippers were born. The umbrella is no more than a variation and it owes its tremendous success to the improvement and popular use of wire line. The old hands on the Chesapeake Bay had to rely on soft lines and sashweights to achieve necessary depth.

Actually, multiple rigs are no Johnny-come-latelies. They've been used since the very beginning of angling history. The ancient Polynesians added feathers (without hooks) ahead of their famed "pearl lures." Inland trout and salmon fishermen have, since the days of Izaak Walton, used two or three dropper flies in addition to the premier offering. Long, long ago, Scandinavians found that a series of small artificial baits rigged above a heavy drail would take more fish than a single tempter. The years spin on, but each of these combinations is represented by similar or improved versions on Atomic Age waters.

For example, Pacific coast sportsmen use strings of feather- and yarn-dressed lures to hook rockfish close to the bottom. North Atlantic mackerel fishermen design six- to eight-hooked "Christmas tree" rigs to fill live wells with bait. Surf casters who seek striped bass often rig a dropper fly or a simple strip of pork rind on a hook well ahead of a swimming plug or metal wobbler. In many areas trollers find that a lead-headed bucktail jig, positioned ahead of the swimming plug, improves chances of tying into a prize catch.

Nor is this multiple presentation theory confined to shore-based casters and light-tackle trollers. In Nova Scotia, musclemen who seek giant tuna employ a grapevine string of fresh herring. This consists of a whole host of herring tied into a single line at intervals of a few feet, used as a teaser. The startling success of this maneuver in luring giants out of the depths led to a similar string of herring on the angler's leader, with the last bait armed.

Years ago Charley Mayo of Provincetown, Massachusetts—a great tuna fishing skipper—quietly observed this maneuver and adapted it to his home waters. Since mackerel were more abundant than herring, he used them with such success that contemporaries chartered airplanes to reconnoiter and discover the "secret method."

Charley later pioneered the use of grapevine strings of squid for the same purpose. The trick is still much used, often utilizing soft plastic squid in line-astern formation. Mayo led the way here, but he simply used his head to use a method that had been discovered by other humans some centuries back.

Offshore anglers do not sweat with guilt when they stream teasers to lure billfish into a wake, nor is there any suggestion of unsportsmanlike conduct when a string of mullet, balao, or eels is used to excite sailfish or marlin. This stratagem, strangely enough, seems to work best when the ocean is flat calm. Of course only the terminal bait is fitted with a hook, a thing that can cause trouble when other species muscle into the act.

Billfish and tuna invariably wallop Tail-end Charley in a lure string, but excitable characters like dolphin, wahoo, bluefish, and the various sharp-toothed mackerels are likely to attack any segment of the grapevine. This automatically prevents a hook-up and often means disaster if the leader is monofilament rather than wire. If all baits are armed, you get into the old hassle about sportsmanlike conduct—and you will have to accept the inevitable tangle.

Multiple rigs come and go. Back in the 50's there was a great to-do about a thing called the "junk-lure." It employed two or three hooks and looked like nothing any self-respecting game fish would touch. The head of this contraption was a standard trolling feather. Attached to this was a piece of swivel chain about a foot or 18 inches long, with plastic skirts tied in at regular intervals. A limber strip of pork rind graced the terminal hook. Junk-lures harvested striped bass and blues at a phenomenal rate during a couple of seasons; thereafter they were pretty much forgotten.

When you think about it, the spinner and fly or the spinner and trailing bait is a multiple lure. Although one hook is standard, the gamester is lured into attacking by the flash of the spinner. On the

Pacific coast this technique is varied by the use of king-sized spoons called Herring Dodgers, first introduced by Les Davis. They are big and, naturally, highly visible. The battlers come up to investigate flash or color, then are vectored in on the bait that trails behind.

Similarly, the Southern popping-cork combination is a multiple rig. This consists of a cork rigged ahead of a single hook which is sweetened with bait such as a minnow or a shrimp—usually the latter. The cork is popped on the surface: game species come to investigate the commotion and are then intrigued by the edible trailing bait. In some cases the cork has evolved into a small popping plug armed with hooks: thereupon doubles are possible.

Northern pollock and striped bass fishermen work the same stunt when they employ a dropper or trailing bucktail jig with a surface plug. Both lures are artificials, yet both are highly effective. Many game fish can be taken on such combinations.

Multiple rigs can be deadly, but they possess built-in disadvantages. Most of them are prone to tangle or foul during a cast, or even when trolling. Obviously, the more hooks used, the greater the chance of fouling. When two or more fish strike at the same time they are able to pull one against the other—as well as against the pressure exerted by the rodsman. Unless terminal gear is stout and the basic tackle is heavy, such a rig becomes self-defeating. If heavy, it is a meat-fisherman's instrument: if light, it is a constant source of frustration. There are variations which offer compromises.

Are such rigs sporting? This is a matter of opinion and of semantics. We are complimented by those anglers who write to ask that *we* "outlaw the things." Certainly we (the authors) cannot dictate to state or federal government agencies, nor would we wish to do so. If a majority of marine sportsmen feel that specific game fish should not be taken with multiple rigs, then they need only marshal their numbers to petition legislators for some sort of hook-and-line law, similar to those posted in many inland states, to limit the number of hooks that can be used by a single angler.

This is a ticklish operation where a specific gamester is also recognized as a commercial, renewable resource. If state and federal government allows exploitation by commercial fishermen, any restriction imposed on so-called sport fishermen (actually small-time commercials with rod and line) becomes an exercise in futility. The law must apply equally to all concerned.

Over the years we have argued that the International Game Fish Association should recognize treble-hooked plugs as sporting lures, and we feel that some new definitions which would take the onus off wire line should be incorporated into the IGFA rules. The plug is a sportsman's tool, and so is wire—within reasonable limits. The multiple-hooked rig is another kettle of fish.

While nothing we can say individually or as a team of marine writers bears telling weight, we suggest that multiple-hooked rigs should, at the very least, be banned in any angling tournament. Perhaps the outside limit, in any such decision, would be two hooks on a single line.

Again we struggle with semantics. What is a single hook? In some states where inland anglers are limited to two hooks, a plug which is armed with three trebles is considered a single lure and, thereby, a single "hook." We'll buy that, arguing that the lure is designed to catch no more than one fish at a time.

Maybe that's the answer, so far as sportsmen are concerned. If we seek good, clean excitement, instead of fish flesh to be sold at so much per pound, then any bait or lure should be designed to take one at a time. Where commercially oriented species are concerned, and where the law allows—it's your ball game and your conscience.

14

THE MIGHTY MIDGETS

LIGHT TACKLE AND TINY LURES HAVE DOMINATED EXHIBITS AT recent American Fishing Tackle Manufacturers Association trade shows. The nation, it would seem, is experiencing a trend toward miniaturization in every item of equipment pertaining to sport fishing.

This is important to the salt water angler, and so is another show observation: marine tackle is commanding an ever-increasing share of interest, even from jobbers in the Middle West. Paraphrasing an old bromide—50,000 Kansans can't be wrong.

Or can they?

Sometimes a fad sweeps all before it, until such time as cool heads prevail. There is, certainly, a great need for light gear and tiny artificials. Perhaps, in view of the revolution that spinning has wrought in this land of the brave, miniaturization is most important.

However, the skilled and practical angler must view this concept with a measure of caution. There are pitfalls to be avoided; there are certain conclusions that do not prove out in the hard light of dawn on a fishing ground.

Spinning is a light-tackle method: it happens to be both pleasant and effective, although not, under all circumstances, as effective as other methods.

Spinning, at least to that point which permits the practical casting and retrieving of a lure, is easily mastered—hence its adoption by the multitudes and its tremendous contribution to the sport. Nonetheless, fixed spool tackle is highly specialized. (If you want to be technical, so is every other fishing combination in this watery world.)

The thing about spinning is that it is designed to cast light lures on light lines: it is, basically and absolutely, a light-tackle rig.

Those who insist on using this combination for everything from flipping a fly to trolling a balao are extremists. They are, in fact, zealots who fail to understand the mechanics of angling.

This chapter does not intend to minimize the importance of spinning, so veterans who are now breathing heavily can relax. Fixed spool is a magnificent development, and it will not go away if we ignore it. Nor, on the other hand, will spinning supersede other types of tackle if we laud it to the heavens. The sole reason for laboring this point is the fact that miniaturization of lures is tied to spinning.

This is both a curse and a blessing, depending on your preference in marine tackle. If you're a spin-caster, applaud the innovation. After all, it was designed with you in mind. You, as an atom in the mass of statistics which reflect public demand, have insisted on lures that will cast—and catch fish—on the lightest of lines.

Since the fixed-spool captive can't practically employ large and relatively heavy lures, lighter and tinier artificials have become necessary. In many instances these tidbits are superior to the big baits of an almost forgotten generation. Game fish feed on small baits, hence they wallop the miniature offerings now served up in such great volume.

But there is another side to this coin. Unfortunately for light-tackle buffs, many of the great gamesters also dote on large servings—in which case the midgets are ignored. When big fish want big baits, light-tackle anglers weep bitter tears as the lads with heavier outfits tie into trophy battlers.

Obviously, the complete angler on salt water carries tackle calibrated to his need—which often means one light and one heavy combination in areas where the sought-after species may be selective, or where some other factor dictates use of one or the other rig. Regulars habitually tote a number of different outfits, using that which seems best suited to existing conditions.

The trend toward lighter gear and the miniaturization of lures has created another problem—a scarcity of the large and heavy artificials that some anglers find effective. With Kib Bramhall, *Salt Water Sportsman*'s advertising manager, we fished the coast of Rhode Island in the company of a friend who manufactures lures. Art Lavallee (Acme Tackle) accepted our compliments on one of his new spin-sized poppers, and snorted indignantly when we asked whether he'd produce the lure in high surf size and weight.

"Let's face it," Art growled, "you and Kib are the only two

guys left in this world who still want big plugs for striper fishing!"

If nothing else, Lavallee's gravel-voiced quip indicates a trend. While salt water anglers continue to score with big baits, and while demand for these artificials will continue into the foreseeable future, there is no doubt that midgets are best sellers. Manufacturers aren't likely to spend time and money in research, development and production of lures that are in small demand—even if said lures are deadly fish takers. No firm strives to achieve bankruptcy.

To a certain extent, light tackle has become a status symbol. It seems obvious that any angler who uses a featherweight rod, a tiny reel, spiderweb line and a miniature reel must be a genuine sportsman who gives the fish every chance to escape. Maybe so—and maybe no!

Tiny lures do not guarantee sportsmanship in fishing. Indeed, a fly tied on a 1/0 hook may be far deadlier than a 9/0 forged barb, depending on the rod, reel, and line employed.

A salt water fly rod, for example, is a formidable weapon, for it boasts so resilient a tip that break-offs are held to an absolute minimum. Long and limber spinning rods also cushion the line and prevent breakage. This is just as it should be when tackle is well matched.

The point, of course, is that one cannot effectively employ a tiny lure on a heavy rod-line combination. Ignoring for a moment the initial difficulty of casting a light bait on a big rod, one faces serious problems after a game fish strikes and begins to wage war. Because there is so little cushioning effect from a stiff rod tip, fine wire hooks on midget lures tend to straighten, screw-eye hook hangers pull out—sometimes the plug simply breaks into pieces.

If one chooses to match a midget lure and a heavy casting rod, the only insurance is a light drag setting. This, of course, guarantees imbalance. Surf casters who recognize the frequent effectiveness of small artificials constantly experiment in an attempt to produce the impossible.

One popular idea is end-to-end rigging and the substitution of heavy wire hooks for those originally installed. This seldom succeeds, because the plug's weight balance is changed and its action is affected. Often end-to-end rigging is quite difficult, because so many of the miniatures are molded in hard plastic.

All of which boils down to a logical solution: if you desire to enjoy the benefits of the midget lure, employ a rod calculated to throw mere fractions of ounces, a line light enough to enhance the action of such artificials, and a reel with a silk-smooth drag.

Forget the true midgets when you choose a conventional high surf squidding outfit, a heavy two-handed spinning rod, a beefed-up popping or marine bait-casting stick. Remember that no one rod, reel and line is all-purpose: that's why the real professionals employ a wide range of outfits, each suited to a specific task.

The fire beneath all this smoke about tiny lures is there all right, and it's plenty hot. While manufacturers produce some real dogs, a surprising number of the new midgets live up to advance publicity. In many cases tackle makers have scaled down old favorites and offered them in the miniature range. There is, in addition, much copying of ancient standards. Once in a blue moon a copy actually outperforms the original, but this is the exception to prove a rule.

Wood, a variety of hard plastics, and many new soft plastics lend themselves to the fabrication of tiny lures. Those artificials produced by long established and reputable firms are thoroughly tested before they are shipped to the sporting goods shops. As a result, the "lure that catches more fishermen than fish" is something of a rarity.

Now and then, it is true, some promoter launches a bait that is "guaranteed to catch fish," but which actually is worthless. Such lures rarely remain on the market, for fishermen quickly get the word. On a few occasions, during the past thirty years, *Salt Water Sportsman* has deemed it wise to cancel advertising schedules ordered by the quick-buck boys with their astonishing creations. So far as we're concerned, such ads should be relegated to the limbo of "pictures that men like" and "Kickapoo cancer cure."

While replacement of hooks, end-to-end wiring, and weighting of midget lures invariably destroys the bait's balance, and thereby its appeal to game fish, the practical angler may experiment with minor adjustments of wobble plate (if the lure has one) and eye loop. Worth noting is the fact that these adjustments may be made on plugs of any size.

Anglers since Adam have questioned the action built into any lure by its manufacturers. A tackle concern may have employed design engineers, metallurgists, field testers and experts galore to determine the exact curve of a spoon which will insure seductive action in the water. No matter, the ultimate consumer, a fisherman, will bend that spoon to his own requirements.

There's nothing particularly ridiculous about this, for the angler may be entirely right. Surf casters often bend metal squids to insure action on a required slow or rapid retrieve. Surface swimming plugs can be made to flurry on top, or dive. Wiggling action can be speeded or slowed.

The trick here is to know what you're doing, or at least to experiment until the desired action is obtained. After a lure has been adjusted, cast or troll it a short distance to observe action.

One secret of success which seems to elude many anglers is a simple bending of the eye loop on a surface-swimming plug. Some of these plugs work best when they wriggle along on top, yet on other occasions become killers when induced to swim at a depth of eight inches to a foot. Bend the eye loop *up* if you want the swimming plug to dive; bend it *down* if you prefer top-water action. No other adjustment need be made.

There is one other gimmick, short of adding lead weights at the balance of a plug, to take it deeper than it is designed to swim. Many of the modern lures are constructed of hard plastic, with air spaces to insure flotation. A couple of tiny holes, drilled through the body of the plug, will permit water to enter and add casting weight. Buoyancy is diminished, and so is action—but not drastically in most cases.

Changing the angle of a wobble plate will change a plug's swimming action. Indeed, after an active game fish has walloped such a lure, adjustments may be necessary to insure the original action of the bait. Similarly, the addition of bucktail trailers or bucktail-dressed tail hooks always slows the action of a swimming plug. Sometimes this is very effective, but the angler should always understand that a trailing "feather" diminishes the built-in action of the lure.

Practically all artificial baits work best when they are not burdened with excessive hardware. When monofilament lines are used, and where sharp-toothed game is not anticipated, it is usually wise to bend the line directly to the lure. A snap or snap swivel, although handy in changing baits, may add just enough weight to spoil lure action. Even when using a leader, if you must use a snap, make it a light one—with no string of swivels. Artificials designed to be cast should not spin, therefore swivels may be kept at an absolute minimum.

Trollers are advised to disregard this advice. Lures fished behind a boat usually require swivels—if not keels—to defeat line twist, but note that swivels are best placed between line and leader, not right at the lure itself.

If you must use a light wire leader while fishing a midget lure for sharp-toothed fishes, insist on glint-free leader material and a flat black or neutral-colored swivel. Bright chrome or brass swivels often draw strikes from bluefish, Spanish mackerel and other saber-toothed tigers.

Thanks to the current popularity of light tackle in salt water fishing, miniature lures will be in good supply during the foreseeable future. Use them with the proper rod, reel and line—and you'll catch fish.

But don't write off heavy gear and the big baits that have caught so many record gamesters. There's a time and a place for all things—even on the sea front. Light tackle means nothing at all until you match it with a specific fish.

15

THE HOME MECHANIC

ANYONE WITH A PINCH OF COMMON SENSE AND A FLAIR FOR HOME mechanics can make plugs, tin squids, or bucktail jigs that will catch fish. If time is no object, there is even a good possibility that such craftsmen can save themselves a buck or two. Nonetheless, we always wonder about talented and high-salaried people who spend hours manufacturing facsimiles of lures they could buy at a pittance.

The answer, logically, lies in satisfaction derived from personal achievement. We know tycoons who wrap and finish their own rods, tie flies, and create a host of lures in superbly equipped cellar workshops. Money is no object, so we deal with a somewhat expensive hobby. This is a healthy state of affairs.

Not so healthy is the situation of the optimist who spends cash he can ill afford to fashion and patent a new departure. This is, generally, a loser's game: hence it appears most attractive to certain types. Categories roughly include the neophyte who fancies himself a genius, and the truly inventive expert who understands the odds.

Make no mistake, it is a gamble to attempt stumping the big firms. Lure manufacturers employ specialists who have devoted their lives to the fabrication of wooden, plastic, and metal fish attractors. These technicians seldom miss a bet and they forever probe the unknown. Moreover, the old and well-established firms employ an edge in quality control. When one of their bright young men blueprints a new design, a host of equally bright devil's advocates are called in to detail problems. Finally, if the lure is deemed possibly salable, it is first tested (secretly) by field experts.

Established lure manufacturers never market an artificial bait until it has first passed a series of severe tests. Although they rarely "guarantee" a lure's effectiveness, you can bet that anything placed on the open market by a reputable firm is worth its weight in salt. Miracle lures are suspect: they are in the same league as "Four complete outfits, together with tackle box, net, gaff and lure assortment!" for some ridiculous fee like $3.98. The stuff has to be junk, and it is.

We do not intend to discourage invention, for the record indicates that occasional masters of angling create something that is a local killer. If the tempter has something very unusual in its design, the chances are better than good that one of the national manufacturers will buy it, copy it—or that the local maker will form a small company and struggle toward success. Some of the big wheels in lure-making launched their careers with a few borrowed dollars and an idea. They're exceptions.

Since entirely new ideas are blue moon affairs, it is far likelier that some smart fisherman will alter an existing lure to make it more effective. For example, back in the early 50's three Cape Cod surf casters re-rigged a well-known surface plug so that it would swim backward and simulate a squid. Success was immediate, and Bob Pond, maker of the famed Atom plug, promptly issued the new "Reverse Atom." Unfortunately, demand has never extended beyond the borders of northern New England. Manufacturers do not amass riches on regional triumphs.

Granting that marine angling is an infant science, the individual inventor's field narrows with each succeeding year. It isn't necessarily so, but usually the unsung genius spends a good deal of time and money in a patent search—to discover that somebody else has registered the same idea, or something so close that it cannot be duplicated. In our own salad days we poured cash down the drain in a futile attempt to patent a lure type. Who hasn't?

Some questionably smart operators, aware of the intricacies of patenting, simply produce a tempter and mark it *patent pending*. This is illegal in the first place. It means nothing, and the idea is to make a bundle before anyone else copies and markets the "killer." We do not suggest this maneuver, yet we note that certain manufacturers make a business of incorporating slight change in the design of any successful lure, to get away with what amounts to outright duplication.

This is the point upon which name brand becomes important. If you desire the original, insist upon it. The prototype may cost a few pennies more, but you get exactly what you yearn for. You also get the promise of an established firm: if the lure disintegrates, the company makes good.

It is only fair to note, in this connection, that occasional copies prove more effective than the originals. This is an exception, but it has happened often enough to be noteworthy. Probably, when the unforeseen occurs, designers have really incorporated a clever variation.

Annually, tremendous amounts of money are gambled away by new corporations formed to market a home inventor's well-promoted dream bait. As recognized laborers in the vineyards of salt water angling, we are bombarded with a succession of such artificials, and we can only declare that misses are far more plentiful than direct hits.

The fact that we are asked to serve as field testers indicates good faith on the part of the plungers. They really believe that they have something of value, and it is no pleasure for us to point out faults that would be obvious to any regular on the boats or the beaches.

Obvious errors in design lie in the field of engineering. New departures may look like nothing any sensible fish would strike, but the lure is worth testing if it is designed to absorb the punishment meted out to any marine artificial. Some very great lures seemed ridiculous at first sight.

Condolences are extended to inventors and backers who mass-produce expensive artificials that at the very outset have the unenviable chances of a wax bat in hell. These include the brain children of inland artists who cannot visualize the power of ocean game fish and who therefore provide rigging that a fresh water bluegill might happily demolish.

Also included are lures evidently blueprinted by a dreamer—without any of that basic field testing of prototypes which is so necessary to the development of a practical artificial. Curiously, fired-up inventors often find angels who will finance production and advertising. Such a company is doomed from the beginning. The charlatans, occasionally people of good faith and little angling intelligence, rarely succeed for very long. They always lose a bucket of money.

All of which gets back to the home mechanic who desires to make his own lures and, possibly, his fortune. This is a universal hobby, and there's nothing reprehensible about it—so long as the hobbyist recognizes his own limitations. If you have developed something strange and wonderful, more power to you. But note that the strange-and-wonderful is a very rare bird. Remember that the reputable manufacturers heed Mowgli's instructions: "Look well, oh wolves!"

For the home mechanic who has no immaculate dream of producing a new secret weapon, all of the basic lures—with the possible exception of those fabricated of hard and soft plastics—are quite feasible. The resulting tempters may not be as perfectly balanced and finished as those turned out by quality-control machinery, but they will catch fish.

Popping plugs are easiest of all, with balance the major consideration. Long ago, when striped bass fishing became a major sport on the North Atlantic coast, anglers made commendable poppers from lengths of broom handle. The design remains popular, and some old-timers still regard any popper as a "broomstick plug."

Some of the better manufacturers still miss the boat in regards to basic poppers. Such a lure should be tail-heavy to implement casting. It should be slim, streamlined, and should tend to sink at the stern until the retrieve is initiated. Unlike an inland black bass popper, the usual marine version is retrieved fairly rapidly. It is a noisy, speedy, erratic lure—an artificial that can be cast to maximum distance and worked to produce lots of noise and commotion.

This requirement is varied to a certain extent with the fish sought. Some great game fish of the sea are most likely to take a stop-and-go retrieve—but you'll find that "slow" in the briny would be classified as very fast back in the watery boondocks of our hinterland.

Granting performance requirements on specific game fish, the popper probably is the simplest of all lures to manufacture in a home workshop. Load it aft, cut a slanting dish-face that will insure commotion—and you have it made.

Swimmers are more complex, because balance, air characteristics, and action must be incorporated into a single plug. You will need a lure that casts well and then swims like something the game fish wants to inhale. Heavy, well-streamlined lures are fine casters, but light and buoyant baits offer better action in the water. Obviously, there is a need for compromise.

Once upon a time, recognizing this conflict, we built a surface swimming plug with a hinged lip which would fold back during the cast and thus insure better air characteristics. A 38-pound striped bass gobbled this masterpiece on the first heave, and we thought we'd invented a true killer. Unfortunately the finny tribes assiduously avoided this plug on subsequent occasions.

Best bet is to ignore tricks and stick with standard wobble plates. These can be cut out of aluminum sheeting, or they can be purchased from dealers who offer plug components.

Weighting is another tricky business. No swimming plug succumbs very gracefully to weighting at the tail—to insure a maximum-distance cast. You may heave closer to the horizon, but action will be impaired. This trick works only where such a lure is used in a furious rip or in a strong tidal current. Additional weight should be added at the balance, if at all.

Inventive anglers forever regale us with bucktail jigs made from such easy-to-find components as a single buckshot or a steel bolt cut down to proper size, dressed with bucktail, feathers—or even strips of chamois. These will catch fish, but they are far inferior to the professionally fashioned offering. Molds can be made with plaster of Paris, bronze, or steel. Most of the better home-made bucktail heads are turned out by people with access to sophisticated machine tools. We know citizens who employ moon-rocket materials and ultramodern tools to fabricate jigs.

No comment, aside from the fact that commercial firms produce similar jig-heads of plebeian lead, so carefully shaped and balanced that they are superior to haphazardly molded heads of exotic metals. Maybe there is some special satisfaction in catching a fish-shaped fish on some ore that has been compounded at great cost to take a space ship to the moon!

Tin squids, now made of so many different metals that "tin" is a misnomer, remain in the bailiwick of the home mechanic. Again, a mold must be constructed, either of plaster of Paris or metal. There is some question whether the soft glow of pure block tin is not superior to plated lead or stainless steel. Jigs, at any rate, have always been more of a home mechanic's project than plugs, bucktails and artificial flies.

Actually, there is another lure, sandwiched between plugs and flies, that intrigues do-it-yourselfers, This is the salt water feather jig—and we use the term because no other is immediately applicable.

The feather jig is nothing but a streamlined lump of lead to which is attached a dressing of feathers, bucktail, or nylon filaments. It is easy to construct: all you need is a cigar-shaped weight of lead with an after surface which lends itself to the tying-in of feathers, bucktail or nylon strands. Such lures are ideal for trolling and they are easy to manufacture in a home workshop. All you need is a dowel of lead through which a hole has been drilled, plus the necessary dressing.

Feather jigs are no problem for home mechanics, although there is some reason to doubt that they could not be purchased at a cost that would discourage home manufacture. The design is simple and materials are cheap. All it takes is time and work. Nowadays, nylon filaments supersede bucktail and feathers. If we make our own, we probably wind up in the red. It would be better to buy the standards.

Finally, there are salt water flies for those who insist upon catching marine game fish with the long wand. Several firms offer great feather attractors, but the usual romanticist insists upon making his own. Patterns are vague, yet every feather merchant has his own ideas—proof that we have yet to enter an era of great marine fly casting. Our oceanic Hewitts have yet to be named, hence the field is wide open.

Whatever the lure, we deal with a frontier. Marine game fishing is new and it will prosper during the coming years. Pioneering anglers, who are still beginners, will break through almost insurmountable odds to initiate new lures and new techniques. It was ever thus.

Those who dream of great advances may be first-class nuts, but who can say they are not prophets? No science halts. No progress is becalmed. A very few talented people always see beyond the present and manage to blueprint the future. It's a rocky road, and one that is rarely forecast. We can only warn that new departures are rare and that any advance must be based on a complete knowledge of the past, plus an understanding of present needs.

Those who dream of showers of gold for their inventive efforts are deluding themselves. The home workshop approach can be fun, but never imagine that it will save any appreciable strain on the pocketbook.

16

LURE IN MOTION

THERE ARE PEOPLE IN THIS WATERY WORLD WHO WORSHIP SPEED alone. When one of this peculiar group heads through a school of surfaced fish in a craft that is more motor than hull, assembled anglers long for a pocket-sized torpedo. Fishermen generally condemn speed, and do so in unprintable terms. However, the marine angler can do worse than consider speed as it applies to his own sport.

We refer, of course, to the speed with which a lure or bait moves through the water. The subject is far from simple, yet those who have even a fundamental grasp of the factors involved will catch more fish than those who do not. Included in the equation must be species sought, time of year and day, angling methods employed—and the lure itself.

Look first at the species. There are extremes, ranging from the streamlined wahoo, which is supposed to be one of the fastest fish that swims, to the black drum—crunching its way over an oyster bed. Obviously, the chances of a wahoo hitting a crushed clam on the bottom are slim. Similarly, it is difficult to imagine a drum speeding after a trolled feather which is moving along at a brisk seven knots.

In general, the faster any fish moves through the water during its normal feeding activities, the faster a lure should be moved to insure results. Note that word *normal.* There are times when even the most sedate grouper will dash about like a school tuna, and others when a racy mackerel appears to browse along like a demented sea cow. Nature provides clues to normal fish speed: the more streamlined the body, the swifter the fish—and the more rapidly a lure designed to catch it should be moved through the water.

As is true of any angling generality, exceptions are numerous.

Swordfish and marlins, according to all rules of design, are built for speed—yet they are often baited while lolling on the surface. Moreover, the bait is swung in front of these great gladiators at a comparatively leisurely rate. All things considered, however, the rule holds true in a majority of cases.

Obviously, an angler wishing to take advantage of this rule will hike the speed of his boat, or will step up retrieves when casting, if he seeks any rapidly moving, predaceous species. For the more sedentary fish, he will slow down, or even present a bait in one position.

Unfortunately the time of year complicates things. During the early season, when waters are cool or when a migratory species first reaches any given area, game fish tend to feed upon the easiest prey at hand. In most cases such forage moves at a lower rate of speed, if it moves at all, than it will later in the year. Bait fish are also apt to school at greater depths in the spring, rising to the surface as water temperatures zoom.

It follows that an early-season angler, all other things being equal, should fish slow and deep. This actually is a blessing, for it is difficult to present a deep-running lure, either trolled or cast, at high speed. Nature, for a wonder, apparently cooperates with the angler.

As the summer sun climbs, all things increase their pace. During this period, and again during the early fall, fishing may be classified as normal. High-speed fish hit rapidly moving baits, medium-speed gamesters feed at moderate velocity, and the usual sluggards munch away at their usual relaxed pace. A knowing angler matches action to that desired by his quarry.

Naturally, so-called *normal* periods vary with species. The peak of normalcy, if there is such a thing, may be attained in April for one species which favors cold water, while another—fond of warm seas—may not be really comfortable until July or August in northern latitudes. Again, this is helpful to the fisherman, for if all fish hit avidly during a period encompassing a few weeks, and then became inactive for months at a time, coastal angling would be a feast or famine proposition.

Although variance in seasonal weather, with changes in temperatures of both air and water, has some effect upon the exact date when each species may become normally active, it is surprising to see how closely fish follow the calendar. By studying his quarry's seasonal pattern, an angler can time his trips to insure maximum success. *Salt Water Sportsman*'s "Coastal Fishfinder" department calls the shots on arrival, peak and departure of many species frequenting American coasts, and does so with surprising accuracy. No divination is involved: the predictions are based on actual arrival, peak and departure dates over a span of years. In some cases arrival and departure can be plotted to a calendar date. Such information, coupled with the immediate information supplied by local rod and gun writers, and with an eye to the weather, should permit a clever angler to set his speed limits.

During the height of summer vacation periods, which do not necessarily coincide with good fishing, the speed pattern often changes. Fish that prefer cool waters tend to go deep when the temperature rises, and they avoid great activity in bright sunlight. Unfortunately for anglers, the species most sought after are still apt to be full of zip, so that the fast-moving types will still seek fast-moving baits. Presentation may be difficult when you have to plumb the depths.

In these circumstances, time of day—or night—can make a considerable difference. Dawn and dusk become the witching hours, for at these times the fish are not overly bothered by heat or light from the sun. Normal speeds of lure presentation are the rule. Night fishermen, particularly those who ply the surf, come into their own at this time. After dark, chances are improved when a lure is worked more slowly than it would be in daylight. For example, a slow-moving swimming plug is a better nighttime lure than a speeding surface popper which succeeds during the day.

Even during the hot weather season, however, an eye should be kept peeled for cloud cover. We well remember one dawn on an overcast day when fishing was nothing short of fantastic. The hour before sunrise was stretched—from the fish's point of view—to almost an hour after sunrise, due to overhead murk. We had a ball. That evening, clouds cleared away and a full moon shone brightly during the night.

The following dawn, full of hope, we were out again—and caught nothing. The fish evidently had been feeding happily by the gentle light of the moon. At the first flush of a clear dawn they retired to digest their meal. A few half-hearted swirls were the only signs that they were still there.

A cloudy, rainy, or unseasonably cool day with much fog can trigger exceptionally good hot weather fishing. Curiously, the period just before or just after a line storm is likely to see good sport, and retrieves can be every bit as rapid as they would be under the noonday sun.

When autumn rolls around, things return to normal—and things include the speed of retrieve. Migratory game fish—most species migrate to a certain extent—are extremely active. Therefore trolling and retrieving of cast lures can be stepped up to a pace which is faster than that employed at any other time of year. The travelers are accumulating fat for a long trip or for a winter of comparative inactivity. They tend to feed on swimming baits at or near the surface, and these baits often are speeding along on migrations of their own. Even bottom feeders may be taken nearer the surface at this time of year.

When winter descends on the northern coastal regions, the feeding cycle swings full circle. Once again a deep, slow presentation is the best bet if you would rack up a good catch. After a spell of warm weather speed may be slightly increased, but the quarry, by and large, will not exert itself to collect a meal.

Obvously, the method of fishing used will have a great deal of bearing on the speed at which a lure is presented. An angler rowing a skiff cannot hope to troll at a rate fast enough to entice a tuna from the depths. On the other hand, the owner of a big sport cruiser will have difficulty taking seatrout from the sod banks of a tidal creek. The power plant and size of trolling craft automatically sets limits on speed. The best rule is to start at a pace suggested by the factors involved; then, if this speed fails to produce, make a change.

One indicator that helps to determine whether to increase or decrease speed when trolling is the action of any bait that may be sighted. If feeding fish are observed among this bait, so much the better. When the forage species are moving rapidly, the boat should move equally rapidly; if moving slowly, the boat should be throttled down. A further point in this connection: small bait moves more slowly than large. Although tiny bait species may appear to dart about very rapidly, they actually are not moving through the water nearly as fast as similar bait of twice the size. Trolling speed should be altered accordingly.

Too many boat fishermen stick to trolling whether sport is good or bad. This is a mistake. By casting from their floating platforms, the anglers might make alterations in lure speeds which are impossible by straight dragging. A fisherman operating from a large cruiser can kill the engine completely, cast, allow his lure to sink and bump bottom at a speed far slower than when under way. Drifting will produce similar results in a weak current, and this involves no casting at all.

Similarly, anyone fishing from a low-powered craft can cast when under way, then reel like crazy. The lure speed will be far greater than that possible when trolling at a high rate. Although maximum speed may be achieved by casting directly over the stern, and then reeling in, this is often awkward and also may result in too much of a good thing. The cast should be made off the quarter. There will be added speed as the lure swings in toward the wake, together with variations both in the angle of lure presentation and the speed itself. This technique often produces when others fail.

When using rate of retrieve as a method of changing lure speed, the reel itself must be taken into account. The smaller the reel spool, all other things being equal, the slower the retrieve rate. Big game and trolling models usually boast a lower gear ratio between handle and spool than those designed primarily for casting. Watching a successful fellow angler and turning your own reel handle in exact coordination with his is a fruitless exercise unless you and he employ the same size and type of tackle.

At times the short-based caster discovers that, no matter how fast he reels, the lure simply does not move fast enough to induce a strike. Swirls behind or around the hooks are good indications of this unhappy circumstance. The trick then is to cast, engage the reel handle the moment the lure hits the water, start the retrieve, lift the rod tip smartly, and take a few steps backward. Reel, rod, and legwork often will impart just enough additional lure speed to achieve the desired results.

One word of warning: make sure that the path is clear of obstructions. We have taken many a tumble by failing to heed this warning ourselves. In addition, the rapid lifting of the rod tip and the immediate retrieve can be used to advantage when fishing from a boat. The footwork should be omitted!

Design and size of both natural and artificial baits have a limiting effect upon the use of high speeds to take game fish. A very large bait cannot be trolled at full throttle without placing heavy strain on the gear used. When big-game fishing, for example, a whole bonito will snap the line of an outrigger pin at high speeds. If trolled on a flat line it tends to dive and skip to such an extent that the angler has difficulty in handling the rod and in preventing line loops from being thrown around the tip. Besides, the bait soon tears itself apart.

Under such conditions, fishermen have the choice of slowing down or of using smaller and more streamlined natural baits. One compromise, often neglected, is to use a very wide strip bait. This gives the appearance of size and bulk, yet may be moved at high speed without undue strain on outrigger or tackle.

Speed capabilities are equally important in the selection of artificial lures. Those designed to be worked slowly often will spin or skitter over the surface when fished fast. Similarly, a lure made for rapid trolling or retrieve may have no action at all when fished at a leisurely pace. If doubtful about the action of any lure and its best fishing speed, take the ultimate step—read the manufacturer's instructions!

All too often, fishermen ignore obvious indications that a change in fishing speed will insure better results. One typical example of this is the occasion when fish are hooked fairly consistently as a boat is turned while trolling, yet are not taken when cruising in a straight line. It seems obvious that trolled lures slow down and sink deeper on the turn. By throttling down on the straight run, the same presentation can be made over a far longer period.

Another example is provided by the caster who, at the end of his retrieve, reels in the last few yards of line at high speed—and gives added speed to the lure by raising his rod tip to lift the tempter clear of the water. When a fish strikes at this particular moment, the angler is apt to exclaim that the fish followed the lure right up to beach or boat. Chances are better than even that the fish did nothing of the sort and was simply enticed to strike by the more rapidly moving plug, jig, or what have you.

Or, you can go the other way. Anglers often are amazed when, after picking out a backlash or a line slough, they get a hook-up even though the hooks themselves have been motionless for some time. It should be obvious that, at this moment in time, the quarry wanted something moving at a very slow rate of speed, or even inching along the bottom. The smart fisherman will put two and two together.

Speed in trolling or retrieving a cast lure is important. Keep it in mind. Meanwhile, note that no single component which goes into the description of so mythical a character as the complete angler is all-inclusive.

17

BAIT RIGS

SOME ANGLERS OF OUR ACQUAINTANCE CLING TO THE ILLUSION that it is more difficult to fish an artificial lure than a natural bait. They're right only when beginners place full confidence in bait, without really understanding its use and presentation. Where skill is roughly equal, we have the impression that a bait fisherman enjoys greater tactical flexibility than his purist colleague.

Certainly the amateur on salt water invariably chooses bait. He reasons that such tempters as seaworms and squids, various forage fish, shrimps, and crabs are more likely to attract game fish than a reasonable facsimile made of wood, metal, or plastic. And he is right!

Unfortunately, the equation undergoes considerable change when a tyro flunks selection of bait, tackle, and presentation. Perhaps more than the advocate of artificial lures, the highly successful bait fisherman must be a specialist.

Anyone can drape a hook with the flesh of a clam, a shrimp or a seaworm—and catch an occasional fish. Not everyone can insure consistent success with such morsels. Doing so is an art in itself, and an art that has been relegated to obscurity by the champions of the artificial.

Some beginners never progress beyond the basics: they dwell in a rosy world of "fisherman's luck" and they assume that chance is more important than skill. The hooks of these happy warriors are ill-chosen and usually dull. Their terminal tackle is atrocious and their presentation crude. A fish, to be captured, must engage in some aquatic version of Russian roulette.

A minority of elite bait fishermen study their quarry and the natural forage available, match tackle to the job at hand—and regularly get into the record books with big fish. These experts are students of their sport, and they are every bit as skillful as the great anglers who choose to catch gamesters on artificials alone.

Without examining each species, and then discussing size ranges found on various American seaboards, it is quite futile to list proper hook sizes for each occasion. Generally speaking, anglers on the Atlantic coast gravitate toward hooks which are too large. Note that hook size, length of shank and bend are equally important, and then seek out that which is most effective for your particular need.

For example, the O'Shaughnessy bend probably comes closest to being all-purpose, but Eagle Claw types often wreak greater havoc when soft baits are used. Small, long-shanked hooks are preferred for winter flounder fishing, because this species has a small mouth and is not spooked by the long shank which facilitates unhooking. Siwash or Pacific salmon bends are well chosen for use on small to medium-sized, soft-mouthed jumping fish. Heavy Sobeys or Martus may be most effective on big game, sharks, or corpulent black sea bass: their primary boasts are bulk and strength.

Any hook which is to be used with light tackle should be made of fine wire, if only because it is difficult to drive a heavy point home with a limber rod and elastic line. In this connection, and in any other, hooks should be needle-sharp. The dull hook is an invitation to disaster. A hook hone works wonders with tiny, light wire barbs; a flat machinist's file is more satisfactory for touching up heavier hooks, such as those from 1/0 on up.

For successful fishing with natural bait, keep hardware to an absolute minimum. If the rig calls for swivels and snaps, be sure that these are the lightest deemed practical. Sinkers should be just heavy enough to hold bottom in the tidal currents encountered. Use monofilament leaders for fish that lack cutting teeth, and wire for those with sharp teeth.

Sinkers are part of every bait fisherman's arsenal, and we have examined them in Chapter 7. However, there are occasions in live-lining where the sinker is not used, and there are times when a float, or a series of floats, will produce.

In one important variation, a float is used to bring the bait above the bottom and thus place it beyond the reach of trash fish. Some call this the "Jersey doodlebug," and Jersey men add a measure of attraction by painting the cork some bright color, usually red, yellow or orange, and fitting it with bucktail dressing. A simple cork float, rigged ahead of the bait, may suffice.

High-low rigs feature a sinker at the terminal end of the leader, with two or three droppers spaced at intervals above it, each armed with a hook. This can be an effective combination when one species is feeding on or close to the bottom and another is cruising at a slightly higher level.

Hundreds of combinations have been dreamed up for specific game fish under unusual conditions, and it is always worthwhile to study such variations in order to put them into use where the normal approach fails to pay off.

Bait presentation is the great stumbling block for beginners. In the final analysis everything depends on offering a tempter so naturally and so subtly that it is accepted as bona-fide. Here again, one must take the fish into consideration and second-guess its immediate preference in foodstuffs.

Some salt water gamesters are sharp-eyed and suspicious: for them the bait must be absolutely lifelike. Others will settle for unnatural bits and chunks: indeed small pieces of food which waft the right scent into surrounding waters may be most effective.

Winter flounders and tautog may fall for very short chunks of seaworm threaded over the bend of a hook, while a long, naturally streamed worm may result in short strikes and failure while seeking the nibbler. Striped bass usually prefer naturally streamed worms, although there are occasions when bunched-up squirmers are accepted. Don't ask us why!

Most of the literature exhorts a fisherman to use nothing but fresh bait, the fresher the better. In marine angling, it has always been stylish to make one exception: rigged eels are supposed to be much more tempting when they smell to high heaven. We are not quite sure that this is good reasoning, but we know that spoiled bait can be extremely effective.

Every now and then, for reasons which escape logic, those species that feed on seaworms seem to prefer a rancid offering to that which is vibrant and squirming. Cod and haddock will take baits which are much the worse for wear—indeed, haddock seem to delight in gulping a stinking tidbit.

Some years ago one of our readers submitted a lengthy article which was *not* printed in *Salt Water Sportsman,* much to his dismay. He told of a fruitless striped bass fishing trip which was made successful by the attention of a family dog. The mutt lifted a leg and liberally sprinkled the party's supply of seaworms. Thereafter bass launched an all-out attack and the catch was worth recalling. We do not recommend such treatment: indeed, having heard of it once, we hope we never encounter the phenomenon again!

Often a half-dozen small bait fish, such as sand eels or sperling, can be presented en masse. Usual technique is to thread one bait fish up over the shank of the hook, and then suspend four or five others from the bend by hooking them through the eye sockets. This is an effective method when gamesters are feeding on the particular small bait used.

In southern waters the large shrimp is a deadly bait. For live presentation they should be hooked through the tail or horn. Horn-hooking is good sense, for the bait is then presented in a lifelike manner and attitude. However, one must be careful not to pierce the brain and thus kill the bait. Drive the point through a clear spot: if the dark spot aft of the horn is punctured, the shrimp will die quickly.

Tiny grass shrimp, much used as chum and bait in the Chesapeake Bay and northward, are threaded on the hook three to four at a time and are almost always fished in a slick of live shrimp. In this case the hook itself should be small, usually ranging from number 2 to 1/0.

Fiddler crabs and many other crustaceans are deadly baits for marine game fish. The fiddler has one big claw which usually is broken before being used as bait. The hook is worked up through the socket and out the dorsal shell. The barb should be exposed to insure hooking when a fish bites.

Other crabs, such as the small calico, the larger green or blue-claw varieties, may be used whole or quartered, depending upon size and the fish sought. Soft crabs, popular as bait in some areas, must be secured to the hook with fine netting or elastic bands. At the turn of the century anglers used small, live lobsters and lobster tails as bait for striped bass. It is unlikely that this practice will ever be resumed, owing to the cost of legal-sized lobsters and laws prohibiting possession of so-called shorts.

An astonishing variety of natural baits are used to catch marine game fish, and just as many hooking methods are employed. Rigs depend on size of bait and action required. West coast anchovies, which should swim rapidly, are hooked through the gill collar. East coast herring or mackerel are pinned through the skin just ahead of the dorsal fin. There are variations galore.

A strong bait fish such as an alewife can be used with a fish-finder rig by thrusting the point of the hook through the tough gristle under the gills, just ahead of the pectoral fins. This permits the bait to swim upright in the current, even though it is anchored by a sinker some 18 or 20 inches below.

When herring or mackerel are to be live-lined, without weight—but occasionally with a float—the best hooking area is just ahead of the dorsal fin. This keeps the bait slightly off balance, so that it keeps struggling, pursues an erratic course—and thus intrigues hungry game fish.

On a live-lined bait of this type—particularly a large bait—one must use some care in selecting hooks. There is a wide difference of opinion, and all of the favored combinations work. Some prefer a single large barb, such as an 8/0 O'Shaughnessy, while others feel that the single 6/0 to 7/0 Siwash is best. In recent years there has been a switch to very small trebles—light wire hooks in the 1/0 bracket. These, according to their champions, are more easily swallowed by game fish and then insure a hook-up.

Single beaked hooks are frowned upon by most of the regulars, primarily because they may turn in and bury their points in the body of the bait. Stingers, in some cases, are recommended.

The "stinger" is simply a second hook, attached to a short trace of leader material and laced through the tail of the bait. When baits are large, such stingers do not seriously handicap their swimming ability, and certainly save a percentage of short strikers.

Another technique used with some success in recent years is to employ a live bait fish together with a trailing dead bait, such as a sewed-on squid. Here the live fishlet provides action for the dead one—which must be rigged with considerable care so that it appears alive when dragged around. A trailing pork rind may serve the same purpose.

In every fishing area certain baits are considered most effective, but the smart operator ignores custom and studies his immediate problem. In the New England area, striped bass fishermen have discovered that big bass will often grab a small pollock as readily as they'll take a herring or a mackerel. Norfolk spot account for big channel bass, and pigfish are esteemed by snook. Small game fish of all kinds are eaten with glee by larger game fish.

Eels are snacks for many marine fighters, from stripers to snook and white marlin. Eels can be rigged whole, or fished alive. If you plan to work them while they are still wriggling, pass a hook up through the edge of an eye socket and out through the gill cover. Thus pinned, an eel can be cast and then retrieved slowly, or it can be fished just over the bottom by means of a float. A strike requires careful free-spooling, so that the predator can run with its quarry, halt, and swallow it.

Live bait fishing is not confined to small or medium-sized battlers. Some of the best catches of huge game fish are made on bait. The trolled bonito, flying fish, and balao are natural baits of tremendous importance to the offshore fisherman.

Wherever a man fishes in salt water a whole host of creatures are ready to serve as bait. It is the angler's task to determine just which of these morsels is most effective at a given time, and then to employ tackle which displays the bait to best advantage.

Selection of a proper bait may begin at the seaside tackle shop, for proprietors usually know which offerings are most in demand. However, it is common knowledge that certain game fish can be highly selective. Once committed to feeding on a particular seafood they often spurn all others. If you can determine the bait most in demand at that magic hour, obtain such a bait and use it well—the outcome is never in doubt.

18

BAIT ON ICE

TIME FLAPS ITS SABLE WINGS MORE RAPIDLY THAN WE THINK these days. One of our friends dropped by the other morning and stated flatly that we had never published anything concerning the preservation of natural baits. We bridled in our best horselike manner, but when we investigated, discovered that almost four years have passed since we tackled the subject in detail.

Undoubtedly, one reason we felt that the discussion had been more recent is the fact that we receive letters on the subject each week and our replies have fallen into a sort of pattern that is so familiar we feel that the subject has been covered. The pattern, with elaborations and improvements, is given below to forestall additional letters asking for this information.

The ideal preserved bait retains its flexibility, natural color, toughness and aroma—the latter meaning natural aroma and not an odor caused by deterioration. Unfortunately, for the average angler to procure a solution or solid pack that insures such results is next to impossible. Refrigeration is the best short-term solution, but competition with the lady of the house for icebox space can become keen. Also, even the freshest of natural baits become a little tired after a week in the cooler.

A deep freeze is the next alternative. Whole fish, squid, shrimp, eels, and the like may be kept for long periods if they are quick-frozen and stored in sealed packages. It is wise to clean larger baits that are to be preserved in this manner. Many small packages are to be preferred over one large one, for refreezing unused surpluses is not satisfactory. Once deterioration starts, after a bait has been thawed, it will continue even in the freezer. Note also that this method tends to soften bait because it breaks down the tissue cells.

Bivalves, such as clams and mussels, should never be frozen in the shell. Extreme cold causes the muscles holding the shells together to gape—a helpful hint if you are having trouble opening clams for eating purposes. Bacterial action will start and the shellfish will spoil if kept in its natural state. Shuck out the meats, wash them in a brine solution, and then package them for freezing if this type of bait is your favorite.

Unfortunately the "dry freeze" process is not available to the home bait keeper. In this process, water is removed from the animal as it is frozen. When the job is completed, the bait may be kept without refrigeration and, to bring it back to its natural state, it is simply soaked in water. Such bait is, or has been, commercially available in several forms.

Pickling solutions or solid packs are what most anglers seek for a variety of natural baits. With these, no special care need be taken once the bait has been treated. It is therefore ready for use at any time. Plastic containers, rather than glass, are recommended for large fish and eels—for a broken jar can make a tackle box, boat, or beach buggy very unpleasant to the nose for many weeks after it has been broken.

There is one primary rule when preparing any liquid solution for such pickling: boil the water for at least ten minutes before using it. This will kill any bacteria that may be lurking, ready to attack the bait's flesh the moment they have a chance. The water should be allowed to cool sufficiently so that it does not cook whatever is immersed in it.

Most widely used of all preservatives for home pickling is common salt. Ordinary table salt is the least desirable, for it contains additives to eliminate caking of the finished product. Kosher and cooking salt are more coarsely ground, contain no additives, and are to be preferred. Both are available at any modern grocery store or supermarket. Salt solutions and salt packs tend to toughen most baits, which often is an advantage.

To make a satisfactory brine solution, allow water to boil for ten minutes, then keep adding salt and stirring until no more of the chemical is dissolved. Chemists call such a point "saturation," which means that further salt will simply sink to the bottom of the container. If the solution will float a whole egg—be sure to leave the shell intact—it has reached the saturation point.

Small bait fish may be kept almost indefinitely in such a solution. Larger baits should either be cleaned, or a knife inserted into the body cavity so that the liquid can penetrate completely. Odor of the solution surrounding the pickled bait can be reduced by changing the brine from time to time. However, this odor apparently does not reduce fish-catching effectiveness.

Packing bait in plain salt, without water added, will also preserve it for a long period. However, since salt draws off liquid from the bait itself, such baits will often appear shriveled after a week or two. Soaking these in fresh or salt water for a few minutes will restore their original shape.

Addition of common household borax to a salt pack will help to keep baits limber, but don't use too much of it. We have experimented with this combination a good deal and find that three parts of salt to one part of borax produces the best results. With greater concentrations of borax, the body cavities of such baits as eels and larger fish will rot.

A pack new to us was described by Bob Banghart, a Los Angeles nurseryman and surf fishing enthusiast, who says that the system is an old Japanese trick. He takes mackerel filets and sprinkles them with a fifty-fifty mixture of salt and sugar. The filets are then placed in a container with a layer of the mixture, a layer of the filets, another layer of salt and sugar, and so on. When the mackerel flesh turns slightly pink, it is ready for use and is an excellent bait for surf perch. This pack does not keep the filets indefinitely, but is good for several weeks.

Another effective mackerel pack uses no salt whatever. Outdoor writer Roland Patterson's "candied mackerel" is layered in a mixture of blood meal, water, and sugar. (Blood meal can be purchased from garden supply centers: it is used in the culture of roses and other plants.)

It is evident that sugar attracts some species of game fish, and perhaps a bit of it added to any of the solutions we have mentioned might add to their effectiveness. However, the blood meal, sugar, and water mixture is not intended to keep mackerel filets over any considerable period of time. Such a pack could be frozen, of course, and used immediately after thawing. If such bait strips are to be stored over any period of time, then they'd best be heavily salted.

Museums throughout the world preserve many of their marine specimens in a formaldehyde solution. There is no doubt about the effectiveness of this, but the odor produced is horrible. Anglers who wish to play around with this chemical should take care not to inhale its fumes excessively and not to allow it to remain on the human hide for any length of time.

Formalin is the trade name for a solution that is 40 per cent straight formaldehyde and 60 per cent distilled water. It may be purchased at any drugstore. For use as a bait-preserving liquid, combine one part of formalin with nine parts of distilled or boiled water. If the bait is very large, it should be "fixed" in a solution double that strength for about ten days, then transferred to the one-to-nine bottle.

Baits prepared in this manner lose much of their natural coloring. They also are toughened considerably, which is an advantage for the big-game man who wants a durable skip bait. Oddly enough, most big-game species do not appear to object to the odor of formaldehyde—in fact, some claim that billfish are attracted by it. Small species, however, definitely do object to the smell and rarely will take such a tempter.

Baits fixed in formaldehyde and formalin tend to become fixed in the position they occupy in a jar or container filled with the chemical. This is a definite handicap and the angler should keep it in mind. Keep baits straight and well aligned in the pickling jar, or they'll emerge crooked and impervious to any straightening efforts.

There are various other solutions which may be used to pickle baits. One of these, known to us as the "Burlingame Cocktail" in honor of the man who developed it—the late Mark W. Burlingame—consists of one-half ounce of formalin, three ounces of glycerin, and 20 ounces of distilled or boiled water. Soak the bait in this solution for a minimum of ten days, then place it in brine. Colors will be better preserved and the bait will remain more limber.

If the bait concerned is to be bleached slightly, another mix consists of one part Chlorox or other commercial laundry bleach, one part formalin, two parts glycerin, and ten parts distilled or boiled water. This solution is particularly good for filets that are to be converted into strip baits at a later date. As in the case of the Burlingame Cocktail, the filets may be soaked for ten days or two weeks, and then transferred to brine.

Those who haunt medical laboratories always think of alcohol as a preservative, since many medical specimens float about in the stuff for years on end. For the angler, alcohol has a good many disadvantages. It is expensive in the first place, for pure grain alcohol with water and perhaps a bit of glycerin added gets the best results. Second, it evaporates quickly once the container has been opened—and fishermen want a container that can be opened with a minimum of fuss. Finally, colors of some baits, particularly shrimps and crustaceans of all sorts, are changed radically the moment they sop up enough alcohol to have a preservative effect.

We recommend that alcohol be used for medicinal or beverage purposes to suit the fisherman's taste, and not for preserving bait.

Shrimp, crabs, and squid present particular problems. Although all three may be preserved in solutions or packs, they soon turn red and, as often as not, deteriorate rapidly. Sometimes a red shrimp, crab, or squid will draw strikes: often it will not. The only answer thus far is the deep freeze.

The deep freeze is also the answer for large blocks of ground chum, used by many tuna fishermen and bluefish anglers. Texture, color, and—to a lesser degree—freshness, is not a major problem with chum. The main purpose of the stuff is to attract game fish to the area where an angler can catch them. If the actual bait used by the angler is fresher and more appealing than the chum itself, it has a better chance of success.

Although fishermen usually think of liquids or packs for keeping bait, there is another way in which certain types may be preserved. This involves what might be called curing—for want of a better description. Early settlers in this country did a good deal of fish curing to supply themselves with a source of food that would last through the winter months. Some of this is still done, but the technique is unknown to many: it may be applied to the preservation of bait fish.

In tropical climates, almost any fish may be utilized, but in most areas of the United States, species which have little oil in their flesh should be selected. Any member of the herring family, with the exception of the oily menhaden, is a good choice.

Scale the fish and remove entrails and gills, but leave the head on for reasons which will be evident in a moment. Split the body from the belly side almost in two. Leave skin and enough flesh along the back so that the fish remains in one piece. Sprinkle salt liberally over all surfaces. If it is raining, stop right there—place the bait in the refrigerator and wait until the sun is shining strong and bright.

String the future bait up through mouth and gills. (Now you see why the head is left on.) Leave space so that no bait touches its neighbor. Hang the whole string out just like clothes on a line on washday. A hot, breezy day is best. Naturally, such a tempting meal should be well out of the reach of wandering house cats.

In an amazingly short time, the surface flesh of fish prepared in this way will dry sufficiently so that flies and other insects will be discouraged. In tropical areas we have seen this happen in a matter of one hour. However, the curing process to be complete takes at least a week. Examination of the cured fish from time to time, to determine whether or not there are still any soft spots, will indicate when such baits are ready for storage.

Storage is simple enough. The dried fish is almost as indestructible as leather. If kept away from dampness, it may be stacked like cordwood. Prior to use, it should be soaked overnight in water. Bones are almost entirely dissolved in the curing process, so baits prepared in this manner are a bit soft for skipping, but can be used to good advantage as cut bait and for drifting.

This same system may be used on filets or strips of larger species. In the New England area, dried cod was a staple food for export in years gone by. For reasons lost in antiquity, strips of this fish were called "Scully-Jo," and youngsters along the coast chomped on these strips in much the same manner as those of today eat Popsicles. A soaked bit of "Scully-Jo" doubled in brass as a bait for bottom fish, thus completing some sort of complicated life cycle.

Returning to liquid preservative solutions for a moment, many anglers like to rig baits before placing them in the preservative. Rustproof hooks, swivels, and rigging wire should be used whenever possible. If such hooks and fittings are not readily available, drop a penny or bit of copper into the container holding the rigs, and rusting will be slowed down. In some cases the hooks actually will become lightly copper-plated if this is done.

However, particularly when a brine solution is used, hooks and swivels may weaken through crystallization induced by electrolysis, even when they do not rust. Therefore, if the rig has been soaking for months, test it thoroughly before use. It is better to have it break in your hands than to have it break when a potential world record catch has it in mouth.

When natural bait is scarce along any section of the coast—and this happens at times almost everywhere—a supply of the preserved article can be very useful. The do-it-yourself angler can use any of the methods we have described to insure that he has a suitable bait at the right moment. Those who prefer to let others do the work may purchase preserved baits from any well-equipped tackle store.

19

OFF-BEAT CHUM

ACCOUNTS OF RECOVERY OF VARIOUS STRANGE OBJECTS FROM THE stomachs of fish appear in daily newspapers at regular intervals. Some mercenary cod may have swallowed a diamond ring, a halibut with a sense of timing engulfed a watch, or a grouper (with dental problems?) is found to have consumed a set of false teeth. All, it appears, is grist to the gastronomical mill if a fish is interested enough.

This can be rather frustrating to an angler who has spent hours trying to tempt such fish with the best of recommended lures or baits. However, some of the off-beat items that are not found naturally in the marine environment can be put to good use by imaginative anglers. Those listed in following paragraphs have been, and are, used as chum—or to supplement chum—in salt water fishing.

Some of the strange tempters are more popular than others, of course. Ordinary corn, either cooked, canned, or fresh off the cob, has become a standard chum used by many winter flounder fishermen. Dried corn may also be used, but often it does not sink to the level where fish are feeding. In our limited experience with this type of baiting, the yellower the corn kernels are, the better they seem to work.

It is difficult to understand why any flounder should develop an appetite for such fare. Obviously corn in its natural state is not found below the sea's surface, yet the flatties gobble it with delight. Color evidently is important as an attractor. Texture, taste and perhaps the action of individual kernels as they sink may be involved in the final successful results.

Another classic example of this strange attraction of terrestrial food products to various ocean species is bread. Toss a piece of hard bread into the vicinity of a coral or limestone reef in semitropical or tropical waters: usually a host of small fish, among them pompano and small sheepshead, will attack the baker's product the moment it hits the water and will devour it down to the last crumb.

Under these circumstances we have experimented in an attempt to determine whether color and texture were the major factors in attraction. Bits of foam plastic, cloth, wood, and various other materials that might have the general appearance of the staff of life were tossed seaward—an operation that probably induced doubts about our sanity on the part of observing native anglers.

Usually, the fish ignore such offerings, unless bread has been offered first. Even when this had been done, most of the substitutes were given a quick glance but were not actually touched. Some species will—in a feeding frenzy—grasp the inedible product, and expel it immediately. In this case texture and color apparently were less important that odor and taste.

Next, take the case of rolled oats. Uncooked, this product is favored by northern weakfishermen who wish to "stretch" their supply of grass shrimp when chumming. We have used it for this purpose on many occasions, and rarely has a particle of rolled oats been found in the stomach of a catch—although the grass shrimp often were there.

There is no proof, but we believe that the color and action of the rolled oats as it sinks does the work. Each particle wobbles down through the water, in much the same manner as a leaf falls from a tree. Undoubtedly light is reflected, the fish is attracted to the glitter—and finds shrimp to feed upon. Perhaps bits of tinsel would do a comparable job, but rolled oats are cheaper and more readily available.

Although we have never tried it, we have been assured by those who have done so that cooked potato is an excellent chum stretcher. The number of marine species which count potato in their regular oceanic diet certainly must be minimal, so—again—success may be assured by eye appeal that brings fish within range of a more natural offering.

When canned cat and dog foods are considered, the appeal is more obvious. These items contain oils and animal proteins which may well be similar to the natural feed found in the ocean. Almost any game fish is attracted to such a chum. Keep the slick going by punching several holes in a can of cat or dog food, and by lowering it over the side on a line. Water and tidal current will wash out a steady driblet of material.

Similarly, lettuce and garden peas may tempt the Pacific opaleye, a species which nibbles on various marine vegetable growths, as well as on animal life. Like the pig, to which it bears no resemblance whatever, the opaleye can be considered omnivorous. This does not explain why many of the mackerels will eat cooked peas in a chum line, and evidently eat them with relish. Mackerel are not vegetarians at all.

Like the ring, watch, and false teeth mentioned at the outset, all additives or attractors used need not be edible. Sand or fine gravel is a common mixer employed by those who are chumming with ground natural bait. Whether or not the sand acts as a reflector of light is a moot point. There is no question that oil and particles of chum cling to it and therefore sink fairly rapidly. This action sets up a vertical chum line at varying depths in addition to the horizontal slick.

There are other ways to do this. One of the oldest methods is to fill a paper bag with the ground fish or whatever else is used. Add a rock or several handfuls of gravel, enough to sink the whole package, and lower it over the side. When the bag has reached the desired depths, a sudden jerk on the cord that secures it will cause the weight to break through the paper—and the chum will scatter.

The same effect may be achieved by a caster who wraps chum in a piece of light tissue paper. This will hold together long enough to make the cast or throw the package, complete with small rock for weight, into the desired area. The paper then disintegrates. Addition of such a tasty, instant chum pot—tied about a foot above a hook adorned with natural bait—insures automatic chumming in the precise area where the basic lure is located.

Today, there is a new material which is even better than tissue paper for this purpose. Pharmaceutical houses supply sheets of water-soluble plastic that looks much like ordinary cellophane. The material is the same as that used in capsules which are swallowed by humans to cure their various ills. Within a minute after hitting the water, the plastic film dissolves and its contents are scattered. This water-soluble material is handy for wrapping tender baits, such as salmon eggs, seaworms, and mussels which tend to fly off the hook during a cast. Note that drugstores do not ordinarily handle the stuff: look for it in pharmaceutical houses, as mentioned. Note also that the plastic film must be kept tightly sealed against moisture, a requirement sometimes difficult for any angler.

With many cleverly prepared and natural types of chum available to the average fishermen, few are willing to experiment.

Selection of prepared foods to use on fish for this purpose is largely a matter of guesswork, although there are some guidelines. Just how corn, peas, bread, and other items originally found their way into the world of sportfishing is a mystery lost in antiquity.

Some of these selections undoubtedly came from the fresh water angling world. Corn, for example, has been a well-known carp bait over a period of centuries. Perhaps some enterprising soul who had little knowledge of the feeding habits of his quarry simply figured that salt water species might also be interested in such an offering. In other cases, discoveries may well have been accidental.

It seems evident that action, color, odor, and taste all play a part in attracting fish to unusual materials. In some cases, such as that of beef blood and blood meal, odor and taste are all-important; action is completely lacking and color probably has little effect. On a trip with one enthusiast, where sharks were being stalked, dried blood chum ran low and the sharker added several quarts of tomato juice to the slick. The color effect was not bad, but the results were! It was an expensive experiment, and sharks left immediately.

In other cases, action and color apparently are the deciding factors so far as fish are concerned. Both dolphin and bluefish, and perhaps many other species as well, will strike a speedily trolled banana peel which has been cut in the shape of a strip bait. Chances are slight that the quarry has ever become fond of the tang of banana oil. Therefore odor and taste do not enter the equation.

Consider the fact that one of salt water's noblest gamesters, the tarpon, can become a regular garbage hound. Many anglers, particularly those fishing out of Gulf of Mexico ports, have found it expedient to follow garbage scows that dump their contents well offshore. Someone scientifically inclined, with plenty of time on his hands, might determine whether the silver king prefers old coffee grounds or a snack of moldy orange peel.

When standard chum runs out and substitutes are being sought, it seems evident that certain criteria should be observed. First, select something that boasts a color which contrasts with the surrounding water. Second, if possible, select a substance that sinks with a fluttering motion, such as the rolled oats previously mentioned. Finally, bet on a substance that emits oil, gravy, or what have you. This last choice is most difficult of all, because it is evident that humans cannot determine what tastes and odors appeal to fish. It is a question of trial and error.

There is another point that should be mentioned. Chumming with foodstuffs such as bread may not attract game fish immediately. However, the bread will create a concentration of vegetarians, such as mullet and assorted minnows, and these, in turn, draw larger game to the area. In effect, you will be chumming to attract a storm of bait.

Any well-educated salt water fisherman knows that it pays to be an opportunist. Try something different. Who knows what mysterious allure lies in the containers so brilliantly displayed in American supermarkets!

20

STRIP BAITS

ALTHOUGH WE TEND TO USE ARTIFICIALS, THERE COMES A TIME when our artistic instincts and the fussiness of the fish we are seeking combine to force us into preparing one of the most effective trolling baits to be found. Armed with a keen-edged knife and the dedication of a sculptor, we go to work on a small dead fish to produce a strip bait.

Definitions are important in the field of marine angling, and we plan to be very specific in what is meant by a strip bait. Some anglers call the natural lure a cut bait; others generalize and place it under the term "skip bait." Actually, a strip bait is obviously cut and it may well skip when trolled. However, in our angling lexicon, a cut bait is a chunk, glob, or what have you placed on a hook and still-fished from the beach or from a boat. A skip bait can be a whole creature, part of it, or even an artificial trolled in such a manner that it rises on the top of the water and, as the name implies, skips. A skittered bait, in case you are interested, is one that moves through the water in the same manner, but the movement is imparted to it by rod action or by wind. The angler does not move around himself.

A true strip bait is a sliver cut from any bait creature. It can be primarily a strip of flesh, as when the bait is cut from a whole squid, or it can be both flesh and skin, as when cut from the belly of a bonito. Usually this carver's work of art is cut longitudinally from the creature, but there are times when the bait supply is low and the cutting must be done perpendicular to what might be called the mean axis of the bait.

Every skipper and angler who uses strip bait has his own particular method of cutting the strip itself. Shapes, sizes, and tapers vary with the personal tastes of the fishermen and, of course, with the game fish sought. The basic strip when viewed from the top is rounded at the head and tapers to a point at the rear. Length is approximately eight times the width at the widest point. Thickness may vary from a full inch down to skin thickness.

Although basic shapes are legion, the various bevels and trimmings in thickness are the characteristics which allow every angler to use his imagination to the full. Some insist that the very center of the strip should be thickest, while others maintain that the portion at the strip's head should be—and so on. The main purpose of such artistry is to obtain the maximum possible action when the lure is trolled through the water. The more the strip wriggles and shimmies, the better it will be as a game fish attractor.

The only point upon which strip bait designers agree is that the hook should ride with the shank down and the point up. It is almost impossible to balance such a lure so that it rides with the hook point down. Unfortunately, a poorly cut strip may ride sideways or spin. When this happens, go back to work with a knife or cut another until proper balance is achieved.

Some push the hook point through the head of the strip and troll the tempter in this manner. This works well enough in an emergency when haste is required. However, short strikes may result and, in addition, the strip is likely to tear loose after a short time.

A safety-pin twist in leader wire is the usual method for affixing a strip. The snap is put through a small hole at the head of the strip. The hook point is then thrust through the strip itself so that the bait lies smoothly between snap and hook bend. Some prefer to use a regular terminal snap or snap swivel between leader and hook. This is a requirement if cable wire or nylon leader material is favored. Even with such rigs, short strikes may follow and an additional trailing hook may be added—even though it cuts down some of the action.

The hook eye itself may have the leader wire twisted through it in such a manner that the hook is comparatively rigid. More action is obtained by having the hook attached by a simple loop. The trouble with this is that, as the bait strip skips around, it tends to double back on the leader and foul.

As far as size of the strip is concerned, it can vary from a scant two inches for snapper bluefish, on up to 20 inches or more for marlin and tuna. The average strip for offshore fishing ranges between 12 and 18 inches. For inshore and bay trolling, lengths average six to ten inches. It is better to err on the side of excessive length than to cut the strip short. The longer it is, the more wiggle it will have.

Almost any fish that swims, plus squid, may be used for fashioning a strip bait. Members of the mackerel family are favored simply because their flesh is firmer than that of many other species, such as the herrings. However, salmon fishermen of the Pacific coast choose the herrings because they are the natural food of the quarry sought, and also because the strip exudes a considerable quantity of oil. This acts as an attractor in its own right.

Oddly enough, strips cut from members of the family of the species sought seem to be particularly effective. Thus a piece of fluke, suitably carved, is an excellent choice for catching fluke; bits of bonito and mackerel will take bonito and mackerel—as well as their close cousins, the tunas. We have never heard of anyone using a marlin strip for marlin or a salmon strip for salmon, but it might be worth trying!

When rigging the strip, there are two schools of thought on whether the skin should be facing downward to the ocean floor or upward to the sky. Those who select the first method claim that the skin's color is more readily visible to the game fish than the flesh. The opposite camp says the flesh has more appeal because it is more tasty. We happen to belong to the second school, but for a special reason. It is easier to prepare a well-balanced strip when the flesh is down than when it is up.

Traditionally, strips are cut from the belly of a bait fish and they are therefore predominantly white. However, anglers who break this tradition are often pleasantly surprised. A strip cut from the dark back of a mackerel, for example, can be very effective when the weather is dull or cloudy. The rule—if it can be called a rule—seems to be: use a light strip on a bright day and a dark one on a dull day. The reasoning is similar to that which prompts night fishermen to select black plugs—the outline of the lure is distinguished against the sky more readily by the fish beneath.

Primarily a strip bait is a surface lure. It should be fished at a speed sufficient to keep it on top of the waves. It may dive from time to time, but most of its action is a fluttering one over the surface. A wake of bubbles caused by this type of lure can be spotted by game species lurking in the depths. Edges beveled thin seem to increase the amount of wake and also increase the fluttering action.

Occasionally a submerged strip can be highly effective. Any

weight to make the lure run underwater should be added between line and leader, rather than at the eye of the hook when fishing in this manner. The strip itself, of course, must be perfectly balanced to prevent spinning. Trolling speed is reduced or the strip will plane, skid or dive. In very calm weather, when game fish are apt to follow, but not take, a surface lure, the submerged strip often is a killer.

The basic trolled strip bait is highly effective. Its many adaptations in conjunction with other lures or with other methods of angling are equally so. For example, the common Jap feather type of lure may be given further appeal by adding a three to six inch strip of bait directly to the hook. Some anglers even go so far as to decorate all hooks on a plug with lengths of strip bait. This makes casting the result something like heaving a spider through the air, yet the practice still prevails. For our money, if strips are added to plugs, they should be one per plug and should be affixed to the tail hook only. Purists may shudder over this addition, but we are not—and never have been—members of the purist party. We happen to like to catch fish.

Both still fishermen and drift fishermen may use strips to good advantage. For the former, reading a rig from the bottom up, first comes a sinker, next a hook with a cut or chunk bait, finally a hook with a strip bait. This top hook should be either on a stiff snell or on a spreader so that it will stand clear of the line or leader. The bait will then flutter in the current in an enticing manner.

The old-time fluke fishermen of Long Island, New York, learned that a strip was one of the deadliest baits available when drifting. It still is, and the strip is usually from the belly of the fluke itself, as previously described. Some drift this behind a weighted spinner just above the ocean floor. Others forget about the spinner and use only a sinker 18 to 24 inches ahead of the hook. The sinker bumps bottom and stirs up tiny puffs of mud or sand. It is followed by the strip riding slightly off bottom and this, in turn, is presumably followed by the fluke. To insure that fouling is kept to a minimum, many use a tiny cork float at the hook eye so that the strip rides several inches above the sinker's line of travel.

Pier and bridge fishermen can live-line a strip bait with telling effect. The baited hook is lowered into the current and allowed to drift out a considerable distance. A split shot or tiny clamp-on sinker is sometimes required on the leader to keep the strip riding properly. Often strikes result when the line is being let out, so no slack should be permitted. When well away from the bridge or pier structure, the reel gear is engaged and the strip is reeled in with short jerks of the rod tip. This will cause the bait to play on the surface of the water just as it does when trolled. Strikes often come when the strip is right next to the pilings and it is therefore wise to dabble the strip for a moment before lifting it clear of the water or allowing it to drift out again for a repeat performance.

If an angler is not artistically inclined or interested in carving, tackle manufacturers have cooperated to make his life easy. Today it is possible to purchase strip baits made from the natural creature and bottled. If something more permanent is desired, there are all sizes and shapes of pork rind available, in many different colors. Finally, the latest addition to the strip-bait clan is a whole series of these lures made from special soft, limber plastics. These also come in a variety of sizes, shapes, and colors. In brief, the tackle makers know a good thing when they see it.

21
CALLING ALL MATES

MATES ON CHARTER BOATS ARE UNDERPAID, BUT SOME OF THEM do right well financially. In addition to their dollar an hour average, the better practitioners collect a succession of healthy tips. We feel no compulsion to write a field manual for mates, but it is high time for somebody to outline standards.

Tipping has always bothered those who go aboard sport fishing boats. No angler wants to be a cheap skate, and few desire to become patsies by offering too much in the way of lagniappe. There is no norm, other than the standard 10 percent for services rendered.

That, of course, is the key: "for services rendered."

Charter skippers, generally, find it difficult to hire efficient mates. Those who are lucky enough to sign on retired seafaring men who take pride in their craft, or vacationing college boys who are similarly impressed by the necessity for excellence, have no complaints.

Unfortunately, for every crack mate there are three who deem this job a summer vacation. These lackadaisical characters drive the skipper right out of his alleged mind: he'd fire 'em immediately if he could find a replacement before the next patron arrives on the scene.

Patrons are confused. Most of them know that the mate is supposed to be a general font of knowledge and a whirlwind of service. They are surprised to encounter a crewman who is slow, inept, and surly. At the dock, such customers finger their wallets and wonder how much they are obliged to tip.

The answer is—nothing!

There is no obligation to tip. A gratuity indicates satisfaction, and service should be such that the fisherman is pleased. Those who are neglected, plagued with poor terminal tackle, forced to wait for basic amenities or deprived of attention should pay the skipper's agreed-upon fee and go home, never to return.

On the other hand, a mate who is efficient deserves his 10 percent stipend—or more if you can afford it. The good mate can make your trip a glorious adventure and can insure the catching of fish that would otherwise have been lost. In some cases the mate is more important than the skipper, for he is the fine link between boat, angler, and fish.

Good mates are very close to their skippers: they know exactly what is required and maintain an almost telepathic communication with the master. Thumps, delivered by an imperious heel on a flying bridge, code certain actions. Words are unnecessary.

Don't try to decipher these communications, for they are part of the captain-mate relationship. Do evaluate the mate. See whether he is attending to his job and your needs. The mate is a maitre d' on the high seas: his task is to make you feel like visiting royalty. He should be a craftsman with rigging, a helper when necessary, and a general jack of all trades in the cockpit.

Experienced anglers may shrug off the suggestions of a mate when it comes to rigging tackle or setting a proper fighting drag. This is their prerogative, yet even the most erudite of marine fishermen require certain services.

These include the proper handling of fighting chairs and harness—on the double when things happen fast. One looks for sharp gaffs and ready nets. An angler should never find it necessary to criticize the handling of a leader wire or the rigging of a bait.

Before we continue this combined diatribe and praise of mates in general, let no angler entertain the false notion that a mate is a servant or slavey. Good mates are proud men, expert at their trade and obliged to take no guff from ill-mannered patrons. Treat the crewman as an equal and he will serve you well.

Unless previously agreed upon, no boat is expected to provide free food and drink. Usually it is the angler's responsibility to tote dinner and to include enough to host the skipper and mate.

Nor is it the mate's primary mission to prepare sandwiches and drinks, either soft or hard—but a majority of good crewmen will do this cheerfully. Obviously, any mate who drinks too much firewater on a charter trip becomes a liability.

Invariably, a time is set for the initiation of a sport fishing trip. If the mate is tardy, one may miss a tide and even miss a tussle with a great gamester. Sleepy crewmen have delayed and thus ruined trips. The sluggards deserve no tips. In fact, they really deserve a cold dunking at the Deep Six. If this were not against the law it might be standard operating procedure—with the skipper's blessing.

Since the mate is a general factotum aboard any sport fishing boat, it is his task to meet anglers as they arrive at the dock, to remain in the near, but respectful background as his skipper greets patrons, to tote duffel aboard and provide chairs for the weary, to offer advice when asked, and to suggest techniques when he is aware that his sports are amateurs. All this must be done subtly and diplomatically.

The crack mate is alert and helpful. Whether opening a beer for the muscle-head who sees each cruise as a relaxing water haul, or providing anti-motion-sickness pills for the lady who cringes at the very thought of the sea, he must be quick on the trigger and geared to the desire of his patrons. Service is the watchword, and it must be service with a smile.

People who charter boats want to fish. Therefore, the mate should never engage in personal fishing unless he is specifically asked to participate in the game. He is paid to guide, to instruct, to aid the paying angler—not to get in the way.

That "aid" is a flexible thing. Experienced fishermen may want to do things for themselves, but they'll still keep a weather eye on the mate. In fact, the semi-pro may create more problems than the first-timer, for old hands can spot any slight fluff on the part of a crewman.

By the same token, a mate who *works* for the regulars is practically assured of a tip. Ancient anglers appreciate efficiency and service aboard a boat: some of them have served as skippers or mates, and they recognize the difficulties involved.

Once, booked out of Rock Harbor, Orleans, Massachusetts, we observed a mate who was knee-high to a lobster. Although he was a little guy, he knew his business. First, he was there at the zero hour and eager to stow tackle. The coffee pot was bubbling before the dock lines were cast off.

In action, this youngster tended each rod, hovering like a bait-famished tern, yet never getting in the way. His hooks were sharp and he quietly tested each line with thumb and forefinger to detect possible nicks or frays. We caught fish, and the mate caught a healthy tip. Perhaps more important, we have advised many anglers to book that particular boat.

Only a skipper knows how good his mate can be. The best are wedded to the boat: they take great pride in fish hooked and landed. Because this is so, a crack performer leaves little to chance: his gaffs are needle-sharp and his tackle is properly maintained. The work day does not begin with the arrival of patrons, nor does it end with their departure.

Exceptional mates are great scroungers: they know everyone in the area and manage to procure squid, balao, or whatever bait is needed, from local commercial fishermen just prior to a trip offshore. In many cases the mate employs his so-called leisure hours in cast-netting mullet or trapping eels which will be used to tempt great game fish.

If rigging is necessary the crewman whips out sailmakers' needles and thread the night before a booking. Baits are prepared and iced, so there'll be no delay out beyond harbor bounds. Additional fresh bait is iced for emergency use.

Back at the dock, after a long day on blue water, the red-eyed mate's work is far from done. Now the vessel is dirty, littered with trash and fish slime. The tackle is thrown hell-west and crooked. Gaffs are dull and lines may need cutting back. Soft drinks are lacking and the galley is short of bacon and eggs.

It is the mate's task to maintain his gear, to restock the larder, and to swab down—without being told to do so. He must have everything in readiness for another dawn and another patron. (The skipper, meanwhile, is dining with his latest booking, wondering whether he'll get a couple of hours of sack time before casting off.)

Mates are regularly recruited from vacationing high school boys and college students, ex-skippers, or retired fishermen who thought they could swallow the anchor, plus occasional physicists who are enamored of the sea and taking sabbatical leave. All may be efficient—or impossibly inept. The charter skipper who engages these helpers is the big winner—or loser.

A poor mate is a distinct liability, for his every action discourages patrons. A good one is priceless: he won't get rich, but he'll make a living wage, learn much of the sea and more of human nature.

Efficient mates are destined for success in life (if they have not already achieved fame and are absorbing the good medicine of the sea). They must understand humankind and, within that short period between casting off and reaching the fishing grounds, must evaluate patrons.

Rank amateurs require heavy tackle and drags preset to safe fighting tensions. There is a need, here, for diplomatic coaching and advice. Often, indeed, it is necessary for the mate to set a hook and then hand the rod to his charge. This, of course, is frowned upon by the august International Game Fish Association, as it should be where record fish are concerned—but beginners need help.

Experienced anglers are quickly spotted. They know exactly what they want and require only basic services. Usually the semi-pro's tote their own tackle and know how to use it. There'll be no "setting the hook" for these lads, and if the rigging of bait requires consultation, the angler must be allowed to make his wants known.

The offshore veteran appreciates a good mate, but he doesn't want elementary advice or the usual wet-nursing. He demands a steady hand on the chair and he expects clean, precise gaffing at the end of a battle. He wants a dousing with cool, salt water when that is necessary, and he wants the professional employment of practical gear.

How about the skipper himself? Modern charter captains expect no tip for themselves and, if they receive one, often turn it over to the mate. There are two exceptions. The first is when the skipper is a one-man operation with no mate involved. Then a tip for good service rendered is in order. The second is the once-in-a-lifetime occasion when you break a world's record that you have been seeking for years without end. At that point the sky is the limit!

22
OUTRIGGER COUNTRY

IN THE COOL OF THE EVENING WHEN A GROUP OF BIG-GAME FISHermen gather to wash down their successes or failures with a little of this and a good deal of that, mention casually that some specific angler or guide invented the outrigger. The name of your choice can be from the living or the dead. It will have the same effect—explosive!

Just why many fishermen are so touchy on this particular point is a mystery we have never been able to fathom. The fact of the matter is that the basic idea of the outrigger, used to present a lure or bait in an area outside a boat's wake, may well be as old as fishing itself. Trollers operating before the days of the internal combustion engine were familiar with the technique. Polynesians in the Pacific made use of the idea, and undoubtedly old Uglug, the caveman, developed a crude outrigger for his floating log.

Present-day outriggers of sophisticated construction may be a far cry from the stiff pole used by old-time bluefishermen trolling from a catboat, yet the purpose served is basically the same. The idea is to expand the width of the boat itself, if you will, in order to cover a wider path with more lures as the craft moves through the water. A secondary consideration, although some consider it more important than any other, is presentation of the lure itself in an enticing manner.

Undoubtedly the first outriggers were simply rigid poles extended from the cockpit of a boat at right angles to its keel. Tied into the end of such a pole was a small pulley and a loop of outhaul line running through this. While several fishing lines might be trolled directly over the transom, additional ones could be clipped to the outhaul and, as noted above, the area of water covered was increased. It should be noted at this point that presentation of many lures, rather than one or two, brings better results when seeking some of the schooling species of fish. The basic outrigger serves this purpose.

As big-game fishing developed, anglers began to experiment with flexible outriggers. Tradition has it that Pacific coast fishermen off Catalina were first to concentrate on use of the device primarily for presentation, rather than for extension of the water covered. Noting that marlin fed on flying fish, they attached long, limber bamboo poles to their craft and trolled baits from stout lines attached to the pole tips. As their craft rolled and as the pole flexed, the bait jumped and skipped like the marlin's favorite meal. When a fish was raised by this method, the angler then dropped his own bait astern, complete with hook, and the outriggers were swung in so that the fish had only one choice.

The next step was a logical one. Since a fish often mauled the outrigger bait before it could be withdrawn, and then ignored the flat line streamed directly over the stern, it was obvious that the hooked tempter should be fixed to the outrigger in some manner. All sorts of experiments followed, ranging from light thread used to tie fishing lines to the outhaul, through complicated release knots and simple spring clothespins. The plan, in all cases, was to hold the line to the outhaul against normal trolling pressure, and then release it when a fish struck.

Once the idea of outrigger use had caught on and had been proved successful, particularly with billfish, designers ran wild. Theoretically, an extremely long outrigger would give the most natural action to the bait. It was soon discovered, however, that the rolling and pitching of the boat concerned often whipped the lure around so much that it cartwheeled, tangled, tore loose from the hook—or could not be held in the snap device employed.

Firm in the conviction that it was necessary to get the lure as far away from the boat's wake as possible for best success, anglers developed all sorts of stays and braces to cut down the whipping action of long outriggers. Some of these would have put to shame the aerials used by ham radio operators. Bamboo was the basic material and, for a time, good natural cane brought premium prices from members of the sport fishing fleet—if the sticks were long enough!

Several things then happened more or less simultaneously. First, anglers discovered that reasonable action given to the bait by a comparatively short outrigger might be expected. In many cases, getting the lure away from the side of the boat was not the ultimate solution. Equally good results could be insured simply by dropping the hook farther back astern. Although many modern fishermen do not realize it, this still holds true, particularly when the weather is calm and the water is clear.

The other major factor that revised outrigger construction was the development of glass fiber and tough, light metals. Bamboo, which was subject to rot, splintering, and constant care has practically vanished from the large-boat scene, although it is still used by those in small craft who seek a cheap material for a quick rig. Glass fiber and aluminum alloys now dominate in offshore waters.

Although modern materials and design have advanced since the outrigger first became popular in sport fishing, the basic principles of selection for any given craft still hold true. An angler should first determine whether he plans to use the device primarily to allow more anglers to fish from the cockpit, or to present baits to a particular species. If the former, then a fairly short outrigger will suffice; it will be more easily handled and will require minimum attention. If the latter, advice should be sought from qualified marine architects and experienced skippers. Some 30-foot boats can handle outriggers of their own length—if the craft is broad of beam. Other 30-footers, fitted with long outriggers, will wallow to such an extent that shorter poles are indicated.

In all cases, fittings at the base of the outrigger itself should be of the best quality and should be heavy enough to withstand punishment in heavy weather. The strain produced by a whipping pole in high seas is far greater than the average layman realizes. In addition, the locking system used to hold the fittings in place when the outrigger is swung out or in should be comparatively simple. Trying to juggle a complicated mechanism while balancing on a slippery deck can be not only dangerous but fatal.

In times gone by, small pulleys were used for the outhaul line. These had a nasty habit of jamming at crucial moments. Today, simple plastic or metal rings have replaced the pulleys. The line most favored by anglers is heavy monofilament, which runs smoothly and which does not fray out. The snap, clip or other device used to hold the actual fishing line in place is tied into the outhaul.

The common spring clothespin was standard for use in this manner for many years. For light lures it worked well enough—and still does. By using large swivels between the pin itself and the outhaul line, tendency of the snap to tangle or get out of alignment can be minimized.

However, such pins were found to be too weak to hold heavy

baits or to troll at high speeds. Their strength can be increased by wrapping the jaws with a rubber band. Slipping the pin directly onto the line tends to fray the line at the contact point, and anglers discovered that wrapping a cigarette paper around this point helped. In addition, twisting, but *not* knotting, a loop into the fishing line at the clip point adds holding power.

Fishermen soon began to develop all sorts of release devices for outriggers. Today there are several excellent types on the market, and almost all of these permit adjustment of the pin's holding power for different sizes of lures. In addition, they are designed to minimize fouling as the outrigger bait skips about in the water. Those who use outriggers extensively are well advised to invest in these, and to forget about the old-fashioned clothespin.

The varied uses for outriggers, both on large and small craft, have expanded steadily as the years have passed—and undoubtedly will expand further in the future. The charter skipper, anxious to furnish sport for a maximum number of people, can troll four or even more lines with the outrigger's aid, say one or more from each of the 'riggers, plus a couple of flat lines right off the transom. The great danger in such multiple trolling is entanglement. We have seen a dolphin take an outrigger-presented lure, then leap and dive in such a manner that it wove all other lines into a bit of lacework that had to be seen to be believed.

Normally, flat lines over the stern are snubbed in so that they ride on the second wave of the wake while the outrigger lures skip several yards in back of and to one side of these tempters. This system tends to minimize tangling when the boat turns. A notable exception is when flat lines are weighted or fished a good deal deeper than those streamed from the outriggers.

On the Kona coast of Hawaii, outriggers are used in a rather unique manner. They are not swung outboard at all, but are kept in the upright position. Flat lines over the transom are fished close astern while those from the outriggers skip far behind in the boat's wake. Obviously this use does not cover a wide swath of water, but it seems to work well on both blue marlin and yellowfin tuna.

When drifting, or even when still fishing at anchor, outriggers may be put to work advantageously. Swing the rigger into trolling position and clip a line in place. The outhaul line may then be adjusted to carry the bait any desired distance from the boat's side where it will not foul other lines fished close aboard.

When fishing in this manner, a plastic ring may be slid over the fishing line itself. The ring is then pinned into the clip and the angler may adjust depth and distance to his bait simply by letting out or reeling in line. On the strike, the ring pulls free, slides down the line, and causes no trouble during the ensuing battle. This system originally was tried when trolling, for it was felt that the angler could maneuver his lure with greater ease. However, unless the trolling speed is very slow and the water calm, such a system puts an excessive whipping strain on the rod tip.

Outriggers are by no means confined to large sportfishing cruisers. They can be used to advantage even from small outboard craft, either when drifting or still fishing, as noted above, or when trolling. Often only one such device can be handled with ease and, to save weight and space, a jointed or telescoping pole is desirable. Elaborate fittings for the base of the small boat outrigger are not required. A strap or shoe made fast to the cockpit deck will hold the butt and another strap or clamp on the after corner of the stern will brace the outrigger in place. The outrigger itself should be rigged in this manner so that it lies at about a 45-degree angle to the keel when in use.

Many small-boat owners do not bother with an outhaul line, since the outrigger is stowed away the moment there is a strike. Things can get a bit hectic when this occurs, which is another argument for keeping small craft outriggers comparatively short and light.

One specialized use for such a rig, so far as the small boatman is concerned, is initiated when it is desired to troll along the edge of a reef or tidal flat. Water over such areas often is too shallow for proper navigational operations. Even when it is not, the shadow of the boat and the underwater noise of the motor may spook the fish. By trolling along the edge of the shoal and swinging the outrigger over the shallows, the lure is presented to the quarry safely and without undue disturbance.

Apart from the advantages of outrigger use mentioned above, there is another plus for the billfisherman. When there is a strike, the line snaps out of the pin and the loop between rod tip and pin provides what might be termed as an automatic drop-back. This should always be remembered by the anglers concerned, for the traditional count of ten before setting the hook in most cases will be cut in half.

Of course the ten-count system undoubtedly is one of angling's crudest rules of thumb. Every strike is different and only experience will provide knowledge of the crucial moment to set a hook. Often it will be necessary to knock the line out of the pin just prior to a strike. Good fishermen study the situation and react accordingly, and sometimes they fluff the operation. We have been fishing for a good many years and we still miss strikes.

Two warnings must be sounded. The first, and minor one, is that line running from the rod's tiptop to the pin tends to throw a half-hitch around the rod tip if the loop is slack. If too tight, the line will be pulled from the pin when the boat rolls and the outrigger flexes.

The second warning is far more important. *Never* allow any person to stand aft of the line which runs from rod tip to outrigger pin. This rule is commonly observed once line and lure are in proper position, for it is obvious that a strike may whip the line across a portion of the cockpit. Unfortunately it is often ignored when the line is being snapped into the pin and adjusted by the outhaul. Strikes can come during this crucial moment and a fast-moving loop of line can sever a thumb, finger—or even a neck!

Development of the outrigger in modern angling has been rapid. No well-equipped sportfishing craft is without them on the offshore grounds these days. Future developments, in our opinion, will bring outriggers inshore as tools of the small-boat angler.

23
CAR-TOP BOATS

SOMEBODY RECENTLY ASKED HOW BIG A BOAT COULD BE CAR-TOPPED with ease. We thought about it and came up with an arbitrary figure of 12 feet. Later, we began to question this reasoning—which happens to be quite right, provided we are referring to the rugged, deep-hulled tin boats surfmen like to call seaworthy.

For many reasons, though, this is a question that cannot be answered without adding a series of qualifications. For example, some 12-foot skiffs are much too heavy for basic car-topping, while other models ranging up to and beyond 14 feet can be levered aboard with no great effort.

Fourteen feet is far from the ultimate: canoes and john boats ranging up to 18 feet are light and often lend themselves to car-topping. Therefore length is a deceptive measure to use in determining just how much boat can be carried on the roof of a motor vehicle. Weight can be a tricky criterion too, but there you have a reasonably stable range of figures, say anything up to approximately 250 pounds.

Unfortunately, this is just another figure, subject to variation determined by the type of roof rack employed and the physique of the loader. Certainly a craft which is much too heavy for man-handling by a person of small stature or limited strength might be handled with ease by any big, athletic type. Worth noting is the fact that loading can be simplified through the use of patented roller and lift racks, or by platforms that lend themselves to levering.

Perusal of catalogs issued by marine suppliers will provide information on the many types available: they range from the simple, twin-crossbar models precariously attached with rubber suction cups, through heavier crossbars which are designed for latching to rain gutters—on up to a bewildering array of rollers and levering devices.

Obviously, the simplest of crossbars may be quite practical for a very light boat, such as a canoe which is easily lifted on and off by one man. Heavier crossbar rigs of two designs will work well. One is fitted with a roller aft, so that the bow of the skiff can be walked up over the car's roof from the rear.

A second type utilizes hardwood longitudinal stringers connecting fore and aft crossbars. Loading is then initiated from the side rather than the rear of a car. The boat's bow section is simply dropped on one of the stringers, after which it is relatively painless to lift the stern and, with the aid of leverage, walk the hull around and into position.

In addition to design which will facilitate loading and unloading, a practical rack should be well anchored. Rubber suction cups are not sufficient, since they tend to slide and even dry out and pop off the surface. Straps or other fastenings are good insurance with this type of carrier.

Better racks are securely anchored with clamp-down arrangements that fasten into rain gutters. Indeed it is sometimes wise to copper one's bets by driving metal screws through the clamps and into the gutters. Racks on beach buggies or other back country vehicles may be bolted to roofs, and this is most secure—although it doesn't enhance trade-in value if you decide to sell the vehicle at a later date.

Think about two other things when you choose or design a cartop boat carrier. First, blocking—to hold the boat in one position and to prevent sliding sideways, forward or aft. This, of course, assuming that one particular hull will be toted.

Judicious use of blocks will insure that a hull can be very nearly locked in one position. Usually, due to gunwale conformation, the craft will slide backward, out of the restraining blocks, but will not shift forward or sideways. A bowline can be attached to the car's front bumper, or a stern line snugged up to the rack itself, from the transom handles on the boat. Either way, you're secure.

Next, you'll need foolproof tie-downs. Elastic shock cord is favored by many, but it has been known to part. Better use another method, especially when long highway trips are contemplated. Quarter-inch or half-inch rope is safe, albeit a plague to tie and untie. Turnbuckles, jury-rigged to connect boat and rack, are more practical—although we still like additional tie-downs on a long, high-speed journey.

Perhaps our major sin, in writing about car-toppers in the marine angling field, is a tendency to think of relatively big boats which are "seaworthy," and to exclude most of the lightweights originally designed for inland water operations. "Seaworthy" is a relative word, since each hull has its own limitations. A 12-foot skiff with 60-inch beam and freeboard of 23 or 24 inches certainly is able to take more rough water in stride than a similar 12-footer with 16 inches of freeboard and moderate beam.

Similarly, the soft chine and the vee-bottom hull will slide through more confused waters than the shallow, flat-bottomed design. You can be very safe in a rubber raft (if you don't stick a gaff in its flanks), but there isn't much room for duffel and there isn't the comfort of an orthodox boat.

There is, however, a definite place for each of the various designs. The ancient Indian canoe can be a mighty safe and comfortable craft in which to explore a coastal river or sheltered bay. Salt water anglers have used everything from kayaks on up to twin-screw cruisers of heroic proportions. Boating experts emphasize, however, that each craft is ideally suited to a particular sphere of operations and can be a death trap if extended beyond its capabilities.

Experienced anglers and boatmen are well aware of these limitations, yet the Coast Guard's casualty figures annually list unfortunates who pushed their luck with inadequate craft—inadequate, that is, for prevailing conditions.

No car-topper is an all-around sea boat. Much has been written about the tin skiffs used by surfmen, and we plead guilty to a good deal of this verbiage. Paeans of praise about light hulls are excusable, so long as the limited capabilities of such craft are spelled out. None of the little skiffs are designed to challenge heavy seas, pounding surf or vicious rips. If they have any choice in the matter, smart helmsmen never gamble with the elements. Russian roulette is a quicker way to join one's ancestors, and perhaps less painful.

Used within reason, however, the light car-top boat is a wonderful tool. It can be launched in areas where hard-pan ramps are lacking, and it can be portaged where necessary. The car-topper excels in those areas generally regarded as back-of-beyond, and it is for this reason that the type remains popular. Also, for this reason, it follows that the maximum weight or bulk that can be loaded or unloaded from a rooftop rack may be deceptive. It's your aching back, so think about the entire operation, not loading and unloading alone.

Car-toppers in the maximum weight bracket can be stubborn packages when you have to slide them down slippery clay banks to reach the waters of remote brackish creeks. They're much tougher to coax back up the incline at journey's end. Such a hull may be better suited to beach buggy use, where manhandling is lessened by proximity to the water.

There is always a very human tendency to use the most powerful motor a craft will take without splitting its seams. A few surf-launching addicts have now progressed to 35 hp on 14-foot tin boats. If manhandling is contemplated, this is a bit beyond maximum, simply because few men are comfortable lugging kickers that scale more than the approximate 90 pounds of today's 25's. Without a prime mover, air rollers or other aids, launching becomes very hard work. You tote the package, not the motor alone. There is the hull, plus a couple of tanks of fuel, plus all the usual duffel.

Think about this, and study the requirements. In most cases a 5- to 10-hp motor is sufficient to buck a foul tide or wind, yet these power plants are lightweights compared to 20's, 25's, or larger. Moreover, despite the promises of motor makers, these small kickers troll down better than the big ones, they burn less fuel and they take up less room in duffel compartments on the way to and from a fishing ground. Keep weight to a minimum if manhandling will be maximum: it's as simple as that.

Some things you can't do without on salt water, or at least you should not attempt to do without. Wherever winds, tides or currents are likely to be factors, a practical anchor and at least 50 feet of anchor rope will be necessities. The sea's a big place, and it's no fun to be drifting aimlessly, in trouble, with no way to call a halt while you work on a balky motor or wave a tee-shirt to call for help.

Most car-toppers are reasonably good rowing boats; therefore it is wise to include a pair of oars and to count them standard equipment on any trip. Tape a shear pin and cotter pin to the operating handle of your motor, and carry a couple of new spark plugs, plus tools, in a handy tackle box.

Nowadays, buoyant seat cushions or Coast Guard approved jackets are generally required by law. Law or no, they're good insurance. Most of us tempt fate by declining to wear a buoyant jacket, even when the wind howls and the sea roars. Stupidly, we equate the wearing of a bulky jacket with loss of face and an admission of failure.

Nobody's about to revolutionize human emotions, but there is a solution. Several firms now offer flotation jackets which look like ordinary parkas. These garments are warm, reasonably waterproof and extremely light—yet, if you go overboard, they'll float you like a cork raft. Best of all, the new lifesaving jackets don't look like safety vests. Nobody will ever know, unless you tell them!

Charts and compasses too often are associated with big, offshore cruisers—and forgotten aboard car-toppers. Granting that neither chart or compass may be as important on a brackish creek or sheltered bay as in the open ocean, it's a fine feeling to know where you're going when a sudden fog erases the shoreline.

Actually, for limited small-boat use, a compass is more important than a chart—provided the helmsman has a working knowledge of shore points and directions in his mind. If he lacks these, then he needs a chart, period. Plus a workable compass. Visualize the plight of a small-boat skipper working several hundred yards off a known beach when fog obscures all check points. Suddenly, and it is an eery feeling, the helmsman is enclosed in a milky, opaque blanket. If there is no sound of familiar surf, no wail of a foghorn in a known location, then direction-finding is completely frustrated.

In such a situation, a small-boat skipper's need will be some means by which he can steer a rough course toward that point of the compass which he knows insures safety. Traveling, say, westward toward shore is infinitely better than guessing—and possibly outboarding straight out to sea.

An accurate pocket compass, like that used by woodsmen, is better than nothing: indeed it may be far superior to many of the fancy little gimbal-mounted abortions which are sold for small-boat use. The woodsman's compass will indicate a roughly accurate course, and that's about all you can expect in a tiny craft which is pitching and forever veering in the grip of ocean waves and currents. A cheap, gimbal-mounted compass, on the other hand, usually goes into the deep six when somebody grabs an oar or gaff and hooks the thing out of its inadequate mounting.

There are small, compact compasses that are ideally suited for use in a light skiff. We use one which is securely screwed to a wooden bracket which, in turn, clamps over the center seat of a tin boat. It is a compact, no-nonsense instrument, with no delicate mountings or electrical wiring, yet on many occasions when fog has descended on our coast, the unerring lubber line has insured safe landings.

One warning: always check a compass during good visibility to insure that its magnetized needle is not influenced by some mass of metal in the boat. Manufacturers provide instructions for the proper orientation of their instruments, and this should be done at the outset.

Surely any angler who launches a small boat on marine waters should insist on equipment which insures both sport and safety. Just as surely, we've cruised rings around the original question—just how big can a car-topper be?

And we're afraid that any answer will boil down to a paraphrase of Abe Lincoln's remark that a man's legs should be long enough to reach the ground. Weight and bulk are factors, but solutions depend upon proposed use, well designed racks—and the physical fitness of the individual concerned.

24

THE WADE-FISHERMAN

ACADEMIC ANGLERS—WHO SELDOM GET WET—ARE LIKELY TO ASsume that a surf or shore fisherman always casts his baits from the security of terra firma. Actually, the marine shore angler, whether he likes it or not, is a wader. Indeed the land-based sportsman's success or failure often depends on how well he has learned to invade the edges of the oceans.

Whether you challenge the angry surf of the north or the placid flats of our American tropics, expertise in wading is a plus. The specialist, moreover, will dress for the occasion and take full cognizance of certain dangers—which are nullified by fine technique.

The uniform is important, and it will vary with the area to be fished. There is, for example, no pressing need for waders, hip boots and foul-weather tops in the tropics. These are concessions to cold water, a discomfort rarely experienced in, say, the Florida Keys or the warm suds of Baja California.

In the tropics, and especially for those pallid pilgrims from northern cities, canvas tennis shoes, long pants and long-sleeved shirts are logical; plus a hat with sufficient brim to protect neck and ears from a broiling sun. Long-sleeved shirts and pants are sun-guards, but the pants serve a second purpose. Tropical waters often harbor stinging jellyfish and their toxic tentacles are turned by light cotton material. Tennis shoes protect tender feet from sharp coral and from the more serious wounds inflicted by sea urchins.

While boots, waders and foul-weather pants might effect the same protection, such equipment is an abomination in the tropics because of high temperatures. These items of outer clothing are northern, and they are tremendously important to the marine angler. Proper selection and matching of garments for specific tasks insures the success and the enjoyment of wading for game fish. There are several combinations.

Hip boots are much used. They're great for shallow wading where surf is at a minimum. Chest-high waders are called for where the water is deep or where breakers are booming in. In either case, you'll want a practical foul-weather top, preferably with a drawstring hood attached.

The angler who chooses hip boots for work in high surf had best top them with foul-weather pants. If these waterproof pants are snugged down at the ankles, it is surprising to note how well they will defeat spray and even permit wading close to the boot tops.

Such a combination, together with a foul-weather top, can be entirely adequate for surf fishing where wading is held to a minimum, but where spray from breaking waves threatens the angler with periodic wetting. Do not, however, choose hip boots for deep wading in cold water.

There, nothing beats the chest-high wader and the coupled foul-weather top. The latter should be a one-piece garment, with no up-the-front zipper, and with a drawstring rather than a rubberized cord at the waist. For insurance, the deep-wading surf caster can employ a tight belt to bond foul-weather top to waders. So accoutred, an angler can venture over his wader tops for short periods and expect to remain reasonably dry.

Boot foot waders are ideally chosen for sand beach work; they are not very practical for work on rocks and jetties, however. There, an angler should add strap-on ice creepers or customized sandals. Some prefer steel-studded golf shoes. Felt soles, preferred by inland trout and salmon fishermen, are not very effective on the seacoast.

Having chosen a uniform which is adequate for the task at hand, a fisherman must think about operational procedures. In this connection, tropical work is least demanding, if only because seas are warmer. While there are drop-offs and slamming ground swells in southern fishing areas, the problem usually resolves itself into defeating sea urchins, sharp coral, and stinging jellyfish. There is one additional hazard in the south.

There a wade-fisherman may encounter stingrays, fish which frequent light sand, marl, or mud bottoms and lie half-submerged in this cover. The stinger boasts a sharp spine in its tail, and this spine may be driven into the leg or foot of an encroaching human being—unless the ray is given ample warning of the human animal's approach.

Stingrays are not anxious to tangle with mankind: they become a problem only when frightened into action. Therefore the best defense is to shuffle one's feet in progressing over a soft bottom where stingrays may be lying. The rays will flush ahead and nobody will be hurt.

Waders on tropical flats often worry about barracudas and sharks. The 'cuda is no problem and sharks invariably veer off. However, the sportsman who drags a string of bleeding game fish may well find a shark following to nip morsels off the "grapevine." Sharks are unpredictable, so it is wise to get out of the water if they become excited. So far as wade-fishermen are concerned, it is only fair to note that the incidence of shark attack is very low—almost infinitesimal.

Thanks to rough seas, strong currents, cold water and slippery rocks, northern waders face more difficulties than their southern cousins, but tragedy is uncommon. For every unfortunate who is swept off a jetty and lost in boiling seas, a million others fish in safety or get wet, bruised and angry with the elements. Beginners are cautious and veterans learn to copper their bets. There are rules in wading.

The enemies are heavy surf, strong currents, slippery rocks and sudden drop-offs—not always in this order. The perils may be encountered en masse, but rarely. Almost always a surfer courts trouble by wading too far off the beach or by ignoring tidal phases and currents. If fish are breaking just beyond a man's best cast, it is human nature to edge out—and out. The hazards are evident.

On a sand beach waves, depth and strong currents should be taken into consideration. A man can wade just so far until he risks swimming. Practical tactics are further determined by ground swells or combers that pound in at regular intervals. Wave-hopping is an art among the regulars, and it is an art worth cultivating. Briefly, the deep-wader gauges an incoming swell (which would pass right over his head were he to remain firmly anchored) and jumps upward just as the wave reaches him. For a moment or two the wave-hopper is floating free on the crest of the swell. As it passes, racing shoreward, he descends to make contact with the bottom again. An experienced surfman encased in chest-high waders, with a foul-weather top snugged down by a tight belt, can remain surprisingly dry in waters that would inundate a beginner.

The problem is complicated by any strong tidal current. On a sand beach, such a current will sweep sand from under the booted feet of an angler. The first time this happens it is a peculiar experience to feel the bottom melt away. You descend rapidly, and there is just one solution—keep moving. Step forward, sidewise or back, but never remain in one place long enough for the gouging current to work its magic.

Very often the surf caster who is working a point where wind and current creates a rip will find combers advancing from different directions. Such locations are hot spots because the clash of waves and the movement of water tumbles bait and draws game fish. Unfortunately, the turbulence can tumble anglers as well. Constant vigilance insures balance, but we've been dumped on our shoulder blades too often to claim any sure cure defense. Just watch it, friends. Such spots can be treacherous.

For various good reasons, an offshore bar is a banquet table for inshore game fish. Bars often lie just beyond a long cast, hence we all try to reach the payoff spot by wading. This may be impossible on a flood tide, but quite feasible on the ebb. Indeed, on low water, a surfer may actually reach the bar itself by wading through an inshore slough or by following a finger of sand that extends from the beach.

Throngs of eager surf casters do this, and then fish the flood to a calculated time which insures dry passage ashore. Many of us, thrilled by successive strikes, wait too long—and then we're marooned. There are two courses of action, neither very palatable.

Since the bar is reasonably shoal, one may remain there through the course of the tide. Or, one can tread water to reach the high beach. This is not particularly perilous, unless strong currents are racing through the slough between bar and shore, but it will be an experience. You'll tread water and you'll get soaked. The practice is not recommended. In fact, it is discouraged for all but the regular who knows exactly what will happen and does not panic. We've done this too many times, and we don't want to do it again. Uncomfortable.

Surfing a rocky beach posts additional perils, although there is less tendency for the bottom to wash out from under one's feet. Here, even when the angler is equipped with ice creepers or hobs, the bottom will be slippery and irregular. Proper technique entails slow probing, one step at a time—feeling for the unbalanced rock and guarding against the larger boulder that can knock you off balance.

Regulars progress fairly rapidly when they know the bottom contours, but they often use a rod butt as a staff. Clean salt water won't hurt an expensive reel, so it is wise to use the butt as a crutch. Even a very light spinning or fly-casting rod, slapped on the water's surface as you teeter on the brink of falling, can restore equilibrium.

Often the route to an exposed reef is easiest. At that time, fresh and reasonably warm, you face the advancing ground swells and take evasive action when a comber looms. Always turn sidewise to an advancing wave, letting it break against your legs and not full in the breadbasket. Lean forward to maintain balance, and be sure that both feet are anchored at the moment of stress. If the wave is high, lift your arms. The less surface exposed, the less pressure exerted.

Surfmen probably suffer greatest indignities when retreating from a promising location. At the end of a big-deal wade, a return to shore may be anticlimax. We share a mental block about the safety of shoaling water, forgetting that we are tired, perhaps slightly numbed by the cold and dragging a heavy string of fish. The slippery boulders still lie in wait and a prudent man will progress very cautiously, using his rod's butt as a staff. Too many surf casters get dumped in the icy breakers. Few lose their lives as a result, but the experience can be most ego-shattering and uncomfortable.

Brothers who fish rock jetties pursue a more dangerous star. Jetties invariably poke their granite noses into deep water, and into strong currents. Heavy surf lashes these rock piles and they can be decidedly unhealthy in rough weather or during the night. Experienced jetty jockeys know this and take certain precautions: they wear ice creepers and favor the buddy system. Many carry flotation devices, just in case—and this is wise, for a sudden wave on a far-out jetty can sweep a fisherman into deep water. It is logical to copper all bets and to respect the elements.

If the rules of common sense are observed, there is no great danger in surf fishing or wading the ocean's flats. Jetties may pose greater problems, yet smart anglers continue to fish from the rocks while advancing combers send bursts of white spray over their heads. Whatever the shore's conformation, a regular simply studies the sea and the bottom, the weather and the state of tide and current. In the tropics, a man keeps one eye peeled for the possibly dangerous creatures of the sea itself. Marine killers are overrated, yet caution is necessary.

In the surf we're our own worst enemies, and recklessness is the only real threat to life. Let's face it, a marine wade-fisherman treasures that thin flavor of peril which spices a classic sport.

25

PLAYING THE ACROBATS

ANSWERING READERS' INQUIRIES IN THE "MARINE CLINIC" SECTION of *Salt Water Sportsman* is guaranteed to keep a man on his toes. "Clinic," for those who are not readers of the magazine, is a question-and-answer department. Subscribers ask questions and staffers try to provide logical answers. Sometimes our splendid words of advice are considered less than immortal. Indeed, response to any controversial reply can be nothing short of overwhelming.

Sometimes reaction is varied, ranging from assent to bitter disagreement. The answer to a "Marine Clinic" question which asked what to do when a big fish, such as a marlin or shark, jumps, prompted this type of response. We think the subject is worth analysis.

Basically, our reply stated that the type of tackle, the amount of line out at the time of the jump, the direction in which the boat or fish is moving and the species itself all had bearing on whether to drop the rod tip in order to give slack line, insofar as possible, or to lay back on the rod in an attempt to throw the jumper off balance. We were necessarily brief, and therein burgeoned the virus of dissension. Let's take a look at the response, both by letter and in personal conversation, and the areas from which response originated.

"This is the first, and only, sensible written commentary on handling jumping fish I have ever read," says a southern Californian who spends as much time as possible fishing the Baja area in Mexico. He, as is true of all the other responders quoted, is an experienced angler and has fished in many waters other than his home grounds.

"You must lose at least half the fish you hook," says a Texas engineer. "Your idea of the physics involved was disproved long ago. Try tipping the fish over every time and it will become exhausted far more quickly—and no more strain is put on the line."

"Your name has become a dirty word here among the guides," said a Floridian. "They will throw an angler off the boat who does not bow to the fish on the jump."

"Perhaps you are right, but I am still confused and probably always will be," writes a New Jerseyman, who has taken billfish all over the world. "The confusion, I think, arises from the varied circumstances under which a fish may jump. Most of us react instinctively, as you mention, and hope that our reactions are correct."

This last angler has put his finger directly on the crux of the problem. Needless to say, all the commentators supported their individual opinions with many examples and statistics. So did others, who were not so explicit in their basic response. It should also be noted that all those cited said there were occasional exceptions to any rule—a good indication of their angling knowledge. Like ourselves, they know that the word "always" does not belong in the fishing lexicon when tackle and methods are being considered.

"Never say always" is a pretty good rule. "Generally" is a better word to use. In this case we seem to have a knock-down, drag-out battle between specialists who believe in bowing to a jumping fish, and those who prefer to knock the critter flat in midleap. We submit that there are arguments for either extreme. Circumstances, to coin a phrase, alter cases.

Let us agree that there are two separate and distinct factors to consider when a fish jumps—and we will be quick to agree that these factors overlap to a certain extent. First, there is the necessity to keep the hook in the critter's mouth well anchored. Second, there is the equally vital need to prevent breakage of line or leader during this climactic maneuver. Both are equally important in the final result and the trick is to keep both factors in balance so that the barb remains in place while line and leader hold.

The practice of "bowing to a fish" began with Atlantic salmon. This great anadromous battler of the North Atlantic river systems is taken on fly-casting tackle, and because the salmon is cagey about rising to an artificial, light silkworm gut or gossamer nylon leader tippets are essential to its downfall.

An Atlantic salmon is a jumping fish—make no mistake about that—and a large salmon invariably parts a light leader if the angler permits the creature to fall back upon a tight trace. "Bowing" simply throws enough slack into line and leader to prevent solid contact and a resultant break.

This strategy is perfectly applicable to salt water angling where line or leader is too light to withstand the ponderous, crashing descent of a leaping game fish. Any angler who seeks tarpon (or any of the big aerialists) on fly casting or light spinning gear would be an idiot to attempt the tight-line approach when his quarry goes into the air. You bow to a fish when terminal tackle is too light to withstand the tremendous stresses levied on any portion of the equipment during that spectacular maneuver.

By the same token, and this must be qualified because fish are of separate species (some with soft mouths and some with hard), you can overpower and upset a jumper if your tackle is equal to the task. The tarpon that requires "bowing" with a light outfit can be manhandled and upset when deep-hooked on heavy gear. It is hardly logical to stereotype fighting tactics without taking into consideration the potential of the tackle used and the physical makeup of the fish.

Let's consider the fish itself. We will include large and small specimens in all that follows and we will attempt to develop very general rules. Following these generalities when some finny monster clears the water within spitting distance is another problem. Never say always!

Jumping species vary greatly in their ways of taking a bait or lure. One of the marlin tribe, for example, may follow a skip bait for agonizing minutes before taking a slash at it. A bull dolphin or wahoo is likely to grab the offering without hesitation, although they do not always do so. Even among the same species, variations in strike action are tremendous—and this holds whether the bait is trolled, drifted, cast or still-fished. The primary task of the angler is to hook the fish—and veterans work averages.

Each species introduces another variable. Mouth and tooth structures are different. The hard, bonelike jaws of a tarpon cannot be compared with the chopping teeth of a bluefish or the comparatively soft mouth of a broadbill. The trick, so far as any fisherman is concerned, is to get the barb embedded so that it will hold. For the sake of definition and to simplify the discussion, let us assume that the fish has been fairly hooked in the mouth prior to making its first leap.

Unfortunately, no one is able to read a fish's mind. Many attribute human qualities to their quarry and assume that each jump is an attempt to throw the hook. Perhaps—and perhaps not!

A fish may feel that something is wrong, but whether or not it associates the hook with its restricted swimming ability is open to argument.

Reaction of species differs. At times it appears as though the salmons, white marlin, and some of the sharks, to mention a few, connect their inconvenience with the line's drag, rather than with the sting of a hook. Some gamesters jump often—and therefore dissipate their strength—when played on a light drag rather than on heavy pressure.

Obviously, this is human conjecture and cannot be proved conclusively one way or the other. However, there is no question about the fact that one fish may come out of the water like an arrow, while another will shake its head savagely when jumping. If either appears to be falling back upon a light leader or line, it is logical to drop the rod tip to give as much slack as possible so that the terminal connection will remain intact.

It is with the head-shaking category of fishes that all sorts of questions arise. The theory of those who keep a tight line on these species during the jump is that strain will continue on the hook and that the barb will therefore be kept firmly embedded. In addition, if the fish is tipped over while in the air, it will return to the water off balance, will take more time and effort to recover, and therefore will exhaust itself sooner.

A few argue against this premise. They claim that, if a fish is allowed to jump freely once, it will continue to jump often and will thus be brought to gaff or net more quickly. We only agree that a frequent jumper is a quick catch and that an acrobat tipped over at each aerial foray becomes more exhausted than one which is given its head—*tackle permitting.*

As far as throwing the hook is concerned, the argument basically concerns the necessity of keeping a strain on the line in order to hold the barb in place. Here again we have perfectly valid arguments from all points of the compass—and each specialist is quite right! It is only when the expert on a given species and a certain technique applies his reasoning to all other species and methods that we approach an impasse.

A jumping, head-shaking fish may throw a heavy plug, jig, or spoon with the greatest of ease. The lure has weight, and the rapid shifting of that weight often dislodges hooks. Nothing at all happens when the killer is an almost weightless fly: indeed, if the fly is dislodged from one location, and if the angler is "bowing," as he should with light terminal tackle, then the feather artificial is likely to dig into another spot after it is dislodged from the original hold. It may not be thrown clear, as a heavier lure will be. Stu Apte, probably America's foremost authority on tarpon fishing with the fly rod, seems to have proved this beyond the possibility of doubt.

Again, circumstances alter cases. If much line is out—say 100 yards as a figure grabbed out of the air—tension on the hook is going to be fairly heavy no matter what the angler may do. Water resistance on the line makes this so, and the size and type of line will affect the amount of resistance. For example, 12-pound test monofilament will offer less resistance than 80-pound test Dacron braid. The 100-yard figure therefore must be shaded one way or the other when making comparisons.

Some slide-rule anglers among our readers have disputed this fact, but it takes no certificate of learning to *feel* the difference in stress exerted by lines of different tests and compositions. Stone Age man would be able to detect the variables, although he would not recognize the message implied. Some modern anglers, including the slide-rule boys and the academic non-fishermen, are similarly handicapped.

Dropping the tip of a standard offshore trolling rod will yield only about four feet of slack line. By the time this meagre amount of slack has any effect—when 100 yards or more is already off the reel—the acrobatic fish will be back in the water after its jump.

At long range, when an angler lays back on the rod in an attempt to tip the fish over, the effect is even less. The rod tip presumably will be fairly near the perpendicular as the quarry leaves the water. The amount of line that can be retrieved instantly by raising the tip further is a scant two feet—not enough to make much difference one way or the other.

Arguments and theories fly faster as the line is shortened. Because water resistance becomes less, action by the angler becomes more important. Under these conditions, we submit, other factors must be taken into account. Tackle involved is vital.

To illustrate this point, let us consider two extremes. On the one hand we have a shore-based surf fisherman who seeks trophy bluefish, roosterfish, or what have you. He uses a heavy 10 to 11 foot production rod mounting a free-spool reel filled with 36-pound test braid. On the other hand is an angler with a one-handed spinning stick shooting for a record on eight pound test mono for tarpon. He is in a high speed outboard skiff and his guide is ready to crank up the motor to chase whatever may be hooked.

When a surfman hooks a jumper that is big, he must exhaust the fish as soon as possible—or stand a good chance of losing it. His tackle is of sufficient strength to risk laying back on the jump, for that tackle is designed to put the lure where it will reach fish, and not for maximum sport during the ensuing battle. He must do this, and he must use such tackle in order to insure against a broken line or leader.

If the skiff fisherman were to try the same tactics, results would be immediate and unhappy. Here, the angler with light tackle must observe certain niceties. He will bow to the jump of an acrobat and, if his boat is slow in pursuit, he may even have to throw line by stripping it off the reel or by slacking off the drag. Once the hook has been well set, his only hope is to keep excessive pressure off the light monofilament and to employ both boat and technique flawlessly. He cannot afford the slightest of errors.

The extremes cited *are* extremes, yet modifications of them may be applied in other areas. Thus, if it is important to boat a fish rapidly because of deteriorating weather or other hazards, laying back on the jump may be the only solution. If the fish is lightly hooked—which often may be determined on the first leap—such tactics are doomed to failure. Mobility of the angler, ashore or afloat, may dictate any choice.

Of course, things may happen so fast that the fisherman has no control over events or cannot react fast enough to take action. Sometimes, however, movement of both boat and fish may be determined in advance. Let us consider another extreme case.

A boat is traveling due north at a trolling speed of five knots. A wahoo, lurking in the depths, spots the strip bait trolled on a flat line right back of the transom and actually jumps clear on the strike while heading approximately south. The question of hooking the fish is not involved, for it will hook itself. However, if the angler lays back on the rod at this point, something is bound to give—and it won't be the wahoo! Even though it is almost instinctive to raise the rod tip smartly to set the hook, we have learned from bitter experience with this species, under these conditions, that bowing to the fish is the only answer.

Now look at circumstances which might be considered the reverse. A Pacific sailfish has been hooked on medium tackle, has made little fuss about it and is being worked toward the boat—which is lying dead in the water.

Within sight of the cockpit this sail suddenly comes to life, jumps once, twice—and yet again while moving directly toward the angler. Drop the rod tip at that moment and the spindlebeak will land among loops and twists of line and leader to become thoroughly entangled. The solution is to get as much line out of the water as possible and get it back on the reel. Laying back on the rod will help. Incidentally, this situation is not an imaginary one: we have had it happen to us more than once, and with a variety of species.

One factor we have not discussed so far, because it involves great argument, is the holding power of various styles, shapes and sizes of hooks. All of the popular bends now offered to the American public are good. Size must be matched to species sought, and type also depends on species as well as methods employed. There is no happy medium.

Logically, the Siwash bend with its long point and deep barb should be best for jumpers. Actually, it is a fine design for soft-mouthed species such as the Pacific salmon and the Atlantic bluefish but a poor choice for those acrobats with hard jaws. Diamond-ground Martu and Sobey hooks are better suited to action with the big billfish, and a well-sharpened O'Shaughnessy seems to fare well with the smaller jumpers.

Treble hooks are not the death-dealing devices that some think them to be. Lures rigged with such hooks result in a phenomenal number of missed strikes or thrown baits. A single hook, regardless of its style, holds a jumping fish far more securely than any multiple barb.

The big trick is elementary: it consists in matching tackle to fish, in bowing to those jumpers who may break up terminal tackle through their acrobatic surface maneuvers, and in overpowering those who cannot challenge the gear used.

26

BRIDGE AND PIER FISHING

WHEREVER HE GOES, GLAMOUR ATTENDS THE BIG GAME FISHERMAN. Observers similarly view with awe the light tackle aficionado who pits his skill, plus a threadlike line, against some finny monster of the sea. Traditionally, the surf caster boasts an aura of rugged strength and individuality.

While all this romantic nonsense goes on, a vast legion of practical anglers—unsung, unhonored, and having a very good time indeed—fish happily from assorted bridges and piers.

This group is, without question, the most diversified of any who turn to the oceans for rod and reel sport. Ranging from little tykes hardly able to hold tackle in their hands, to nonagenarians (who may suffer from the same trouble), men and women of all ages may be found indulging in this area of angling. Despite this huge audience, our angling literature contains very little about the techniques which please bridge and pier fishermen, let alone the tackle employed.

This choice is wide, varied, and obviously depends upon the species normally taken in the area concerned. For example, an angler seeking big channel bass from a Virginia pier would use far heavier artillery than his counterpart trying for surf perch along California's southern coast. Basically, two outfits might be considered—one light and one heavy. Between the extremes will be found all sorts of specialized tackle for particular uses.

For handling fish below the five-pound mark, we favor the beefed-up bait casting combination made for salt water. This is a fairly stiff rod measuring between six and six and one-half feet over-all. It is single handed, but has an extension butt which may be braced against the body when playing a fish or when waiting for a bite. The reel should be of the free-spool type, equipped with star drag, with or without level wind—depending upon the angler's preference. This reel should hold approximately 150 yards of 15 to 25 pound test line. More on line type in a moment.

Spinning tackle can be used—and often is—for pier and bridge fishing. However, we suggest the free-spool reel for several reasons. First, most of the fish caught from a pier or bridge have to be derricked up through the air. The mechanical advantage of a conventional reel over a spinning reel, for this type of work, is considerable. Second, a spinning rod is apt to be too limber, not only for hoisting a catch through the atmosphere, but also to keep a hooked fish from wrapping itself around a shell-encrusted piling. Finally, a light spinning outfit is designed primarily for the casting of light lures. In pier and bridge fishing comparatively heavy sinkers are often used with natural bait, so tackle should be suited to method.

Note, of course, that our basic tackle choice is based on the best all-around outfit to be used under the greatest number of circumstances. There are specialists who make very good use of spinning tackle from the spans, but these experts invariably cast lures and either play their quarry far away from the pilings, or have gear beefed up to take expected punishment.

Even when seeking much larger fish than the usual run of bridge and pier fare, we favor the free-spool reel—for the reasons cited. However, the rod should be about seven feet overall, with an 18 inch butt. Action should not be as stiff as that found in the offshore bottom bouncing stick, for it should boast enough snap to cast when required. The reel should hold about 200 yards of 25 or 36 pound test line, and, again, should feature a star drag.

There is a distinct choice of lines for both light and heavy outfits. When waters are comparatively clear, round monofilament is the majority favorite. Flat or oval mono enjoyed a brief period of popularity some years ago, but they were and are designed for casting with a conventional, revolving spool reel. It is worth noting that overhand casting is prohibited on many piers.

Monofilament has two disadvantages. First, it has considerably more stretch than braided line, a thing that can be a handicap when hoisting a fish clear of the water. The sportsman starts his catch on its way skyward, thinks all is well—and then there is a sag and a snap as fish and terminal tackle fall back into the briny. True, this may happen with braided nylon or Dacron, but the "feel" of these braids offers a better indication of dangerous tensions. Anglers who can gauge the breaking point, and avoid it, call for bridge gaffs or nets before they get in trouble.

The second point in favor of braid when fishing the big spans is its tendency to "advertise" abrasion. Monofilament can be nicked by brief encounters with pilings and abutments, yet only by drawing the line through the fingers will such injuries be detected. Braided line, on the other hand, "picks out" and the abrasions thus advertise themselves visually so that repairs can be made before a prized fish is lost. No matter which type of line is used, it is well to check the terminal section very frequently.

Bridge and pier fishing techniques vary with the species sought, of course, but there are a few general methods which apply in most cases. For example, many feel that a long cast is necessary, hence they endanger their neighbors by whirling hooks, baits, and lures in all directions. Generally, long casts are a mistake. Fish gather around any structure built over the water for two major reasons—an abundance of food, and shade. The food is found close to the structures because underwater growth, minute water animals and the like hug pilings and abutments. Larger species feed on these midgets, so the smart angler works his lure or bait close to the obstructions.

Obviously, such technique entails some danger. Chances of fouling line or leader are good if a fish is hooked. The risk, however, is calculated and worth taking. The tackle we recommend is sufficiently stout to maintain control of the ordinary catch under the usual conditions.

Shade, the second factor to be considered from a fish's point of view, is of major importance when bridge fishing, albeit a minor consideration on a pier. Any bridge span throws a cool shadow in which many species like to lie, their noses facing into the tidal flow. In addition, because current is forced through a comparatively narrow channel, there is apt to be a deep hole under the bridge itself. Some species, particularly the bottom feeders, will lie on the perimeter of this hole: others, among them such much sought-after predators as the tarpon and striped bass, prefer to hold right at the edge of the shadow line.

The fish will be found, almost always, facing into the tide on the up-current side of the bridge. They use the shadow line as a camouflaged sanctuary, from which to dash out and pin the hapless bait tumbling down with the currents, and they work this dodge at all hours of the day and night—although nighttime is more productive for an angler hunting tarpon, snook, spotted seatrout or striped bass, to name a few. Seatrout, perhaps just to be contrary, often will lie in the current *behind* a bridge, while the others seem to feel, passionately, that it's what's up front that counts.

Taking these shadow line battlers on artificial lures has become a highly specialized art. Plugs, jigs and many of the new soft plastic lures are used at all depths, but the trick is to cast and work them so that they swim into the shadowed area, and sometimes well under the bridge. Those who catch trophy striped bass in this way use cut-down surf rods and squidding reels loaded with stout braided lines. If a fish chooses to dart back under the bridge, it is horsed out. If, on the other hand, it runs up-current, then no such dangerous tactics are necessary. The quarry is played out and then led to the nearest abutment for landing.

Tarpon, more often than striped bass, will turn and run down-current through the bridge pilings. This invariably means a cut-off, especially on the light tackle employed by thousands of thrill-conscious anglers in the South. It is enough for them to hook one silver king after another, to exult at those tremendous leaps—and shrug off the usual hard-mouthed fish's throwing of the hook. Tarpon addicts boast about losing a tackle box full of plugs in a single night!

For those who want to copper their bets, it is always better to fish from a side abutment rather than the bridge span itself—assuming that such an abutment is within casting range of a channel edge or particularly good guzzle. With the line closer to the water than it would be from the span, contact with above-surface obstacles are at least avoided. The pilings remain treacherous and a fish that powers on through is an odds-on favorite to escape.

One ingenious method of overcoming this problem was developed some years ago by Roy Martin of Panama City Beach, Florida. Roy leads a stout cord right through the bridge span he intends to fish. One end of this cord is fastened securely to a down-current bridge rail: the other end is tied to his rod and reel. When a fish is hooked from the shadow line, Roy plays it normally if it chooses to run up against the current. If, as is usually the case, the fish heads on down through the span, Roy sets the hook and then startles fellow fishermen by throwing his tackle overboard!

Martin then scrambles to the other side of the bridge, hauls in the cord he has tied there, recovers his rod and reel—and the battle is on! Needless to say, such technique requires cooperation from those fishing in the vicinity, a paucity of automobile traffic on the bridge—and tackle rugged enough to take the punishment meted out. It also requires a substitute outfit in case the haul-in cord fouls and breaks!

Current can be a blessing as well as a curse for those who fish from fixed structures over the water. Live-lining is most successful when the current runs swiftly. This method consists of lowering a bait or lure into the water with little or no weight attached. With the reel in free spool, line is allowed to pay off naturally. After every few yards of line flow out, the reel's clutch is engaged and the rod is twitched once or twice, after which more line is streamed.

Be sure to keep your thumb on the spool when line is being stripped. A strike can come at any time and, if the thumb is not used as a brake until the clutch can be engaged, the mother of all backlashes will result. Some hardy souls use their thumbs only during the paying out process and twitch the rod with thumbs clamped down hard. We used to do the same until a heavy tarpon blistered our thumb, backlashed the reel's spool, broke the line—and almost ran off with a rod and reel.

Again, trolling wire close to the pilings of Virginia's Chesapeake Bay Bridge in November, we were streaming wire with a swimming plug as the tempter. A large striped bass struck just as the wire was about to be played out completely, and the key loop knot connecting wire and backing gouged, rather than burned, a formerly healthy right thumb. Adding insult to injury, the fish then tore a 4/0 treble out of the center of the plug after we had managed to slip the clutch into gear, and escaped—undoubtedly sneering at Yankee anglers who try to tame Rebel bass.

Once the line has been let out to a point well down-current of bridge or pier, the lure or bait is then retrieved very slowly, with rod action in between each crank of the reel handle. Speed of retrieve may be changed to suit the species sought—and to insure the best action of the lure used—but, on the average, a slow bring-back is the best strike producer. The tempter obviously simulates a bait creature battling up against the current. Few natural baits can make good time against such a force of water, so we simply imitate nature.

Live-lining is commonly practiced with lures or baits that ride on or close to the surface. At times, when fish are deep in bright, hot weather, weighted lures may prove successful. If natural bait is selected, the weight should be placed between line and leader, rather than at the hook.

Often extremely deep holes are found near a bridge or pier. A modification of the live-lining technique may be used in such cases. Rig a fish-finder or sliding sinker on the line. Place a large swivel between line and leader, as is normal with such a rig, and at the terminal end of the leader tie in an unweighted lure or a hook baited with some natural fodder.

Lower the whole works—do not cast—until bottom is reached. Then let out line in exactly the same way as you would do when live-lining on the surface. The hook will ride almost on bottom, but chances of fouling will be minimized.

One excellent piece of equipment for the bridge and pier angler is the common float or bobber. When presenting a natural bait from any land-based structure, it is often extremely difficult to place the bait in the right place at the proper depth. Feeding out line may get the hook in the right spot near, for example, an eddy next to a piling, but wayward currents will wrap the leader around an obstruction or the hook will ride at too great a depth. A float answers this problem handily. Bait depth can be controlled exactly and, simply by watching the float itself, hook and line may be manipulated so that they clear obstructions.

In many areas the float is used as part of the lure. By giving the rod tip action, the bobber is made to pop along the surface. Game fish come up to investigate this disturbance, spot the bait suspended below it—and grab a mouthful never to be forgotten.

Floats are also particularly useful when live bait is used exclusively. The bait is kept at proper depth and also kept clear of weeds as when cut or dead bait is used, but there is an added advantage—little or no added weight from the line. Without a float, this weight tends to drag the bait sideways or downward and to kill it quickly.

Another technique, originally developed for live bait fishing, may be used with dead bait and with a variety of artificial lures. The angler lowers his offering to the desired depths, then strolls along the walkway. This is, in effect, trolling—with the path of travel perpendicular to the current flow. There is, however, no motor noise and commotion. This technique, for reasons best known to the fish, seems to be most effective after dark. The pier or bridge, logically, must be uncrowded.

Although pier operators shudder at casters, and although speeding Cadillac convertibles have been hooked by bridge fishermen attempting to lob lures seaward, there are times when casting from such structures produces well. One of the classic examples of this occurs during the spring cobia run along the northern coast of the Gulf of Mexico. Waters are clear in many of these areas and the fish may be seen as they work their way along the beach. Pier fishermen wait until their quarry is within range, then shower the big chocolate-colored bruisers with lures, baits, curses —and blessings!

Extreme care must be taken in any such casting. As noted, many pier operators forbid such efforts and the angler must be content to flip his lure underhand while the rod's tip is pointed straight down. Many pier veterans have developed this flipping skill to a fine art.

Actually, the practice of holding the rod tip down, rather than up, is a good one to develop in this type of fishing. If the rod tip is high and the fish makes a sudden dash underfoot, as it were, it is easy to put such a bend in the stick that it will snap. No such difficulty arises if the rod is held tip down: it may then be raised slowly as the quarry is fought to the point of exhaustion and is circling right below the triumphant angler.

Small battlers may then be hoisted to the bridge or pier span. The larger ones resent such treatment, and usually are landed with a bridge gaff or bridge net. The former is a three or four-pronged grapnel tied to the end of a stout line. A ring snap secures gaff and cord to the angler's line and gravity then lowers the contraption to the tired fish. Bridge nets are similarly secured to long, strong cords and somewhat resemble an inverted umbrella. Both tools insure against heartaches when a trophy fish is played out and must be winched through the air.

One final point, which cannot be worked into this dissertation in any logical sequence, but which should be emphasized. If you are a shark fishing specialist, make sure that others on the pier or bridge are interested in the same type of sport. Chumming for sharks can ruin fishing for other species. Also, a big shark, once hooked, can tie up neighboring anglers for a considerable period of time. Sport's great, but courtesy makes us sportsmen.

27
DEEP JIGGING

COMMERCIAL FISHERMEN FROM SEATTLE TO SCANDINAVIA HAVE known for years that bottom fish can be caught, sometimes in amazing quantities, by the simple process of lowering a weighted, flashing, or bright-colored lure to the ocean floor and moving it up and down in an erratic manner. Despite this intelligence, every now and then some angling scribe—and we have been guilty—will announce that he has discovered a new method of taking a species which presumably could be tempted only by a natural bait in the depths. All of which underscores the fact that mighty little is really new under the marine sun.

Deep jigging in the handline world falls into two categories. The first consists of lowering a shiny drail over the side and working it up and down until the quarry either strikes or is foul-hooked. The second involves casting the lure well away and then retrieving it, again in a series of sharp jerks. According to old time commercial men, the lure is classified as a "ripper" when tossed and pulled back. That interesting part of technical terminology can be produced when wanted in order to startle fishing friends. (We expect no extra charge for the data.) Use of the ripper method simply insures greater range; technique is basic. Indeed, in angling, techniques often are combined: the idea is to get the lure down to the bottom and then to give it action which will result in a strike.

Although it is possible to adapt a variety of lures to deep jigging, the two types which need no adaptation, and which therefore are most popular, are the metal jigs and the lead-headed bucktails. All of these may be dressed with feathers, nylon, plastics, and various other materials. The bucktail is particularly well adapted to deep jiggling, since its hook barb rides upward, a thing which helps to prevent fouling on bottom.

Deep jigging is best performed from a platform on or over the water. For the shore-based, a bridge, pier or high breakwater serves the purpose. Afloat, anything from a skiff to a twin-screw cruiser or a party boat works well. No matter what the platform, the primary mission is to send the lure to the bottom, and then to move it up and down in a series of short jerks imparted by rod action. If casting, the same series of jerks are employed on the retrieve.

As far as tackle is concerned, the size of fish anticipated must be taken into consideration. However, no matter what the size may be, a fairly stiff rod is to be preferred over a weepy one. A soft stick simply will not impart sufficient action to the lure, particularly if a long line is used. The line itself should feature the lowest possible water-resistance factor, and therefore monofilament tops the list. A good mono with minimum stretch factor is preferred. Choice of a spinning or free-spool reel is largely a matter of personal conviction. We feel that the conventional winch is deadliest, but spin-casters have proved that their tackle is quite equal to the task. Whatever the basic gear, there are refinements.

When using a boat, it is better to drift than to anchor. Not only is more water covered, but also a hooked fish will not alarm all others in the vicinity as it takes its last trip skyward. Once a payoff area has been covered, the motor can be cranked up and the boat piloted back to a point where it will drift over the same spot again. Note that both wind and current must be taken into consideration to determine the course of the drifting craft.

Whether drifting and jigging, or casting and retrieving in the aforementioned manner, the lure should be presented on the upcurrent side of the craft. Even though the shadow of the boat may alarm some fish, this risk is worthwhile when opposed to the nuisance of having the line slide under the hull. Several casters, incidentally, can stand side by side without fear of hooking one another, since casts are made straight away from the boat's side.

When deep-jigging, the angler should "feel for bottom" at regular intervals. This means that the lure must be lowered until it hits the ocean floor, then lifted smartly. In a rapid current, often it is best to eliminate casting because time, and consequently fishing area, elapses while the hook is either in the air or somewhere else where the fish are not.

If the drift rate is comparatively slow and the water is fairly shallow, casting will cover more ground and therefore chances of a strike are increased. The rule is to let the jig hit bottom, take up slack line, twitch the rod tip, let the jig settle once more after reeling in a little line—then give the rod another twitch. Reel, jerk, reel is the order of the day. If transmitting such instructions to a companion, make sure he understands that "jerk" is a verb, not a noun!

The most efficient way of performing this routine from a floating platform is to keep the rod horizontal, on the same plane as the sea's surface, while reeling. The jerks can be imparted more easily in this attitude. A strike is apt to come just after the lure has been twitched forward and hops off the ocean floor. If the rod tip is high at that moment, there is little "striking room" left unless the angler steps backward. Trying to step backward in a small boat can become something less than habit forming.

Rhythm of the rate of retrieve and rod action depends a great deal upon the weight of the lure, the depth of water fished and the speed of drift. A little experimentation will determine the proper rate for the conditions at hand. Ideally, a jig should just touch bottom without fouling after each twitch of the rod tip. The small puff of sand or mud raised by contact acts as an attractor.

Be sure to fish the jig right up to the side of the boat. Often a bottom fish will follow a lure right to the surface and will make a pass at it just before it is lifted clear. This is particularly true when angling is essayed around a bridge piling or other subsurface obstruction.

The shore-based caster does not have as much latitude in his operations, but the same general principles apply. If casting from the beach or from a low-lying structure, it is almost essential to keep the rod above the horizontal on the retrieve to prevent fouling bottom. Twitching the rod tip carries it in an arc more nearly perpendicular to the surface than is the case when boat fishing. However, on a strike, it is simple enough to step backward in order to tighten line quickly to set the hook. Check that which is immediately to your rear before initiating any footwork. A piece of driftwood or a rock in the wrong place can cause an unfortunate tumble at a crucial moment.

No matter what the fishing platform may be, at times currents will be so strong that the jig will not hit bottom at the end of the cast unless line is allowed to run off the reel's spool. With a spinning outfit, the bail should be left open under these circumstances and the line kept under control by placing the index finger lightly on the edge of the spool. With a free-spool rig, light thumbing produces the same effects.

In general, lures armed with gang or multiple hooks should be avoided for deep jigging, because they hang bottom too often. Even with bucktail-type tempters, which ride with the hook point up, lure loss is comparatively high due to fouling. For this reason it is wise to have the connecting point the weakest link in the whole tackle chain. This may be accomplished by using a leader somewhat lighter than the line itself, or by tying a knot which does *not* boast nearly 100 per cent efficiency. We favor the figure-of-eight in such cases. Then, when the hook is firmly fixed in some underwater obstruction, only the lure is sacrificed when heavy pressure has to be applied.

Getting down to optimum depths can be a problem where currents are strong. There, an angler has to employ heavy, streamlined lures and lines which feature least water resistance. It is quite possible to stream a hundred yards of improper line behind a light lure—and never touch down in 100 feet of water. By "improper," we mean line which is too heavy and water-resistant for the business at hand. Such a line will belly in the current, buoy up the lure, and generally defeat the needs of deep jigging.

As current accelerates, weight of lure must be increased proportionately. To a greater or lesser extent, this is true at any depth—but you seldom experience real difficulty in the shallows. Probing a bottom 100 feet below one's boat is an education in itself. At slack tide a four ounce jig may perform well on 30 pound test monofilament line. As the current builds, six, eight and even ten ounce tempters become buoyant. True, the lighter the line, the lighter a feasible jig—but there is a point at which the whole thing becomes academic. Deep jigging can also be hard work.

Once, on the tip of Cape Cod, Joe Brooks decided that he'd like to take the fish that had given its name to this narrow land in Massachusetts. Curiously, although he had conquered a good share of the world's marine gamesters, Joe had never battled a cod on its home grounds.

We took him out in a surf boat, into the very waters that had first seen England's *Mayflower* in 1620. There, within sight of Provincetown's Pilgrim's Monument, Brooks dropped a chrome-plated jig into the 100 foot depths at the head of Race Point Run. Almost immediately he snagged a codfish, and then another. They were fish in the 10 to 15 pound class, and they fought like all codfish—like an engine block with a wiggle. Joe, who has battled the world's great gamesters, had only one comment when we came ashore. He said: "That's hard work!"

Deep jigging can be specialized when the quarry is a schooling species, such as members of the mackerel family. There is one method, which does not involve casting, taken directly from the commercial fishing book. A sinker, or drail, which has a hook built into it, is lowered over the side. Above this terminal lure is rigged a series of small tempters spaced along the line or leader. Small diamond jigs, bucktails or plastic worm lures are favored. When the terminal weight hits bottom, the whole "Christmas tree" conglomeration is jigged up and down.

Although hardly sporting in a classic sense, multiple catches may be made by waiting for a short period after the first fish has been hooked. An angler feels successive bumps as new customers tie in. The system is popular among those who are trying to load the live well or bait box with fresh and lively attractors for larger game.

This technique may be adapted to determine at what level any particular game species is feeding. One or more lures are rigged above that on the terminal end of the leader. Actually, a total of three lures is about all that can be handled easily without tangling. The hooks should be spaced between 18 and 24 inches apart. When lowered to the bottom—and do not cast unless you want trouble—the assortment is then twitched up and down. Quite obviously, the hook which collects a fish after the strike is apt to indicate the depth at which its fellows are swimming.

In offshore waters, where depths are apt to be extreme, deep jigging techniques undergo a bit of change, but success can be phenomenal. Again, drifting is preferred to slow trolling or anchoring. However, sufficient way is kept on the boat to head it into the seas—just as a matter of comfort. Light tackle can be used, but casting is comparatively unimportant. Here the system involves the presentation of a lure, which can range from a half ounce up to three or more ounces, in a vertical rather than a horizontal plane. In brief, the angler is fishing from the bottom up to the surface, rather than hopping the lure along the bottom itself.

The jig is lowered to the bottom with the line kept under control by finger or thumb. Once the hook hits bottom, the reel-jerk-reel procedure starts. Because a great deal of line is often out, the sweep of the rod on the "jerk" part of the operation is extensive—and exhausting.

Hits may come at any stage of the retrieve. Off the Florida coast, where this method has become fine art, species ranging from groupers to sailfish, from amberjack to king mackerel have been taken. Indeed, a small specimen hooked at or near bottom may be engulfed by a larger predator on the way up. It seems apparent that almost any fish will fall for a deep jig fished in this manner.

The hazards of fouling on bottom are minimized far offshore because the hook makes only one contact on each descent. However, toothed species and extremely heavy specimens may be hooked. Therefore leaders with light breaking strain, suggested for shallow water angling, are to be avoided. Wire may solve the problem, but wire is more visible to the fish and undoubtedly slows the action of the lure. Heavy monofilament leaders, generally those in the 60 pound test bracket, are the usual choice.

Because light is dim in the depths, lure color becomes important. Bucktail type jigs are favored over metal squids, and neutral shades should be avoided. Yellow, white, fluorescents, and those colors decorated with tinsel or Mylar seem to produce best.

At times, due to wind or current, it is necessary to troll slowly while deep jigging. In such cases, of course, the lure is presented in the horizontal plane. In order to keep the hook at or near bottom, a shot of wire line may be helpful. However, be sure that the wire is all out and that soft-braided backing takes the strain at the rod's tiptop. Constant jigging can crystallize wire in short order, so that it breaks at the most inopportune moment.

When fish are playing hard to get on the surface, deep jigging can save the day. The method requires effort, but effort is often well rewarded—often with species that are considered to be the sole target of natural bait fishermen.

28

TO STRIKE A FISH

MENTION THE WORD "STRIKE" TO THOSE UNFAMILIAR WITH FISHing and, in this day and age, they conjure up images of labor troubles. To an angler, however, the word has several meanings and all of them are important.

As a noun, strike signifies the blow dealt a lure or bait by a fish in its attempt to gobble up the offering. As a verb, it has two meanings: the first applies to the fish itself hitting the lure; the second applies to the angler as he jerks the rod sharply to set the hook after feeling his quarry. It is this last definition that will concern us in what follows.

Much has been written about striking a fish and, unfortunately, a great deal of it has been written by people who either are not anglers at all, or are poor ones. Every time we read about someone who strikes a fish "again and again" to set the hook, we shudder—and marvel at the excellence of modern tackle which can take such unnecessary punishment and survive.

In the great majority of cases when a lure is moving rapidly, as when trolling fast, lifting the rod tip sharply to strike the fish and drive the hook barb home is largely a waste of time. The fish will be hooked anyway.

If a skeptic doubts this, let him put the rod in a holder when fish are plentiful and note how many are hooked over a given period of time. Then have the doubter hold the rod himself and tabulate the results. We have tried this experiment many times under high-speed trolling conditions and we have never been able to see any appreciable difference in the number of fish hooked by either method. From the point of view of angling pleasure, let us hasten to add, we prefer to hold the rod. Our guess is that a rod holder gets very little thrill from feeling that savage whack when a fish hits, but we do!

If an angler holding the rod is inexperienced, the rod in the holder actually will get best results. The reason is simple enough. When a fish hits, the force of its strike will cause an inept angler to lower the rod tip, allowing slack line during an important atom of time during which the hook point may slip free. A more experienced operator will almost instinctively haul back on the rod, allow no slack, and will therefore insure a hook-up.

There are certain exceptions to this general rule, as there are exceptions to any rule. Many of the billfishes at times will lash at a fast trolled bait with their bills, then turn and grab the bait as it drops back. At other times they will rush the lure and gulp it down immediately. Obviously, the angler must be alert and observing—ready to strike only when conditions warrant.

Another exception is that when a particularly large natural bait is used. In such cases iron self-control is needed—and we must admit that we too seldom have it! The fish grabs the bait, moves off with it, pauses to turn the bait so that it may be swallowed more easily, and then starts moving again. That is the time to lean back on the rod. It is easy to write about, but controlling a wild impulse to strike too soon when fishing is the sign of an expert—or of a natural fisherman who has no nerves at all!

There is a lot more to angling than trolling, however, and the system used in striking must be tempered to the species sought, the lures or baits used, the method of fishing and the conditions at the time. A champion caster may win medals and cups, but if he does not know when and how to strike at the moment a fish hits he had best stick to the tournament field.

Considering species first, several factors must be considered. Assuming that hooks are sharp and of proper size and shape, it is still evident that it is more difficult to set the barb in the hard mouth of a tarpon than in the soft lips of a cod. Too hard a striking action on a soft-mouthed species can do more harm than good. The hook may well tear the quarry's flesh, and it will then "buttonhole"—that is, carve a lengthy slit so that the hook barb is likely to work free during the ensuing battle.

Hooking a hard-mouthed fish is, to a certain extent, a matter of luck. If the hook point hits teeth, bone or other natural plating, chances are it will never penetrate. Once it does go home in a softer area, the hook is apt to hold very well. However, if the "striking again and again" method is used, this additional sudden pressure on the bend may actually spring the barb loose. Note that the action of striking on the part of the angler just as the fish hits serves to take up slack line. Striking again and again after the line is taut merely adds unnecessary and dangerous pressure: the tackle is strained to its limit.

Toughness of the jaws of a fish is one thing to consider when striking. The way in which the fish takes a bait is another. Some species grab hooks with wild abandon, whereas others nibble gently. For example, a blood-crazed shark can be struck almost instantly—and successfully. On the other hand, a channel bass may pick up a bait, toy with it for agonizing moments, drop it, pick it up again—and finally shift it back to its crushing teeth. Then, and only then, should the angler strike. Finally, there is the famous case of the sheepshead. Old-timers claim that sheepshead should be struck *just before they bite!*

Knowing the feeding methods of the species sought is a great advantage and will result in a general knowledge of when to strike. Unfortunately, any given species can change its gobbling pattern at will. We well remember some Nova Scotian striped bass that took herring from a hook like a winter flounder sucking up sea-worms—instead of hitting with the thump usually associated with stripers. Similarly, there was a day on the beach when black drum in Georgia were walloping lures in the surf—like bluefish! Usually these huge bottom-browsers munch clams and "smash" baits only in the lurid fiction of outdoor writers who are describing a first encounter.

When things change—as they will on the sea front—a good angler will adjust his reaction on striking to the circumstances. Often, however, several fish are missed before the fisherman can really believe that they are behaving in an unusual manner. It pays to maintain an open mind and to be flexible.

When lures are being used in high speed trolling, as previously noted, there is no great emphasis on striking: the fish will do it for you. A high speed rate of retrieve in casting has the same effect. With the lure going rapidly one way, and the fish going another, setting a hook may almost be automatic.

When a lure is fished slowly, the picture changes. A fish that grabs a slow-moving natural bait or artificial will, almost immediately, realize that the hooky object is not a tasty morsel of food—and he will drop it quickly. A fast, hard strike is therefore the proper reaction the moment a bump is felt on a slowly moved lure.

The general tendency when using surface lures is to strike too soon. Often the fish may be seen approaching the lure, or maybe he cartwheels wildly or splashes before actually opening his mouth.

One common reaction is to tweak the hook out of reach before the quarry can grab it. A French-Canadian guide we know, on a Gaspé river, says: "Pull on the salmon when the salmon pulls on you!" His advice is good in many cases around the world. Such a fish should actually be felt before setting back on the rod. In most cases the lure should have disappeared beneath the surface, and the line made taut, before the angler strikes.

One angler we know claims that the best way to strike a fish when it can be seen taking the lure is to close your eyes and wait until a tug is felt. This is carrying the system a bit far, but it is worth noting that striped bass buffs often land more linesides on surface plugs at night than during the day. At night these happy warriors can't see the progressive phases of the surface strike, so they wait until the bulk of the hooked fish is apparent.

Natural bait presents additional problems. Feeding habits of the fish, as mentioned, make a tremendous difference as far as time of striking is concerned. So does the bait itself. A whole crab will be munched a bit before the fish tries to swallow it, and the strike should therefore be delayed. On the other hand a tiny, soft bait like an anchovy will be gobbled down in one gulp and the strike must be rapid before the fish feels the hook and spits it out. In general, the tougher and larger the bait, the more delay there should be in setting the hook.

Purists who scoff at bait users and stick solely to artificials are not necessarily more skillful in the art of angling. Their expertise simply lies in a different area of the sport. Striking at exactly the right moment when bait fishing takes experience and a high degree of adroitness.

Trolling at low speeds presents new problems. Here, the forward motion of the boat will not automatically set the hook unless the fish is moving rapidly or swimming in a direction opposite to the boat's course. In this event the unattended rod will not make nearly as many catches as one hand-held by an angler. In addition, the longer the line astern, the greater the arc through which the rod tip must pass when the strike is essayed.

When drifting, still fishing or live-lining—allowing the bait or lure to be carried out by the current and then retrieved—suit the strike to the species and the tempters used. As is the case when slow trolling, the more line out, the greater the effort which must be put into the striking action on the part of the angler. Except in the case of surface lures, mentioned earlier, the caster will strike the moment he feels a tap. As is true with other methods of fishing, the faster the lure is moving and the shorter the line which is being used, the less the striking arc required.

Circumstances alter cases in fishing as well as in everything else. Sometimes it is possible to determine whether or not a fish is approaching bait or lure from the side or from the rear. Often someone on the flying bridge of a sport fishing boat can see this very clearly. Casters, from piers or even right at sea level when the water is clear, can determine this also. If the quarry is following the hook, as in the case with a surface lure, the tendency is to strike too early. Although the fish will turn one way or the other after it has taken the offering, there is a split second when its mouth is closing and when it is swimming in the same direction as the lure. To strike at this precise moment will pull the hook clear. Therefore, pause very briefly before laying back on the rod.

Bonefish offer a perfect example: they are nervous, high-strung, and prone to move like an up-tight butterfly across a tropical flat. Yet when a bonefish takes a lure or bait, it seems to hesitate for a breath-catching moment before turning away. This is normal, because it is the gray ghost's habit to grab a morsel and then toss it back into the crushers in its throat. If you strike too soon, you may well jerk the hook free. Therefore, although every nerve in your body is screaming, you wait until the bone darts forward to take the bait, does a curious little circular dance—and then jets away. It is time to lift the rod tip when you feel him. He'll be there—and without any herculean strike—because his mouth is both soft and tough.

Night fishing offers a particular problem. Although darkness might well be considered ideal when using a surface lure—since it has the same effect as closing your eyes—this is not always the case. For reasons best known to themselves, fish seem to take an after-dark hook in a more leisurely manner than they do during daylight hours, and they often seem to play with a lure.

Among night fishermen, one school of thought holds that striking should be initiated immediately after a tap is felt, in the hope of hooking the fish somewhere or other about the mouth or head. The other, which we follow in the main, is to drop the rod tip slightly on the first light tap and then strike hard when a solid thump indicates greater interest. There may be several taps before the final solid belt—and we are first to admit that our plan of action is marred by one major fault: that final belt may never come at all!

Fortunately, so far as the night plugger is concerned, the strike is a progressive thing. There may be a succession of taps, but these usually build up to a no-nonsense whack which causes the rod to bend sharply. The fisherman succeeds precisely because he can't see the developing action and let his excitement tweak the hook away.

Many game fish play with baits and lures. By this, we do not mean the type of mouthing done by a channel bass or other picky, finicky feeder. We do mean the adrenalin-inducing strike which knocks a lure out of water time and again. To suggest ideal striking tactics under such conditions would be naïve, because each case is individual. There are rules of thumb.

Usually, when a frantic game fish slashes at a moving lure and misses it, slaps it with a broad tail, or otherwise seems to be playing, two courses of action are best employed. If the quarry really covets the lure, but is missing it because of water conditions and (possibly) poor vision, then an abrupt halt may turn the trick. After rapid action, stop the lure dead. Often the battler will loop up and nail it immediately.

There are other species capable of sniping a target at any speed. These, on occasion, may be playing with the lure because it is progressing too slowly. Speed things up by reeling like crazy—and you may score a smashing strike. Many of the jacks scorn a slow moving bait, but can't resist a rapidly moving tempter.

There are times when no trick in the book seems to result in a hook-up when fish are playing. We remember all too well an occasion off Nantucket Island in Massachusetts when bluefish were knocking surface plugs all over the ocean. How they did it, we could not understand, but the sharp-toothed cusses would grab a plug amidships, submerge with it, wage a savage battle for as long as thirty seconds—and then simply let go. Strike as we would, very few of these playing fish were landed—or even well hooked.

Missed strikes are commonplace. The successful angler analyzes the reasons for such failures and thereby turns future strikes into hooked fish.

29

TIME AND TIDE

COOKS CALL THEM INGREDIENTS, MATHEMATICIANS SPEAK OF VARIables—and fishermen wrangle about conditions. Inland anglers are concerned about temperatures, the effect of approaching weather fronts, and the clarity of water. Marine rodsmen mull these things and more: they have to take into account the regular changing of tides and currents.

So we sigh, slump, and ruminate on the frustrations of our profession when somebody asks: "Which is better—to fish by time, such as dawn and dusk, or to fish by tide, high or low?"

A one-paragraph answer to such a query is impossible, if only because fishermen have pondered the problem for centuries. Even with the space at our disposal we can only hit the high spots and undoubtedly will be rather vague where definite conclusions are concerned. There are, fortunately, a smattering of ingredients, variables and conditions that can be examined.

The first consideration, of course, is the species of fish sought. For example, many of the grouper family feed more avidly during the hours of darkness than during daylight. Pacific yellowtail, on the other hand, appear to be most active during daylight hours. Between these extreme limits in time there is a host of species which seem to vary feeding habits as the spirit moves. A practical angler always studies his chosen quarry to discover as much as possible about its seasonal movements and feeding patterns.

Although studies being made on fish behavior are still in their infancy, the few preliminary findings on record seem to indicate that many so-called game fish exhibit peaks of activity just before dawn and into daylight, and again just before sundown and into darkness. Such activity, all other conditions being equal, includes feeding—and this, of course, means that there is a better chance of success near the hours of sunup and sundown. Therefore, if a fisherman has limited time at his disposal, he might do well to select dawn and dusk for his trips.

Unfortunately, it is not that simple. Take an inshore tidal flat, for example: at dead low tide it will be bone dry or, at best, covered with a thin film of water. At high tide, on the contrary, this flat may be several feet under a clean flood, loaded with bait and playing host to a wide variety of feeding game fish. Ideal tidal phases may fall at midday, and the angler must fish accordingly.

For the offshore boatman, other things must be considered. Not only the species of fish, but also the size of individual specimens must be taken into account. Long-line commercial fishermen have discovered that broadbill swordfish apparently feed more often at night than they do during the day. However, an angler after swords is courting danger if he tries his luck after the sun has gone down. Trying to fight a leaping broadbill and gaff it when alongside is difficult enough in bright daylight.

In point of fact, those seeking big game well offshore are often governed more by the times of current change than by tides, per se. In addition, many offshore species apparently do not feed near the surface until the sun is well up in the sky. This, in general, appears to be true of the billfishes, while members of the tuna tribe tend to hit more readily at dawn than in the full heat and glare of the day.

Light from the sun unquestionably has a good deal to do with periods of fish activity. It should be noted that light from the moon also has an effect. Not too long ago, when fishing from a small boat, we had excellent luck at dawn after a cloudy night. The weather then cleared and, on the following night a full moon waxed above a calm sea. The next dawn, although tidal conditions were ideal in the area fished, produced almost nothing in the way of action. The critters had gorged their fill by moonlight. Such an occurrence is by no means unusual.

In addition to light, heat from the sun causes some complex changes. Both inshore and offshore anglers therefore must consider the geographical area which is to be fished, regardless of the species sought. In tropical and semitropical waters, after a series of broiling hot days, chances of doing well on most game fish at high noon are slim. Bait seeks cooler and deeper water—and the larger predators follow, regardless of the tidal stage. Under such circumstances dawn, dusk, and even the hours of complete darkness should be favored.

In more northern latitudes, the advent of bright, sunny weather after a series of foggy, cold days may well trigger unusual activity among fish of all kinds. Apparently, like birds after a rainstorm, they come out of hiding to warm up, if not to dry off. In such cases, often neither the time of the day nor the phase of tide has any effect and fishermen reap a harvest while their quarry is on a feeding spree.

Barometric pressure undoubtedly affects the feeding habits of game fish, but there are no statistics to indicate the extent of stimulation or depression. Like the inland angler who believes in "fishing the fronts," a marine enthusiast often finds gamesters walloping all offerings just before, and just after, periods of furious weather.

Heat from the sun during a 24 hour period has its effect in all latitudes. However, it has an even greater effect over longer periods of time, for it brings water temperatures up to a point which certain migratory species can tolerate. Even those which make only minor migrations from offshore to inshore grounds move only when water reaches a comfortable temperature, then return to the depths when the aquatic climate becomes too hot for them. In brief, an entire season for one particular species may be ruined—or made a success—by basic changes in water temperatures. Naturally, tides and currents contribute to these changes.

A typical game fish just arrived at any given area in the early season is apt to be more sluggish than at a later date. Since its activities depend to a large extent upon water temperature, daylight hours—when the sun's warmth is most apparent—are apt to produce strikes from such a fish, regardless of the tide.

A notable exception to this general rule of sluggishness is illustrated by members of the tuna family, which are wild as hawks when they first arrive. Extremely active, they do not seem to settle down and feed normally until temperatures rise to summer levels, but the daylight rule still applies.

As summer progresses and waters warm up, both times of tide and day bring changes. The tides increase in importance to the angler as various species fall into what might be called standard feeding patterns. However, dusk, night and dawn fishing insure better results, particularly where inshore species are concerned. Just as a broiling tropical sun causes change in the feeding pattern, midsummer heat in the north may be too great for fishy comfort. At that time of year, perhaps more than any other, the two factors—time and tide—might be considered equally important.

Those who fish inlets and tidal rivers find, by and large, that stage of tide is more important than time of day—once the season has gotten underway. When water is pouring out of any sort of natural impoundment, such as a marsh, salt pond or river mouth, feed of all sorts is carried with it. Game fish gather near bars and other obstructions where the flood of goodies will be tumbled by clashing currents. Of course, if this optimum tidal condition occurs at dawn or dusk the fishing should be ideal—and often is.

For the surf fisherman and others who are shore bound, such ideal conditions are less than plentiful. In sunny, calm weather, we favor fishing at dawn, dusk, and during the night hours along favored beaches, taking the tide as it comes. Naturally, this must be done within reasonable limits. A dead-low slack tide which leaves a gently sloping shore covered by a few inches of water will not host many game fish. Drop-off areas and inshore holes then command attention. The primary reason for choosing twilight conditions is a twofold thing. In summer, when the sun is bright, bait moves offshore during daylight hours in order to avoid winged predators and to escape the temperatures which are generated in shallow water. There are fewer enemies at night, and the environment is more comfortable.

In stormy or overcast weather, this still holds true to a certain degree, but favorable tides should then be considered equally important as time of day. Anyone who has had much shore fishing experience knows that catches are made much later after sunrise on an overcast than on a bright and sunny morning.

The bottom fisherman, seeking species which normally feed at considerable depth, has a different problem. Although light penetrates to the ocean floor where most of the groundfish taken by anglers are found, tide and current are the most important factors to consider. There are notable exceptions, like the groupers mentioned earlier, and, of course, the sportsman must know the habits of the fish he is trying to catch.

Nonetheless, the amount of daylight reaching the ocean floor should not be ignored. Many party boat skippers say that "the fish have heard the noon whistle" when catches slack off about midday. Canny captains spend this quiet period moving to new grounds while their customers do a bit of feeding on their own part.

Contour of the bottom itself should be considered, both with respect to inshore and offshore waters. For example, a gradually sloping beach, with almost no holes or pockets that might hold game fish over a period of time, will not be affected to any great degree by the rise and fall of tide. Water depths all along such a beach will remain comparatively constant, although the distance from a point on shore at which these depths are found will change. In broad daylight, bait rarely works close to the shore under such conditions, so the time slot selected for fishing is paramount.

Oddly enough, the same holds true when water is extremely deep close to the shore. A sharp drop-off, coupled with a fairly smooth bottom, yields best results when the sun is not high in the heavens.

Add rocks, holes, channels and other irregularities on any section of the ocean floor and the picture changes radically. Under such conditions the stage of tide may be far more important than the time of day. Usually a slough, which is nothing more than a deep strip of water running parallel to the beach between an offshore bar and the suds, will hold little in the way of fish life until the tide is high enough to lap over the bar, or pour through a cut in that same bar.

Offshore, irregularities in the bottom are of importance too. Those seeking deep feeding species should play the tides and currents first, placing light intensity in second place, but they should be vitally concerned with bottom contours and cover. A clean bottom is not frequented by game fish: they go where there is weed or rubble or the bare bones of old shipwrecks—for these offer hiding places for bait. Ledges and broken ground will be found more productive than smooth sand, mud or clay in many cases.

Although variations in shore and bottom may not have as much effect on surface-feeding species at first glance, these variations do influence the flow of water currents, thus forming tide rips where predators gather to gobble up tumbling, confused bait. Again, the stage of tide, which builds such rips to peak commotion—from an angler's viewpoint—will be more important than the height of the sun.

With the advent of autumn along many coasts of the United States and South America, fishing often reaches a peak. Then many of the species which migrate over long distances are feeding heavily in order to store energy for their trips. Those which do not travel very far are gluttons too, for they must stockpile fat to fuel them over months of comparatively low activity.

At this time all rules go by the board. Fish may strike at the wrong time, in the wrong place, on the wrong tide. Similarly, hopefuls who have missed a blitz on one day may appear on the next—when conditions are just the same—to find that the ocean is apparently fishless!

So there is no pat answer, in one paragraph or in many. The major key to any choice between time and tide is knowledge of the habits of a species sought, together with background information about the bottom contours, the depth, the most favorable temperatures for success with a given species in a specific area.

No short cuts, no lucky rabbit's foot: the expert is simply a guy who studies his game and perfects his technique.

30
THE LUCKY FISHERMAN

SPORT FISHING LITERATURE WILL ALWAYS DWELL UPON THOSE WHO have a working arrangement with Lady Luck. Some people seem to succeed with shameless regularity, while others labor mightily, only to catch the discarded rubber boots and trash fish of this watery world.

Like the old shell game, things are not always as they seem. There is no such thing as a lucky fisherman! From beginning to end we make our own luck, and skill always tops incantations, four-leaf clovers and merry legerdemain.

Granted, a bumbling amateur may hook and land a trophy fish —or shoot a great buck. If this is luck, make the most of it—but count it an exception to prove a rule. Any sportsman who scores consistently on fish or game is skillful, not lucky.

Folklore and popular romance ignore facts. The boy with a bent pin must emerge triumphant, and the neophyte who is pure in heart (if somewhat lacking in professional technique) forever lands a trophy. In the fairy tales of America, sport fishing remains a sort of cosmic lottery. Too often those of us who know better are brainwashed by this curious hypnosis: rather than seek an answer we sigh and mutter—luck!

Nonsense! When two men are fishing shoulder to shoulder, and one catches most of the fish, that angler is doing something that his companion is not doing. The secret of success may be found in tackle, bait, presentation, or timing, but never in good fortune. The sooner we scoff at luck and concentrate on reason, the sooner we will enjoy comparable success. Perhaps the average, fairly competent angling man knows this, but denies the possibility because it entails loss of face. It takes a bit of intestinal fortitude to admit that a companion has exhibited greater skill, as evidenced by more and larger fish.

Frequently a successful angler happens to use a lure or a tecnique that immediately intrigues the quarry, while his colleagues go hungry. In this situation the victor may have no idea why he is hooking one gamester after another—but the clues are always there. As the unhappy onlooker, on such frustrating occasions, have you studied and evaluated these clues? On-the-spot research can be most profitable.

Case One: We were fishing the Outer Banks of North Carolina, seeking southern spotted seatrout in the company of famed Virginia angler Claude Rogers. The trout were there, and Claude was catching them: we were not.

Rogers, an old friend, a fine angler and no hoarder of secrets, couldn't explain his success. "I'm just casting it out there," he said, "and reeling it in." *It* was a small bucktail jig.

So we quit fishing, moseyed back on the dunes and spent a few minutes watching Claude operate. In no time at all the vital technique was apparent. He flipped the jig seaward, waited a moment or two, and then started to retrieve. We'd been retrieving immediately, before the lure had time to plummet into the depths.

Claude was doing this instinctively, assuming that we were employing identical rhythms. In his mind he was—*just casting it out there and reeling it in.*

Attuned to the same wave lengths, we caught trout on every cast. Luck was no part of that momentous day, but the proper lure, the proper depth and retrieve certainly paid off.

Case Two: Tarpon were surfacing all over Rio Parismina on the east coast of Costa Rica. They came up in shoals, like the bait fish we'd so often seen at Barnegat and Cape Cod, but these "bait fish" weighed 40 to 60 pounds apiece. It was enough to drive an angling man right out of his skull, especially in view of the fact that Carlos Barrantes, Costa Rica's premier sport fisherman, had hooked several while we languished in silent, strikeless misery.

Since the tarpon were right on the surface it seemed logical to tempt them with top-water lures. We tried. The tarpon sneered at us. So finally we got smart and copied Carlos's method: he was using a deep-diving plug. That's what the silver kings wanted!

Case Three: Away out on the tip of Cape Cod in Massachusetts, on a dark night in July, we manned a picket line, surf casting for striped bass. One angler, a lad named Malte Bottscher, was hooking fish after fish. "What're you doing?" we inquired.

"Nothing," he gasped, hooking another big striper. "I'm just throwing it out there and bringing it back."

"Fast or slow?"

"Same as usual," he said—and that meant a slow retrieve, for you *always* slow a plug's retrieve during the night hours. We noted that he was using a surface swimmer which was popular during that season, a red-gold creation. Malte had four bass, and no one else had registered so much as a strike, even though they were using the same lures.

So, as usual in such cases, we quit fishing and sat down on the dunes in a strategic location, so that Bottscher was outlined against the faint glow of starlight. He made a flawless cast, the diminishing whine of the revolving spool bereft of any line snarl. Then he began to retrieve—and that was all we needed!

In game fishing, *never say always!* Striped bass and other marine battlers delight in upsetting the odds. *Usually* retrieves are slowed during the hours of darkness. In this case—excited, unaware of the fact that he had speeded the bring-back, Malte was cranking much faster than he thought, almost at a daytime rate. Suddenly there was a bomb burst of white spray out there in the dark water, and he was in again. For some curious reason, on that one night a fast retrieve insured a thing improperly called luck.

We tried it and we came away with a great catch of stripers. Those who stuck with the orthodox, slow retrieve were skunked on that particular night. It is unlikely that fortune smiled on us, or on Malte Bottscher. He had stumbled upon something that the mercurial bass liked, and we had been shameless enough to copy his technique. An open mind is worthwhile on any fishing ground.

If game fish persist in hitting one man's lure, and not another's, there is a reason. The thinking angler will always ask why and—ten to one—the answer is obvious. Luck is there only when something unforeseen occurs. Often, even the unforeseen proves very logical.

Kib Bramhall, advertising manager of *Salt Water Sportsman* and a talented surf caster, recalls one frustrating day on Martha's Vineyard when a young woman on her first salt water fishing trip seemed to be blessed with luck.

Kib and his clan, all highly skilled, had provided the lady with a spinning outfit—she was too inept to handle conventional gear—and armed it with a Hopkins lure, the popular hammered metal squid which all hands were using on this particular day.

The beginner promptly caught two striped bass and two bluefish, while our experts contrived to smile—even though murder was brewing in their fishless hearts. Because she was so obviously a duffer, they didn't even study her technique. Later, over evening cocktails, the wide-eyed innocent provided an answer.

"I'll never learn to close the bail on a spinning reel after a cast," she confided. "Sometimes it takes me five minutes to start retrieving."

That day, obviously, bass and blues liked the idea of a jig hopping right off bottom and heading toward the surface. The experts had been working their lures far over the heads of fish. Kib and his usually successful friends exchanged stricken glances, tried to grin—and ordered another round of double Scotches!

Since game fish are perverse creatures, often flouting all rules set down by erudite anglers, an open mind is quite as important as adequate tackle. The skillful fisherman who observes that which is taking place, and then matches the winning technique, is assured of a nebulous thing called luck.

It is as simple as a short cast. Every so often one hears tales of a tyro who backlashes, drops a lure 20 feet away from his rod tip—and comes up with a trophy. The battlers happen to be feeding close in, and the proud regular fails to score because he is driving that lure halfway to Spain. Most of us delight in distance casting, and forget that short-range accuracy can be just as important. Now and then some duffer reminds us that fish have fins and they can swim. Moreover, they swim where the bait is—and the bait may be right under our feet!

Bait, certainly, can be all-important. Usually (never say always) a striped bass prefers a naturally streamed seaworm to one which is abbreviated or bunched up on the hook—but not always. A winter flounder or tautog, on the other hand, usually is just as well satisfied with a tiny chunk of worm, and is far more likely to be hooked on the tidbit. But not always!

If any given species is feeding on one particular bait, it may be folly to use another. For reasons best known to themselves, marine gamesters tend to be selective. If Pacific yellowtail ignore your anchovy or mackerel, yet grab the lively squid of a neighboring angler, your continued use of anchovies and mackerel at that moment borders on stubborn ignorance.

Granted, it is much easier to recognize a preferred bait than some nuance in technique, but the game's the same. If your buddy is catching them, and you are not, he is doing something right. He has not assured success by presenting a burnt offering to Poseidon.

Very often a particular choice of tackle is the key. Few marine game fish are leader-shy. In other words, providing that a lure or bait can be given the right action or held in the right position, it will catch as many gamesters when fished on heavy line as on light line. Unfortunately, it is also true that action and positioning are affected by choice of tackle.

Persnickety battlers sometimes exhibit a surprising reaction to coarse tackle. We have demonstrated this to our own satisfaction on many occasions by failing with heavy rigs, and succeeding with much lighter gear *while using identical lures.* In this case, either the fish are line-shy, or there is something in the balance of the lighter tackle that imparts a different, more attractive action to the lure.

Certain lures are designed for use on heavy rigs, and others will not perform well on anything but light tackle. Some small plugs, for example, must be worked on a limber tip and fine monofilament to obtain best results: they become wooden and dead when employed on big sticks.

At the other end of the scale, there are big plugs, metal squids and spoons which require a powerful rod and stout line to induce seductive action. It is virtually impossible to jig a heavy nylon eel on a limber spinning rod, or to cast a bulky plug to the 100 yard range marker with a stick calibrated to handle much smaller offerings. Nor can you set big, heavy wire hooks with an ultralight outfit.

Obviously, no one rod-reel-line combination is adequate for all phases of marine angling. Those who promote one outfit over all others do so for one of two reasons: either they sell the specific rig, or they are so enthralled by its use that they become psychotic and imagine that it is supreme on the sea. There is ample room for every tackle combination.

Technique, which embraces a host of variations, is another matter. You may love your neighbor, or hate his guts, but in marine sport fishing it may be wise to watch him too, especially if the lad is catching two fish to your one. His margin of superiority may be as simple as the color scheme on a lure, an arrangement of terminal tackle or a heavier sinker which holds bottom in a raging surf or a strong current. Maybe he has chanced on a method of impaling a bait on a hook that is, momentarily, exactly suited to the whims of the fish in question.

There are legions of variables, hence no encyclopedia of sport fishing can list all of them. It remains for the individual angler to study his particular angling methods and the fish he seeks, to gain all available information on orthodox tackle and technique, and to maintain the open mind which will take immediate advantage of any irregular situation that may arise.

Luck is an alibi. Skill fills fish boxes.

31

THE MARKERS

THOSE WHO WRITE ALL SORTS OF SAGE ADVICE TO ANGLERS ARE continually repeating the need to look for certain natural signals which indicate the presence of fish. Birds working, bait jumping, irregularities of beach or water all represent such factors; yet, so far as we have been able to determine, nobody has ever written about the man-made signals which have been developed by anglers. These are many, and they are varied.

One of the earliest indicators used by big game anglers, primarily to advertise their triumphs, were signal flags. Originally, these standards were specially made for the purpose, and early types of catch flags are still seen along the coasts of America. Among them were: a rectangular white flag with a dark blue fish—bluefin tuna; rectangular dark blue flag with a white fish—white marlin; rectangular light blue flag with a dark blue fish—blue marlin; triangular pennant, the top half blue and the bottom half red, with a white fish superimposed—broadbill swordfish; rectangular flag, dark blue top, red bottom half, and white fish—sailfish. The fish outlines, in each case, were stylized look-alikes of the species in question.

These traditional signals, although informative, seem a little too fancy for today's average boat owner. Atomic age skippers are more likely to fly a plain, white rectangle to advertise the boating of a major big-game fish. A dark blue silhouette of the species may be added to the white field. In a pinch, a towel serves the purpose.

In some areas where many species of big game are found offshore, solid color flags have particular meaning, such as dark blue for blue marlin, green for yellowfin tuna, and so on. By learning the local custom, a visiting angler can determine who has caught what at a glance. Unfortunately, colored flags to indicate species have never been standardized, mainly because the more common species themselves vary from area to area.

It should be noted that a catch flag traditionally may be flown from a successful boat from the moment it takes a great catch aboard until sunset of the day the fish was landed. After that time, the flag should be struck.

In big game fishing tournaments, there is a certain amount of standardization in the matter of flag use. For example, a rectangular yellow flag indicates that an angler is fighting a fish and therefore exhorts other boats to stand clear. A red flag means that the boat concerned wishes to register an official protest. Usually the white flag, mentioned earlier, shows that a fish has been boated, while a light blue flag boasts that one has been released.

Small-boat skippers have taken a leaf from the book of big game anglers and have adapted flags of all sorts to the quarry they happen to be seeking. Even beach-buggy operators have joined the signaling corps and proudly display bunting from buggy roofs when they are successful. On Cape Cod, at one time, the tradition was so hide-bound that a flag could be flown from a beach buggy only if a striped bass was in the fish box. Tuna, bluefish and other great battlers were not deemed worth the flying of a flag!

Universally, a flag with any colored field and the outline in black and white of *Mephitis mephitis* means just one thing—skunked!

Another flag which is now common along all coasts is one with a red field and white diagonal stripe. This is used by skin-divers to indicate that one or more of their number are operating in the immediate area. It should be noted that neither this flag nor any of the others mentioned are official—that is, they are not included in the "International Code of Signals" book used by mariners throughout the world. They may be considered angling specialties popularized through constant use over the years.

An interesting use of signal flags is found ashore on the Texas coast. In this Gulf of Mexico area, shrimp is a favorite bait. A passing motorist does not have to waste his time and the time of a bait dealer by stopping to ask whether there are shrimp for sale. If the dealer has shrimp on hand, live and kicking, he flies a white flag conspicuously. If he has only dead shrimp he flies a blue flag. No flag at all means no bait at all!

Flag signals are useful, but hand signals are more so—and

probably the art has reached a greater degree of standardization. Some of the more common are listed below.

Elbows close to sides, palms up, then hands raised upwards and outwards: "Any luck?"

Palms down, hands moved back and forth parallel to the water: "No luck." Sometimes, if the fisherman concerned is really disgusted and disgruntled over the day's events, he will merely shake his head in these circumstances.

Hand and arm moved at chest level, fingers and thumb opening and closing to indicate a fish's mouth: "Strike."

Arm raised and lowered, index finger pointing at the water: "Fish sighted."

Arm moved rapidly upward with a circular motion: "Jumping fish sighted."

Same, followed by the "no luck" signal: "Fish hooked, but lost on a jump."

Clenched fist and arm extended as though giving the Black Power salute: "Fish on!" The political implications of this signal we leave to the politicians.

Open hand drawn across the throat: "Fish hooked, but lost."

Thumbs down, using either one or both hands: "No fish sighted, no strikes—and how could it be worse?"

When answering the "Any luck?" signal, the usual method of indicating success is to extend fingers to show the number of fish caught. Most anglers use only one hand for this purpose and do their mathematics in multiples of five, followed by the display of the necessary number of digits to make up the proper total. One boat skipper we know gets into countless arguments with the fleet because he lost his little finger in an accident. His multiplication therefore must be considered a special case!

Signals of the flag and hand variety serve a particular purpose, primarily that of communication among fishermen. If used to their fullest extent, they might well cut down a measure of the babble which is all too common on the airwaves. There are other types of signals, however, which might be roughly compared to the sign studied by a tracker in the backwoods. These are man-made to mark fishing hot spots.

Boat fishermen within sight of land can mark such spots by obtaining cross bearings of prominent landmarks. Coupled with the use of a depth finder, either sonic or manual, the spot in question can be readily located, weather permitting. When out of sight of land, course and distance run, known currents computed and electronic navigational instruments of one sort of another again can do the trick. Often, however, a temporary marker in the open ocean is extremely handy to indicate where fish have been sighted or where there has been a strike.

Small flag buoys, with a short weighted line attached to keep the flag upright, are carried by many of the more eager offshore anglers. These buoys are tossed over the side at the crucial point, then retrieved at leisure. Naturally they will drift to a certain extent, but for practical purposes the amount of drift is slight in the time involved. Some fishermen turn to dye-markers for this same purpose.

A simple and inexpensive marker of this type is a piece of cotton waste or rag soaked in oil. Unless weather conditions are severe, the slight oil slick radiating from the scrap of waste will cover a fairly large area and may be sighted from a considerable distance. One word of warning: do *not* use the oily waste marker when operating close to shore, unless you wish to become unpopular with bathers.

A skipper of our acquaintance has developed this oily waste marking system to a fine point. He keeps several chunks of waste in a covered can, which is partly filled with menhaden oil or with commercial cod-liver oil. His claim is—and his success afloat indicates that the claim may be a sound one—that the slick serves both as a marker and as chum for small bait fish in the area. We have used fist-sized chunks of frozen chum for the same dual purpose—and it works.

At first glance, it would seem that beach fishermen would have no particular difficulty in marking a particular hot spot for later reference. By driving a stake or piece of driftwood into the sand above high tide line, or by constructing a small cairn of rocks, when rocks are available, the surf fisherman should be able to mark a point to which he would like to return.

Unfortunately, the problem is complicated by the fact that beaches are used by more than one fisherman. Picnicing types will grab a highly visible stake for their cooking fires. Youngsters are drawn to a rock cairn as flies to sugar—and they will move the structure or build it into an unrecognizable castle. Some jealous anglers have even been known to move such markers, just to confuse the person who originally placed them.

Surfmen who are wise to the habits of their fellow men mark their hot spots, but do so in a manner known only to themselves or to a selected group. The basic idea behind all such marking methods is to keep the sign level with the beach as a whole. Anything sticking up above ground level will attract beachcombers and kids, often from considerable distances. Bits of driftwood, partly buried in the form of a cross, triangle or any other geometric pattern have a greater survival rate. They can be spotted by the person who is looking for them, yet will be passed over by the casual observer. Stones of particular color or shape placed in similar patterns at ground level serve the same purpose. Shells should not be used, for they are prime attractors of conchologists, whether professionals or amateurs of the sand-pail variety.

As noted, all beach markers should be placed above high tide line if a degree of permanence is desired. Often, however, more temporary markers will do the trick in the course of a day's fishing. Symbols or actual messages written in the sand serve the purpose. For example, companions working along a stretch of beach a considerable distance apart can communicate by this means and by prearranged hand signals. The lead man simply marks the spots where activity of one sort or another has been observed.

Natural terrain features are often used by shore casters, in the same manner as boatmen triangulate a location via check points. An unusually shaped dune, a patch of wild roses, a gnarled bit of driftwood far up on the beach, or the exposed timbers of an old wreck will serve. Observant anglers find that many relatively stable check points are available along any section of coast.

At night, signals by flashing light may be used both by beach and boat anglers. Use of a huge electric torch for this purpose will make the user highly unpopular, particularly on a well-fished beach. However, the beam of a small pencil flashlight can be spotted at an amazing distance. No knowledge of blinker code is needed, for a few simple signals suffice. The basic one should be for one angler to come toward another, assuming that the angler of the first part really wants to attract the attention of the angler of the second part—and they have devised a simple code. Otherwise, competitors may grin and say: "If they hit, I'll blink my eyes three times!"

No discussion of anglers' signals would be complete without mention of, for want of a better term, the anti-signal. Under this heading come the many schemes, born of fertile imaginations, which are used by fishermen to deceive their fellows into thinking that no fish are in the vicinity. While such tactics are not widely used in offshore big game circles, mainly because binoculars may be used to detect whether a neighboring boat is fighting a fish or clearing the line of weeds, they have reached a level of high art in the small boat fleet and in the surf. Operators of mosquito fleet boats, together with shore casters, hate crowding—and obvious success results in instantaneous crowding.

Therefore a sly small boat angler may plunge his whole rod underwater after he has hooked a fish, so that the telltale bend in the stick cannot be observed. Sideways strain will be kept on the quarry, rather than strain from aloft, until it is time to sneak the catch aboard with a minimum of fuss. Some deceivers keep a stringer over the side: upon this, one tiny specimen languishes—while the fish box aboard is brim-full. When asked by one means or another if he has had any luck, this artful dodger holds aloft the stringer and lets the questioner draw his own conclusions without further comment. Note carefully that he is not actually lying!

Surfmen who have dragged heavy catches from the sea will hasten to eradicate any marks made in the sand by the beaching process. They will then bury the catch deep, with a minimum of marking to relocate it when time comes for disinterment. A suspicious neighbor, of course, will look for drag marks, an unreasonable number of footprints at tide line, scuffings in the sand and a fish scale or two. If spotted, he can get his revenge by walking heavily all over the area until he strikes something squishy. Even better, he can back and fill with his beach buggy until the victim cries out in pain as he visualizes his catch being reduced to pulp.

Beach anglers who have fish on have been known to drop their rod tips when others approach, to give the impression that nothing is going on. With a loose reel drag or free-spool controlled by an educated thumb, they apply light pressure on the line and pray that the fish will not make a dramatic run at the wrong moment. Those who are suspicious can win in the long run simply by stopping and waiting until the deceiver can bluff no more without losing his quarry.

Such anti-signals, if truth must be known, are probably more numerous than the come-hither signals and honest communication between anglers. Moves and countermoves under such conditions become a game.

It is interesting to note that he who lies outright is considered to be an outright scamp, while he who can tread a narrow edge of truth, yet still deceive, is something of a hero!

32

HOW TO ZERO IN

CURIOUSLY, SELECTING A PLACE TO FISH IS A MAJOR PROBLEM FOR the average angler. By this, we do not mean that our sportsman will have a nervous breakdown trying to decide whether to cast off the north or the south side of a jetty. The difficulty arises when today's affluent citizen zeros in on a section of coast which is completely unfamiliar, maybe half a continent away.

Before asking others for help, the potential traveler should take a little time to list exactly what he has in mind. First and foremost, of course, is the type of fishing desired. An area famous for offshore big game may be a biological desert as far as an eager surf caster is concerned. Personal tastes vary greatly: the light-tackle enthusiast may be bored to tears with bottom fishing. Obviously, those who might supply answers to questions concerning angling in any area must know something of personal preferences in order to provide first rate intelligence.

With the type of fishing clearly outlined, the next step is to state definitely the time of year to be chosen and the length of time available for the trip. The longer advance notice is given, the more chance the informant has to prepare an accurate reply. In addition, if several choices (re time of year) are possible, this should be noted so that the best possible season for the type of fishing desired can be selected.

Although traveling anglers may be willing to settle for any and all species available when they reach their destination, often particular fishes or groups of fishes are the target. Again, this should be explained when seeking information.

Other items on the agenda should include: the amount of money, within reasonable limits, that can be spent; whether or not non-fishing members of the family will be along; the method of travel preferred—car, plane, train, boat or foot; services required when the destination is reached, such as type of accommodations, guides, boats and tackle, and, finally, the general fishing familiar to the traveler. This last item is helpful to anyone answering inquiries so that he may explain local differences in general approaches to fish and fishing. For example, the party boats of the northeast are a great deal different from those of the Pacific southwest. A Western angler visiting the Atlantic might be a bit bewildered to find no bunks nor galleys aboard. (There are exceptions to every rule.)

Geographical area and time of year naturally affect the fishing available. Marlin do not school off the coast of Maine in December, (indeed we never heard of them schooling there at any time!). Long-finned albacore are unlikely to swarm off southern California in May. In brief, the great game fishes observe seasons everywhere, and some sections of coast are more productive than others, even though these species range (in lesser numbers) elsewhere. If you pay your money to take your choice, you want to go where the action is. Maybe we can help.

Over and above water temperatures, which are vitally important from a fish's point of view, cold, extreme heat, rainy seasons and the like affect the fisherman himself. A good atlas or encyclopedia will provide basic information on what may be expected as far as the broad picture is concerned. For more detailed information, governmental agencies, ranging from local chambers of commerce to consulates, are sources which should be consulted by the traveler.

Unfortunately, chambers of commerce tend to classify just about every area under their jurisdiction as a fisherman's paradise. These hucksters (and we are being charitable) rarely consult angling experts of the area, so there is little in the way of accurate information to answer the questions of specialized anglers.

Careful study of brochures provided, however, will give a good indication of the type of fishing that may be expected. In some cases the literature lists both fish species and peak seasons. Even when they do not, a glance at the photos will give information concerning the type of angling common to the area. As a result, someone wishing to wade tidal flats will not end up peering over the edge of a coastal cliff that plunges down to hundreds of fathoms of ocean water.

Outfitters in any marine fishing area can be magnificent sources of good information, but the trick lies in choosing those tackle dealers who are not imbued with the overall chamber of commerce syndrome that "fishing is always great here." A few are always willing to practice deception: they soon brand themselves as charlatans and never really succeed.

Any tackle dealer who has a glowing reputation on a fishing coast is likely to provide accurate information. Similarly, any charter skipper or guide who has built his business by satisfying regular patrons will tell you the unvarnished truth. These fine professionals want you to catch fish, because then you'll be back—and every time you come back the local economy will benefit.

It follows, therefore, that a famed outfitter, charter skipper or guide is more likely to give you the straight dope than somebody very new to the business and hungry for trade at any cost. This is no hard and fast rule, for guides and tackle dealers all have to start from scratch. A majority of them are honest, and we mention the problem only because that's the way it is, thanks to a few unscrupulous operators.

If you plan a trip to a specific locality which is well serviced, contact a number of local authorities and skippers. Their answers, when compared, should provide logic. Generally you'll get more truth than fiction, so the opportunist will be detected with ease.

Particularly, when traveling to foreign lands, services of a reputable travel agent are strongly recommended. Although few agents are fishermen themselves, they have access to much source material not commonly available to the average angler. In the fields of accommodations, access, climate, and general living conditions to be found, their services are extremely helpful. Many who have not employed the services of a travel agent feel that they must pay some fee when seeking information. Such is not the case. Agents make their commissions on travel service sold, and therefore it is to their advantage to persuade folks to leave home. You pay the same fee whether you order an airline ticket from an agent or from the airline.

Luckily for fishermen, migrations of game species do not usually coincide with migrations of tourists along many coastal areas. Off-season rates, both on transportation facilities and on services after arrival, may well prevail when fishing is at its peak. Angling enthusiasts may have to put up with inconveniences such as lack of name brands, stinging insects, poor swimming conditions and no breeze, but they can save a little money when so doing—and they'll catch a lot more fish.

One word of caution: after the official tourist season has ended, many facilities close their doors or those operating them travel on their own account. Advance reservations for accommodations, boats and guides are always desirable, and they are a necessity if there is any question concerning seasonal operations. A "Closed for the Season" sign on a motel door after a long day's drive can cause strong men to weep.

As far as tackle is concerned, it is always preferable to bring your own. Unfortunately, the need for such gear is in a sort of inverse proportion to the distance traveled—the farther from alleged civilization one goes, the greater the need for personal tackle. In remote areas, both the quality and the quantity of items available are apt to be strictly limited. Tarpon may be knocking the varnish off a popular plug in a Central American river, but you won't find replacements in a corner tackle shop. The nearest well-equipped dealer may be one thousand miles north, and turn right on Flagler Boulevard.

The airlines are understanding, but they pose certain limitations. Propaganda to the contrary, the fly-boys employ some real baggage smashers. You'd best wrap a stout leather strap around a high-impact plastic tackle box to keep it from springing open and strewing lures around a plane's baggage compartment somewhere in flight. Rods can be mangled unless they are well packaged.

One-piece surf rods should be left at home when patronizing the airlines, except in those few cases when small planes are rigged to carry them. This is not only because the rods are difficult to stow, but also because chances of breakage are high. A couple of crumpled guides can spoil any fishing trip. We prefer to hand-carry all rods aboard, if possible. If impossible, a strongly built rod case is the answer, but it must be constructed to withstand considerable punishment in a luggage compartment.

In this connection, it should be noted that a number of tackle companies are now producing fine jointed sticks which we, for want of a better term, call "airplane rods." These can be broken down to lengths which will fit in a reasonably short, tough container and carried in an airplane's luggage compartment. Fenwick even has a high surf rod which is broken down into three pieces, yet which, assembled, is a remarkably practical weapon.

Elimination of unnecessary items of tackle on any long trip always causes us a certain amount of woe. Almost invariably, it seems that the very lure you need on the scene is resting comfortably in the top drawer of your workshop a thousand miles away just as the fish start feeding. The best compromise is to determine, insofar as is possible, just what gear is effective in the area to be visited, then leave behind what must obviously be dead weight. If all available information indicates that tarpon at the hot spot prefer underwater red and white plugs, do not load the tackle box with other types of plugs, bucktails and spoons. No matter what selection you make, there will always be something missing.

In remote areas in particular, remember that local guides or fellow fishermen will welcome extra lures, lines, hooks or other items left over as you are about to return home. Such tackle, which can be replaced easily and cheaply, is often a better builder of good will than base gold. This is especially true when it is obvious that the recipient has no lack of funds, but has great trouble in obtaining even the most common angling gear. Such action also lightens your own load on the return journey—and show us a flying fisherman who does not feel like a camel in labor as he struggles to tote his baggage from the airline office to a waiting car or taxi.

Leaving expensive items of tackle behind, following a trip out of the continental United States, may be quite illegal, thanks to laws touching on duties—but customs men are unlikely to worry about a half-dozen plugs donated to a fellow fisherman in South America. Cameras and other expensive equipment should be covered by a bill of sale or an insurance policy. Don't fool with guns unless you have all necessary papers from the U.S. and from the nation you plan to visit.

Fishermen traveling by beach buggy, camper or trailer are often disappointed when they arrive at the fishing area selected to find that local regulations limit their activities to certain specific areas or forbid them entirely. As traffic on or near beaches has increased, such regulations have become more and more stringent. Check well in advance on just what rules may be in force. Although chambers of commerce, tackle stores and such sources may have a fairly good idea of what local requirements are, it is best to go to those responsible for enforcement, the local police. A letter or call to headquarters in the community concerned may avoid detailed explanations to a judge, later.

If charter or rental craft are involved in the selected area, advance reservations again are strongly recommended. Not only will such reservations insure that the trip will be made, weather permitting, but also chances are that the quality of the boat will be higher than if left to the last minute. It is always wise to check with the skipper or livery operator the day before a planned trip to determine when, where and how fishing should be conducted.

In far distant places, it is often impossible to make advance reservations for boats, simply because the angler has no knowledge of what craft may be available. Even in active fishing ports near home, the turnover of skippers in a single season can be considerable. In such cases, it may be necessary to depend upon the hotel, motel or lodging operators. If fishing is a sport common to the area, these folk will have close working contact with one or more captains.

Although some anglers pride themselves upon the fact that they can catch fish in any area selected without benefit of local advice, we submit that they could catch a great many more fish if they sought such advice. It is very hard to go in cold. A guide, professional or not, who knows the angling scene can save the traveler a tremendous amount of time and trouble. When in a strange area we make it a business to seek out such informants.

A certain amount of compromise is involved in the selection of a fishing area for a vacation, because few of us can take off at a moment's notice for some far corner of the earth. If it takes three days to reach a hot spot and three days to get home again, a week-long trip is shot before it begins. Perhaps it is better to settle for some section close to home. Fortunately, in this day of jet travel, this problem is not as difficult as it used to be.

When it comes to compromise on the species sought, the problem is a bit more vexing. Someone who has set his heart on catching a big channel bass in a winter month, for example, would be hard put to find a variety of waters within reasonable traveling distance where he could satisfy his whim. The alternate solution, in our opinion, is to try fishing in the same manner for some other species that is roughly similar in habits and battling capacity.

Oddly enough, there are close links among anglers who fish for species that may be widely separated geographically. The striped bass man, for example, will find a blood brother in the snook fisherman; the surf perch fanatic of the Pacific speaks the same language as the white perch and spot specialist of the Atlantic, and a billfisherman is a billfisherman whether he works the Atlantic, Pacific, or Gulf. Therefore, although some compromise may be required with respect to an individual species sought because of season or geographical location, usually there need be no compromise on general type and method of angling.

Selecting a place to fish can be made much more simple if the general rules we have outlined are followed. Boiling them down, the solution is: (1) Make up your mind as to exactly what is desired; (2) ask questions and absorb the advice of people on the scene; (3) fit available fishing into the pattern dictated by season and the movement of game fish.

In our opulent, jet-transported society we can travel anywhere at any time, and we can tote all of the artillery needed—but we can't govern the wheeling seasons and the migratory instincts of game fishes. They call the turn, and we do not.

We have fished the marine waters of this hemisphere fairly thoroughly, and we have—paraphrasing the devil—ranged up and down across the world, and back and forth upon its briny waters. Our discoveries are an open book, and we pass on information gathered by others.

But, like that currently popular TV detective Jack Webb, we must have basic information upon which to act.

Just the facts, sir. Just the facts!

33
PLANNING A TRIP

ARTICLES WHICH DEAL WITH SPORT FISHING IN VARIOUS SECTIONS of the Western Hemisphere provide much good information for marine anglers, but we have a sneaking suspicion that basic data often suffers in translation. Undoubtedly there are good and adequate reasons why more space is not allotted to facilities, climate, and specific tackle, yet these nuggets of intelligence are hard to find.

First off, outdoor writers who describe fishing in a new area are apt to assume that a reader understands the need for specialized clothing and equipment in that particular corner of the world. As a result, things that the author considers too obvious to mention may provide serious problems for those who follow him into a sport fishing area.

Planning a sport fishing trip should be as systematic a procedure as the adventure is soul-stirring, especially if the journey is a long one, fairly arduous and expensive. Research via the U.S. mails and telephone-telegraph services should insure satisfaction.

There are many sources of information, including *Salt Water Sportsman* Magazine and similar journals. In most of the highly developed areas chambers of commerce stand ready to offer assistance. Guides and outfitters, on the spot, have all of the answers and it is in the interests of their business to level with a potential customer.

We hold it logical to employ the chamber of commerce as a first contact. Remember that C. of C. representatives are unlikely to be experts on any phase of sport under discussion, but they will make an honest effort to put you in touch with qualified professionals. Initially, you need briefing on the following subjects:

Peak seasons for species sought. It is particularly frustrating to arrive several weeks after a run of great game fish has petered out. In some cases superb angling continues over a period of many months, but techniques differ with the changing seasons. If you're a light-tackle buff who prefers to use surface plugs, it is disconcerting to find that fish are plentiful, but feeding strictly on bottom.

Therefore, after you have located a guide or skipper whose reputation has been attested to by all hands, ask him a series of objective questions. In addition to the optimum time to fish, see whether certain tides are most productive. Sometimes, months ahead, a guide can predict a specific week when your chances of landing a real trophy are extraordinarily good. Depending on species, this peak period may last a week, two weeks—or several months. The guide will know. Chambers of commerce, lacking any malice, often assume that the fish will be in good supply from first encounter until final flurry. Get your data right from the front.

Among other things, you should know weather conditions and average temperatures in the target area, so that you can pack proper clothing and footwear. Northern seas are cold, even in midsummer, yet local guides assume that any visitor will understand a need for warm clothing. Similarly, a tropical outfitter will shake his head in dismay when a pale Yankee totes chest-high waders but forgets sunglasses, wide-brimmed hats, and long-sleeved shirts to protect him from the broiling sun.

Dress warmly in the north and carry foul-weather gear. If you plan to fish the surf, wear waders. Tennis shoes are a better choice of footwear in the tropics, with long cotton pants to ward off the sun—and the tentacles of stinging jellyfish. Hats that shade one's neck and ears, together with long-sleeved shirts, should be worn. Dark sunglasses are essential—polarized if you plan to hunt game fish on a flat.

Tackle is most important, and it is well to know whether rods, reels, lines, and lures will be provided by guide or skipper. In any event, determine the techniques favored in waters you will visit. Successful methods and gear, except in virgin areas where angling has yet to be pioneered, will be the product of trial-and-error research by local professionals. Ponder the pound-test ratings of their outfits and, if you still desire to go much lighter or heavier, inquire why such rigs are chosen. Usually there are good reasons.

Ask about lures or baits that draw strikes, and don't be vague about this. Your pet artificials may start a new trend, but you'll feel mighty unhappy if neighbors are slaughtering fish on deep-diving, red-striped Dunderhead plugs while you have nothing but surface-popping blue Scissorbills in your kit. Your prospective guide can tell you the exact model number, color scheme, and weight of lures that have proved most effective in his area. Take his advice, at least during this planning stage.

Above all, do not essay an outfit which is entirely new to you, unless this is required to land the game fish of a lifetime. Obviously, people who tackle giant tuna for the first time will use gear that seems mammoth compared to what they have employed on lesser fishes. However, tuna tackle need not be entirely unfamiliar if the sportsman has used revolving spool reels in previous trolling.

Our point, and it is particularly applicable in casting, is the fact that a spinning enthusiast who is unfamiliar with the mechanics of bait casting would be asking for trouble were he to switch without learning the skills involved. Wherever possible, use a familiar rig—one that handles naturally.

Within the continental United States there are thousands of remote marine fishing areas which do not boast well stocked tackle shops. In Latin America gear generally is available only in the larger cities, and selection is likely to be haphazard. In planning a trip it is therefore wise to determine the availability of equipment in the target area. Often, happily enough, the better locations are blessed with dealers who carry complete lines. In this event you can afford to travel light and to purchase lures or other accessories on the scene. But, and we emphasize the point, be sure that such outfitters are in business before you shove off.

If not, by all means make every effort to carry everything that is needed. This is an instance where homework will pay big dividends and where your supposedly picayune questions will provide the intelligence needed to be at the right spot, at the right time—and with the ultimate weapons.

By the same token, if you are a nicotine-stained addict who desires a certain brand of cigarettes or a blend of tobacco, better tote a generous supply. Smokes are available everywhere, but specific brands are not, and some foreign leaf makes corn silk taste like ambrosia.

Before you buy an airline ticket, bone up on facilities and living accommodations, boats and the standard of guide service at your destination. Check transportation, not only that which jets you to a remote city, but the connecting tissue which will convey you to a storied fishing location. If you must maintain contact with home base, better inquire about communications. In some areas natives lack so much as homing pigeons!

Sportsmen who travel out of the United States require passports or tourist cards: they also find it necessary to show evidence of recent inoculations. Don't wait until the last moment to acquire these documents and shots. Some of the latter require a period of time to prove positive or negative, and this time must pass before any physician can sign your card.

Having corresponded with responsible people in the area you plan to visit, it should be a simple matter to pack tackle. Obviously, automobile transportation will allow a greater tonnage of equipment, with lots of room for the rod that you might use, but probably will not. Flying is another proposition: there simply isn't room to take more than the essentials.

Frequently, if a guide or charter skipper promises fishing equipment, you will decide to chance his rods, but will pack your own reels, lines, and leaders. The skipper won't be unhappy about this; indeed, he welcomes a patron who prefers to use personal gear. For your part, it is far easier to transport reels than rods—and your own reels contain the line of your choice, unfrayed. They feel comfortable, hence are better tools to use.

Because American sportsmen are nomadic, all manner of salt water fishing rods are now offered in break-down or jointed versions. One firm even produces a heavy surf casting model which breaks down into three sections. Even then, packing is critical. Be very sure that all of your rods are encased in hard plastic or rigid aluminum containers. Those protected only by wooden stiffeners and the usual light canvas bags are likely to arrive with mashed guides or broken tips. The baggage-smashers are still with us.

It is a fact of life, or maybe another manifestation of the Law of General Cussedness, that nobody ever makes a journey without forgetting something important. If planning is systematic, this failure will be minute. Having corresponded with people on the scene, you should be able to prepare a check list of necessities. In the end of it, be assured that items left behind will be those so obvious that you didn't bother to check them off!

Like various articles of clothing: quilted underwear and woolen shirts, heavy socks and boots or waders for the cold North. Like tennis shoes for tropical wading, and clothing light enough to be comfortable, yet sufficiently covering to ward off the searing heat of southern sunshine. Hats may be head-warmers in the North, and head-coolers in the South.

Marine anglers use dark sunglasses in all climates, for reflection forever assaults vision on the sea. Moreover, when it is necessary to see through the surface glare in order to spot game fish before casting to them, then the polarized glass is a must. Without proper sunglasses the salt water angler is seriously handicapped.

Salt water anglers rarely meet venomous snakes, but expeditions into tropical areas where such reptiles are found should be equipped with at least one snakebite kit. One thousand to one, it'll never be used—but the package usurps little space and might, on that thousandth occasion, save a life. Incidentally, the wag's "snakebite medicine," good whiskey, is found just about everywhere—and Latin American beer is delightfully cool and flavorful after a hot day on a jungle river.

In remote areas—North or South—one does well to pack a head net, mosquito bar, and insect repellent, a packet of aspirin tablets, Band-Aids, gauze, and Merthiolate. In the tropics, tablets prescribed by your family doctor will counteract the effects of Montezuma's curse.

These are minor items of insurance, easy to carry and very important when needed. At the very least, tuck a half-dozen Band-Aids in your wallet: they're life-savers when a misplaced hook or the careless handling of a sharp-toothed game fish draws blood.

For the same reason, every sportsman's kit should contain a sharp knife and cutting pliers which are capable of shearing the heaviest hooks used. Trouble has a habit of multiplying when you have no means of coping with it.

Logistics seldom figure in headlines which proclaim an army's success, but all victories are preceded by exact planning and by the stockpiling of necessary materials at a climactic point in time and space. An angler can put this concept to good use.

Whether you intend a week-long sortie on some fishing ground 50 miles away, or an adventure which encompasses jet flight and a probe of unknown waters, success or failure is likely to depend on how well you do your homework.

34

PESTS ON THE COAST

TUB-THUMPERS FOR VARIOUS VACATIONLANDS ARE UNDERSTANDably vocal about sunshine and clear water, vast schools of game fish and scenic vistas guaranteed to produce lyrical exclamation. Not even in fine print will you discover reference to unlovely critters that bite, sting, or otherwise gnaw upon visitors.

Unhappily, no fishing ground is entirely free of pests. North, South, East, or West, there are certain insect, animal, or reptile villains capable of making trouble for human beings. Usually the problem is a minor one and solutions are easily found. Indeed, visitors who travel to metropolitan fun capitals are unlikely to be bothered at all. The better lodges and motels are well screened and adjoining areas are sprayed to discourage biting insects. Thanks to wind and sea, offshore anglers leave the bugs behind.

Unfortunately, a man who desires adventure in the back country where game fishing has not been exploited will find it necessary to live with a host of pests. Rugged anglers find an exploratory trip grand adventure, while others regard it as torture. The former realize that any aboriginal shoreline will boast a full complement of creatures capable of inflicting injury. These range from insects of various kinds to venomous snakes and even carnivorous animals—although the latter rarely challenge human beings.

Obviously, knowledge is a first line of defense. Fear is a byproduct of ignorance, and it can wreck a safari as thoroughly as any hurricane. We recall a week-long trip among the wild, uninhabited islands of Costa Rica's Bay of Parrots, during which an elderly native guide lived with fear because he was sure that jaguars were man-killers. At the guide's insistence, we camped on remote islands to which, in his ignorance, he assumed that *tigres* could not swim. Jaguars were there, of course, and we found their tracks in the fine, volcanic soil. Characteristically, the big cats wanted no part of man.

A northern sportsman is always snake-conscious during his first journey into the tropics. For some curious reason a Yankee—who often boasts a few healthy rattlers in his own hinterland—seems convinced that Florida is alive with murderous reptiles and that Caribbean or South American grounds are squirming with bushmasters. A few tourists are so thoroughly convinced of this that they forego trips into tropical wonderlands.

The fear is ridiculous, for contact with venomous snakes is always the exception. An angler is much more likely to be plagued by biting flies, chiggers, and mosquitoes. In fact, few sportsmen who visit the tropics ever see a dangerous snake.

Again in Costa Rica, we were skidding down a precipitous ravine in the mountainous country north of San Jose, shoulder-deep in jungle growth and grasping at spiny lianas to keep from plunging all the way to a tiny stream which was alive with rainbow trout, when one of us thought about venomous snakes. Carlos Barrantes, our host on this busman's holiday from the seacoast, meant to offer reassurance, but we entertained some reservations about his statement.

"There are no snakes here, but ten kilometers down the river you're sure to get stung!"

That was small solace, but Carlos exuded confidence and we met no savage reptiles, a thing par for the course among anglers, and especially among salt water anglers. Indeed Barrantes had voiced a rule of thumb: if you are guided by a local fisherman, there is little chance that you will blunder into trouble. A man on his own ground is aware of the odds and he will take no chances. His life is quite as valuable as yours.

However, we do not advocate aimless progress through jungle growth, for one must employ some caution in areas where venomous snakes are known to exist. Anglers have been hit, usually because they became overconfident and disdainful of reptiles in thick cover. An ounce of caution is worth a pound of anti-venin, but unreasonable fear is stupid.

Initially, snakes are never anxious to strike a man: in most cases they resist any contact and will slither away long before you approach them. Trouble occurs when abrupt confrontation cancels out retreat. If the reptile, in its defense posture, figures no other way out of a dangerous situation, it will strike. Fear, rather than any malicious intent, is the trigger.

By this token a slow-going, cautious man usually is safe. In southern fishing grounds, cottonmouth moccasins sun themselves on stream banks and on logs and limbs which overhang the water. They are not particularly aggressive and will escape whenever the opportunity is offered. It is the human's prerogative to look where he places his feet and hands, and to avoid running the bow of his boat under thick overhead cover.

In the United States, some 6,500 to 7,000 snakebite cases are reported during each calendar year. Only an estimated 5 per cent of these are sustained by hunters and fishermen. The salt water angler, because he haunts the seaboard where reptiles are scarce, is particularly safe. If a marine fisherman wants to see a snake he will probably have to go to the nearest exhibit where technicians "milk" a variety of venomous species for the benefit of medicine and a paying audience.

Nonetheless, any sportsman who ventures back of beyond in snake country should carry an anti-venin kit. These are available at something close to ten dollars, and although they may never be used are insurance against the one-in-one-thousand misadventure. These kits contain dry serum which remains effective for approximately five years following date of purchase.

We are regularly bombarded with tales of venomous sea snakes around the continental shores of the United States. There simply are none. The true sea snake is a resident of the South Pacific and, although venomous, the creature does not seek out and attack man. You won't find this threatening reptile at Barnegat or Miami, nor at San Francisco or in the Sea of Cortez.

Carnivorous animals, with one possible exception, are no threat in this hemisphere. In spite of folk legends, there is just one beast which is unpredictable, and that is the grizzly bear of the far Pacific Northwest. Salmon fishermen occasionally meet rogue animals, but even these are few and far between.

The black bear of the Atlantic coast is an abject coward unless cornered. Jaguars, the "tigres" of central and South America, avoid humans. Cougars, also present in some remote fishing areas, are never a problem.

Fishermen often think about snakes and big carnivores as major threats, while they discount insects. Actually, bugs are far deadlier than the tooth-and-claw tribes, for they exist in uncounted billions and are most annoying in wilderness waters where big fish have not been exploited. Biting gnats, mosquitoes, and flies are present in all latitudes. Spiders and scorpions are well distributed.

Ticks and a variety of burrowing mites are attracted by human flesh. Defense against these miniature multitudes should be taken into account at all times.

It is popular to consider the tropics a paradise for insects, but this is a generalization. During the short summer months many northern regions swarm with mosquitoes, no-see-ums, and biting flies. The winged legions can make life mighty uncomfortable on any seaboard. They are present from Alaska to Canada's Maritimes, on Cape Cod's beaches, in the Jersey marshes and in the Everglades of Florida.

Coastal fishermen, thanks to sea winds, seldom have to endure the concentrated attack of biting insects, but any period of calm, moist weather can bring these horrors out in droves. The stinging legions are most apparent when you are fishing brackish waters or quiet bays bordered by lush vegetation.

Modern insecticides are the best defenses. These are offered in aerosol bottles or tubes of concentrated bug repellent. Curiously, some repellents work for one man, where another is best suited to a second individual. A few of these concoctions will take the finish off a fly rod, while others discourage insects but do not dissolve hardware wrappings. There is no universal deterrent, so it is wise to experiment and find the one best suited to you.

Smoke may be the best defense. Anglers who puff on pipes, cigars, or cigarettes will discourage some of the buzzing pirates, but in bug country you'll have to do a lot of puffing. Perhaps a combination of smoke, insecticides, and head nets—plus the stoicism of an Indian—is the answer.

On southern fishing grounds, chiggers, or red bugs, are a constant menace. These tiny, ferocious mites burrow under the skin and create an unbearable itch. Various salves are advertised as panaceas, but the best defense is a hot bath immediately after possible contact. Lacking this, it is well to bathe one's ankles and forearms with alcohol or even with kerosene. In most cases the chigger attacks a man's legs and works up to that point where his belt restricts further passage. Anything below the belt—and there are treasured appurtenances in this region—catch hell when red bugs are on a rampage!

Pay particular attention to the lower part of the body, and bathe with alcohol those areas that are most vulnerable. Be prepared.

Chiggers abound in brush areas and, like ticks, make a home in rotting or rotted wood. Therefore keep clear of the boondocks and no not use an old stump or a fallen log as a resting place. The red bug also may be found in Spanish moss, so tourists who delight in sending packets of this romantic-appearing parasite to northern friends often include this nasty little pest as a bonus. Fortunately chiggers do not thrive very close to salt water, so the danger to a marine angler lies en route to the fishing grounds, rather than right on them. Of course chiggers get their licks in when a fisherman works a brackish canal some distance from the sea.

Ticks are equally insidious in their approach: they cling to grass, brush or bark where they wait for some warm-blooded animal, such as man, to prey upon. The damned things are widespread, from the tropics to the North, and they are similar throughout their range. You won't feel any sting, but unless the tick is soon discovered and removed it will dig in like an anxious bulldozer. Bedding down on the ground is one sure-fire way to attract these parasites, and in tick-infested areas it is wise to bathe frequently and to inspect one's person at least once a day. Some ticks are disease carriers and will infect a host with illnesses such as Rocky Mountain spotted fever.

Fishermen in many areas must also worry about scorpions. These cousins to the spiders are no major threat, but they can be mighty troublesome. Soldiers who campaign in lands that play host to scorpions soon learn to check clothing before dressing. For some reason these repulsive little critters will crawl into an empty shoe and sting the foot that is later inserted into it. An angler in the back country should be on guard.

Worth noting is the fact that spiders, scorpions, ticks, and venomous snakes often take refuge in trash piles. It is always unwise, particularly in the tropics, to place your hand under a driftwood plank, a stone, or any other article on the ground. Use a shovel, a pick, or a staff for safety.

As sport fishermen, we all carry more gear than we ever get to use, and most of us manage to forget a few items that become very important in the back country. An aerosol can of the insect repellent that works best for you consumes little space in a tackle box, and it is important. In an emergency, note that ordinary Listerine mouth wash is an excellent bug repellent—although it evaporates quickly and has to be replenished at frequent intervals. Head nets are similarly brief and often are worth their weight in fine gold. To guarantee sleep where the droning multitudes are a problem, camp cots and mosquito bars—available at any outfitter's shop or army surplus store—should be included. At the very least, if you plan a trip away from civilization, tuck a mosquito bar in your duffel bag, and don't forget insect repellent.

No wide-ranging angler ever entirely escapes discomfort, but those who recognize the problem are able to plan some protection. Marine fishing must rank as one of the safest of sports, yet smart operators protect themselves against the little annoyances that can add up to real trouble. It is rarely the spectacularly lethal snakes and mammals of a wilderness that plague outdoorsmen, but rather the ordinary insects, spiny or sharp-toothed fishes, sea urchins, and sharp corals that are bad news for the unwary.

35

WADERS AND BOOTS

SOME YEARS AGO LEE WULFF BURIED ONE OF SPORT FISHING'S MORE persistent myths by jumping off a bridge into a deep stream—while wearing chest-high waders. Wulff, one of America's great anglers and outdoor writers, essayed this particular stunt to prove something well known to veteran anglers: that a man is not doomed if he happens to fall into the water while wearing waders.

Shortly after Wulff's demonstration, we were prospecting an offshore bar at Nauset Beach, Orleans—one of Cape Cod's wonderful striped bass fishing grounds. Because stripers were taking lures as if they were going out of style, it was easy to remain on the bar as a flooding tide filled the gully between that high ridge of sand and the shore. In the end of it, burdened with a rod and a string of fish, we had to tread water to get back to the mainland.

There wasn't any danger, but salt brine was cold as it poured into the waders. Nor was there any tendency to upset, or to be dragged down. Water pressure plastered the rubber to our legs, yet some air must have been trapped, for there was a curiously buoyant feeling as we paddled along toward the high dunes.

One difficulty was apparent in the shallows. There, emerging from the suds like King Neptune, our waders filled and the resultant weight increased to enormous levels. It was necessary to slip our suspenders and let the brine spill out. No danger: simply discomfort. Aside from the weight of the rubber itself, those waders presented nothing in the way of a mortal threat.

Back in World War II, the writers of this book—one in the U.S. Navy and the other in Armored Force—learned much about survival in the sea. We were taught, for example, how to jettison heavy combat boots and other equipment without drowning in the process. (Boots are removed by taking a deep breath, assuming a humped-up "turtle position," and coolly stripping them off.) Perhaps the key to this maneuver lies in keeping cool and refraining from panic, for panic is a major killer of man and beast.

Today, in writing about marine sport fishing, we do not advocate waders as proper garments for boatmen. Indeed, the chest-high article might be a distinct handicap after any impromptu ditching offshore. They'd be hard to discard and their very weight would handicap a swimmer. Nonetheless, an angler should never fear his footwear. It is simply wise to know which types of boots or waders are best for a specific task, and why.

Initially, boots and waders are protective garments, nearly indispensable in cool climates. Where temperatures are low enough to cause discomfort while wading, the knee-length boot, hip boot or chest-high wader always pays its way. These are rarely a necessity in the tropics. There, so far as the sport fisherman is concerned, boots and waders are excess baggage because the water is warm. Tennis shoes and cotton trousers suffice, the one to guard against sharp coral and the needles of sea urchins, the other to provide a measure of warmth, to prevent painful sunburn and to defeat the occasional tentacle of a stinging jellyfish.

Hip boots have served marine anglers for many years and will continue to be favored by a certain percentage of sportsmen during the years which lie ahead. They are ideally suited to the man who does not plan to wade very deep and who desires protection, together with light weight.

If hip boots are worn under foul-weather pants, and especially if the trouser legs of the foul-weather pants are snugged down with a drawstring, they can be a good choice for surf casting. Granted, you can't wade much deeper than the height of the individual boot, but curling waves and spray will be turned back. For marine use boots should be loose-fitting, never of the ankle-fit type. That's because the ankle-fits, while comfortable, are more difficult to pull on or take off. In deep water the difference might mean your life.

Boatmen sometimes employ hip boots turned down to below the knee. A much better type is the rubber half-boot, which is just that —a roomy type which reaches to a point just below the knee and offers some protection in launching a boat or, later, in cat-footing around wet decks. A boatman's half-boot should always feature squeegee soles to prevent slipping, and it should be easy to remove. Again, keep those ankle-fits for upland hunting.

Chest-high waders are for wade-fishermen, period. These are made from a variety of materials and range from the very expensive custom-fitted to the cheap, all-rubber variety and plastics out of foreign factories. All have a definite place in the scheme of things. No single model is all-purpose, although most waders serve a multitude of needs.

If a fisherman plans to do a great deal of walking, then the lightweight models are worth considering. Usually, with anything rated "light," you must worry about toughness and durability. Thin sheets of rubber or plastic will not take as much punishment as heavier sheets, yet the featherweight garment provides greater freedom of action and is most comfortable.

This, of course, is generality. Some of America's foremost manufacturers produce lightweight boots and waders which are extremely tough—and correspondingly expensive. Durability, and the craftsmanship that insures it, costs money. Exact fit—custom tailoring in rubber and plastic—means more money, yet it can add much to the enjoyment of angling. A fisherman must evaluate his needs and reach a decision.

For some, the inexpensive Japanese rubber and plastic wader is a bargain. These imports seldom match the excellence of good U.S. products, but they are adequate for the sometime angler who never puts much mileage on his gear. Stretch rubber waders of the stocking-foot type are very light and comfortable, yet inexpensive. These will not provide the long term trouble-free service of heavier models with attached boot foot. They are great for the occasional angler and for the flying sportsman who must consider weight and bulk.

Finest of all are custom-designed models which dispense with weight wherever this can be done without sacrificing strength and durability. These are offered in exact leg length, chest height and waist measure. Usually there is a small extra charge for custom alterations.

Over-the-counter waders are offered in several leg lengths, so this is hardly a major problem. Major difference between the custom and standard-grade product will lie in the realms of overall weight and waist measurement. Inexpensive waders will be heavy, and they will be barrel-chested to take care of all comers. There is nothing wrong with this, so long as a thin angler is satisfied with a garment that has to be reefed in with a belt.

Indeed, some of the all-rubber waders sold at minimum price are good buys *because* they are heavy and tough. If an angler finds it necessary to walk for great distances, this may be a handicap. If, on the other hand, he wants a tough, rugged wader for grueling service, the cheapie will last quite as long as the more expensive product. It will not be quite as comfortable, but it will offer quite as much protection.

For marine fishing, the slick-surfaced wader is probably far superior to the fabric-faced type, if only because the abrasion of sand raises merry hell with fabric. Therefore, choose rubber or any of the new plastics. Keep the canvas-surfaced models for inland trout and Atlantic salmon angling.

On the sea front, a boot-footed wader is most practical. Stocking foot types, over which one must wear canvas shoes, tend to wear and puncture as sand and pebbles sift into the shoes. On rocky beaches this problem is minimized, but it is a factor to consider.

While boot-footed waders are recommended, the angler who needs to clamber over seaweed-draped rocks will find that some additional equipment is in order. This *does not* mean the felt soles so commonly employed by inland trout and salmon fishermen. Felt is terribly slippery on marine boulders which are covered with slime and weed growth.

Here there is a necessity for steel, and sharp steel at that. Ice creepers are utilized by some rock-hoppers, while others favor custom sandals fitted with spikes. Such accessories usually are available at major tackle shops in areas where rocks are treacherous.

In purchasing waders, or boots, be sure that they fit. It is wise to buy a size larger than your usual size, because heavy socks will be a comfortable and cushioning addition.

Most waders are fitted for belts, which help to keep them slim and trim—but you'll need suspenders. There are custom braces which fill the bill quite adequately, but we like the old-fashioned fireman's galluses which are in stock at any hardware or haberdashery shop. These are tough and inexpensive: moreover they are elasticized and thus provide some give and take when heavy clothing is a necessity in spring and fall.

Using waders, a man also needs a foul-weather top. This not only wards off spray and possible rainfall—it also serves as a seal between wader-top and dashing waves. Some of the brave souls who venture far out on offshore bars and rockpiles owe their comfort to a well snugged-down foul-weather top.

Any good pullover garment will do, so long as it has a drawstring at the bottom to tie it tightly to the waist. An elastic band does not suffice, for it flexes just enough to admit water. You can use a belt for this purpose, and many do—since the belt also anchors a fish stringer, a hand gaff and a priest. Elastic bands are pretty much accepted at the wrists: they're reasonably practical, but if you're working belly-high surf, water will seep in at the wrists to cool your elbows and armpits!

Fastened securely over waders, a good foul-weather top will not provide complete protection against inundation, but it will resist waves and spray—and will even ward off a few moments of over-the-top water during an expedition to an offshore bar. Belted in, without zippers or snap fastenings, you're pretty thoroughly waterproofed.

Any rubber, rubberized or plastic-coated garment is subject to deterioration. If the article is well cared for, this inevitable breakdown may be long delayed. Finally it will take the form of porosity and hairline cracks adjacent to seams. When this happens the rubber, neoprene, or whatever will have lost its inherent elasticity, and there is no cure. Patent sealers or liquid rubber cannot save the porous boot or wader, and patching is then out of the question.

In order to delay this process of deterioration, rubber garments should be dried after every fishing trip and then stored in a cool, dry place. Moisture, including perspiration, tends to rot out the fabric backing inside boots or waders. Hot sunlight will, of course, hasten the destruction.

Salt, in itself, is not dangerous, yet some fishermen like to wash boots or waders with fresh water and a mild detergent following use. The garment is then hung, boot foot up, to dry thoroughly. Boots and waders in storage should always be racked this way.

Hooks often pierce waders, and these miniature holes can be sealed off with liquid rubber. Larger punctures require rubber patches, or whatever material is designated by the manufacturer. Plastic and canvas-faced articles naturally need special patches. Some boot and wader manufacturers provide emergency kits with their products, while others peddle repair items as an accessory. Ordinary rubber patches are to be found at any automotive supply or hardware shop.

Practical boots and waders are an investment in comfort and efficiency, but it does not follow that the most expensive are right for all hands on the marine fishing grounds. Since we usually get what we pay for, the more costly are likely to be superior—but there are arguments for the very light and the very heavy, the inexpensive and the custom article. Check your needs before shopping.

36

THE FISHERMAN'S KNIFE

BACK IN THE DAYS OF WOODEN SHIPS AND IRON MEN, NO SEAFARER felt completely dressed without a knife at his belt. Today's marine angler is quite as dependent upon a practical blade, yet knives too often are taken for granted. A majority of fishermen therefore carry pig-stickers or penknives: neither is very effective for work on or around the water.

Knives, lurid tales to the contrary, are tools rather than weapons. There is no need in our society for the old Arkansas toothpick or Bowie knife, nor for the double-edged, brass-knuckled dagger used by wartime commandos. Actually, the fighting knife is a misfit when applied to outdoor sport.

Manufacturers of cutlery strive to supply demand. Therefore, while makers are fully aware of the designs which are most practical for any given use, they produce those that sell best. In some cases the popular models are ideal for big-game hunting, but poorly chosen for mariners. Even some of the so-called "fishermen's knives" leave much to be desired.

One of the traditional favorites is a clasp knife with a long, thin blade topped by a saw-edged "scaler." The fact that the scaler is impractical (usually too dulled and rounded to serve any purpose other than impeding the smooth progress of the blade in dressing a fish) is ignored. Moreover, unless there is some sort of a locking device built in, this type is prone to fold, or "jackknife," when the scaler is put to use.

Too many of the larger sheath knives also feature that eye-pleasing, but dubious, scaler. Note that you never find this gimmick on the blades of professionals who dress and filet fish for a living. Further note that the pros use different blades for different tasks. An angler may do likewise.

Be assured, in spite of some damning with faint praise, that clasp knives are useful on the sea front. Compact design and light weight are admirable features. Debits include a tendency to corrode or rust and the sometimes dangerous tendency to jackknife at an inopportune time.

Further, when the going is sloppy, where one's hands are wet and fingernails are soft, it is sometimes difficult to open a clasp knife. Finally, once open, the blade will be found too short for many tasks.

Obviously, the straight-shafted sheath type is far more practical for all-around labor: moreover, it is a man-sized tool with a sensible grip. The best belt knives feature blades tailored to fishing rather than big-game hunting.

Unlike a hunter's knife, the angler's blade requires no extraordinary heft or rigidity. Blood drains, built into the inland pigstickers—often to tickle the imagination of amateurs—are unnecessary. Fishermen desire a slim, functional blade, just rigid enough to perform a given task.

However, since tasks vary, no one knife is likely to provide every need on the seacoast. For everyday use a slim-lined, short-bladed model probably rates highest. Something in the four to six inch bracket is sufficient to accomplish most needs ashore or afloat.

Such a knife serves a multitude of purposes: it can be used to prepare strip baits or to cut back fraying mono leaders, to open skimmer clams or—in an emergency—to cut oneself free of tangled lines after an impromptu capsizing on the offshore grounds.

Sheath knives usually are of rather rigid construction. By this token they can be used to dress out fish, but are hardly the finest of tools for filleting. For this office, the marine angler requires another blade, usually one that can be purchased at very low cost.

Professional filleting knives are usually made of high-carbon steel and are equipped with simple, riveted wooden handle grips. The market man considers them expendable and can whip a keen edge onto the blade with a couple of licks from a sharpening steel. The blades are relatively long, slim, and limber so that they will follow the curve of the quarry's rib cage and spinal column. Often, in dressing large fish, initial cuts—to separate dorsal fins and to slice deeply behind the gill plates—will be made with a more rigid blade, after which the filleting knife is employed to separate slabs of pure flesh from bone structure.

Obviously, a practical filleting knife will not serve all purposes, yet it is the best choice for its specialty. Combine it with a shorter, stiffer blade for the workaday world of sport fishing, and you will be well equipped. Fortunately, there are knives that very nearly attain all-purpose excellence.

The Finnish *puuko* type is an ideal example: designed by generations of people who relied on fishing for survival, it is close to the ultimate. If the puuko was used in battle, that is evidence that the Finns are peaceful folk—for this is not a very effective combat weapon.

Basically, the all-around model should feature a man-sized handle and a slim, sharp-pointed, reasonably rigid blade without any fancy blood drains or notched scalers. Hand guards are unnecessary, although they take nothing away from an otherwise well designed tool.

Handles themselves are important—and it is on this point that some turn away from the Finnish type mentioned above. The round handle, when wet and covered with fish slime, tends to turn in the hand at the crucial moment. Almost without exception, true filleting knives boast untreated wooden handles designed to provide a firm grip for the fingers. Long ago, market men learned that a twisting blade can be both inefficient and dangerous.

Materials now used for handles range from wood through leather to metal and plastics. Avoid those that are too smooth, or roughen the surface a bit with coarse sandpaper. Otherwise you may watch as your knife shimmers down through deep water on its way to Davy Jones.

Practically all cutlery manufacturers now offer types ideally suited for use by marine fishermen. Often these are called, in the smaller sizes, "skinning knives," and originally were designed for the use of fur trappers. A few are designated "trout knives." The woodsman's "bull cook" model is a good example of the right type.

Having acquired a blade shape and length that best lends itself to the carving of bait or the rough-dressing of table fish, an angler must select one or two basic metals. These are, roughly, time-honored high-carbon steel and stainless steel. Reputable American makers offer many alloys, and the custom blade may be well worth its healthy price. Object, of course, is the development of a blade which is tough, holds a fine edge and resists—if it does not entirely defeat—the ravages of rust and corrosion.

Stainless steel would seem to be the answer in our field, yet it has never displaced the high-carbon steel article, nor is it likely to do so until such time as the stainless blade proves able to take and hold an edge as well and as long as its competition. Because stainless steel knives require more working over with a stone to keep them reasonably sharp, many believe that a blade forged of this material cannot be honed to a fine edge. This is not true: it simply takes more effort to maintain the harder, more resilient metal at peak cutting efficiency. Some think the game hardly worth the candle.

Therefore professionals still use basic high-carbon steel blades, and wage a constant battle with rust. They feel that the excellence of this material, together with its staying power, is a worthy combination. Stainless cutlery boasts some advantages, but it has yet to be accepted by commercial fisheries workers or by butchers in the hinterlands.

Regardless of obvious faults, jackknives fabricated of stainless steel may be practical tools for a great many marine anglers, precisely because they resist corrosion and rust. Blades may not be as sharp as a man might desire, but neither will they be welded into one immovable lump by rust after a week or so of neglect. In salt water, we prefer the stainless steel clasp knife.

Some marine anglers are intrigued by the scuba diver's knife because it is fitted with a flotation handle and, often, with a stainless blade. Usually, this tool is best reserved for divers instead of surface fishermen. The cork or buoyant composition handle is uncomfortable to grasp, and many of these knives are double-edged. They are, basically, survival tools, hardly practical for the everyday world of beach or boat.

Where the small pocket knife is concerned, sheaths or other containers are so much extra weight. True, some of the large and bulky models are best carried on the belt, but our feeling is that such tools are impractical. If a blade must be belted, then a one-piece, straight-shafted model is far superior to any jackknife. Such a knife is readily available for use, with no fingernail-shattering gymnastics or digging into assorted pockets.

Workable sheaths are most important. The marine angler wants a container that holds his blade securely. There must be no danger of the point cutting through the sheath, and no chance that violent contact with a breaking wave will spill the tool out of its housing. Two basic holsters are favored on the seacoast.

Perhaps the Finnish *puuko* sheath is best, for it is shaped to accept the entire blade and most of the knife's handle. Thus the tool is deep-seated and requires no loops or snaps to keep it in position. Since the *puuko* boasts no hand guards, it can be shoved well into a protective leather sheath.

Most of the other sporting knives now offered to marine anglers feature hand guards—an ancient throwback to the days of battle with swords and daggers. Nowadays the guard serves little good use, and prevents deep seating in a sheath. Straps and metal snaps must be employed to keep the knife well secured.

There is nothing reprehensible about this, saving the fact that most of the metal snaps used in modern knife sheaths are subject to rust and corrosion. It is well to keep them anointed with moisture-repellent chemicals and oil, else they soon degenerate and become inoperable.

Leather, like almost everything else in this world that is subjected to salt water, takes a fearful beating. The best maintenance is saturation with some animal oil, such as a neat's-foot, between trips—followed by thorough drying and further oil baths. Do not, however, assume that the frequent oiling of a leather sheath will automatically protect a knife blade: it will not.

If the knife is forged of high-carbon steel, it should be removed after every trip and allowed to dry. Ideally, the blade should be washed in fresh water prior to drying—but anglers are human and they forget. Immediate drying insures against heavy incrustations of rust, and the thin scale that is so sure to accumulate can be ground off with a rough stone prior to final touching up with a finer carborundum.

Given reasonable care, a fine knife will survive many seasons of surf or boat fishing. Indeed, it may survive a series of leather sheaths, items which suffer tremendous torments under hot sunlight and the dehydrating effects of salt.

Filleting knives are inexpensive: while they serve a definite purpose, few ever possess any character other than the plebeian ability to do a certain job well. Good sheath knives are another thing entirely: they are designed to last a lifetime—if given half a chance. Choose a well-forged and scientifically ground blade, then maintain it after the manner its heredity deserves. You'll enjoy a supremely practical tool.

37

OPTICS FOR ANGLERS

SALT WATER SPORT FISHING, DEPENDING ON YOUR POINT OF VIEW, may be anything from bottom bouncing for flounders to offshore trolling for the great gamesters of the sea. In many cases the angler never sees his catch until it is hauled out of the depths; in others, there is a definite advantage accruing to the operator who can spot his quarry before it strikes.

Various electronic aids have made it possible for a big-boat skipper to detect depth, unusual bottom conformation—even schools of game fish far beneath the surface. No such marvels have been produced for surf casters and skiff fishermen, so the average citizen has to make do with binoculars, spotting 'scopes, and specialized sunglasses.

Fortunately, the close-to-shore angler rarely needs any more sophisticated tools than these: his problem resolves itself into choosing the best available optics for specified tasks.

Perversity of the human animal is obvious when a fisherman shields his body against brilliant sunlight, but neglects to shade his eyes. If you think that sunglasses are an affectation, be advised that prolonged exposure to ordinary white light can, literally, burn holes in your head.

What happens is that gargantuan doses of brilliant light drills holes in the human retina—the photographic-plate membrane which lies at the back of the eye. The first untoward effect is loss of night vision, and it has been estimated that a single day on a sunny beach—sans protective lenses—can diminish an angler's night vision for one week. Spend a full week squinting into the sunny waves, and your night vision will be impaired for nearly one year!

Headache and eye strain on the water is a warning that bright light has begun its potentially deadly work. However, some tough characters may feel no discomfort, even though Old Sol is destroying a measure of their vision.

The solution is obvious: wear sunglasses. These need not be the best available: in fact a drugstore article with flaws in the lenses will be better than nothing, so long as they're dark.

Of course it is always wise to insist on well-ground lenses, and it is therefore logical to purchase sunglasses produced by well-known, reputable firms. If they bear the name of an established company, the glasses will be optically adequate.

Next, if your object is the defeat of that white light which can damage the eyes, be sure that the lenses are dark. Light yellow, blue, pink or green shades may be stylish, but you'll still chance a hole in the head.

Color is important, but no expert can advise you about particular needs. Curiously, it has been found that reaction to color varies with the individual. Usually, the average person is best pleased with a neutral gray or a cool, gray-green hue. A minority find that these induce nausea. Yellow, while some can abide the color, most often triggers mal de mer on the rolling ocean. Shades of tan are more soothing, and a great many anglers think that tan is the best see-through-the-water color. An individual should experiment to determine the most comfortable hue. Finally, make it dark for protection.

Any of the various "dark" sunglasses will defeat white light and make a long day on the beach or the offshore grounds pleasant. However, the angler who desires near-perfection in fishing shades had best choose those which incorporate the polarizing principle. These, in addition to filtering out much of the available white light, also cut surface glare and make it possible to "look through" the water.

Fine polarized glasses are now made of the basic material, which resembles hard plastic, at very low price. The best are "glass sandwiches," in which the polarizing gelatine is compressed between two optically correct glass lenses. You may also buy clip-on types for use with ordinary spectacles. While some expense is involved the glass-sandwich types can be ground to prescription and —more expense—it is even possible to produce polarized bifocals.

Do not assume, however, that the standard, low-priced glass found in a tackle shop or drugstore is an inferior product. It is not: in some respects it is a better article than the very expensive glass sandwich, if only because the polarizing gelatine can be bent into a variety of wrap-around shapes—a thing that would be extremely expensive with glass. The only valid criticism of the inexpensive shade is its tendency to scratch. Lenses should therefore be cleansed with a jet of water prior to any polishing with a soft cloth. If any grit is there, you can bet that application of a polishing cloth will produce scratches.

On the fishing grounds there is a need to defeat peripheral light —that which insists on slipping in around the rims of your sunglasses. Therefore the wrap-around style is best chosen, so long as the glass is not so tightly fitted that it becomes uncomfortable. Tight-fitting shades induce perspiration.

With the glass-sandwich type, or with inexpensive plastic lenses that do not wrap around sufficiently to block peripheral light, there may be a need to fashion "blinders." These can be made of polaroid material and fastened to the frames with epoxy. It is also possible to purchase ready-made blinders, which are manufactured for use with industrial glasses or goggles. These are not readily available and may have to be ordered from one of the major optical companies.

By all means attach some sort of retainer cord to the ear pieces of your favorite sunglasses. This may be a hank of fish line, secured by a few turns of plastic tape, or a nylon rubberized cord, available at any optometrist's shop. You can drill the ends of ear pieces to tie in a retainer cord. At any rate, make some provision to anchor the things. Glasses that haven't been secured by a line around the wearer's neck invariably drop into the deep six at some point during a fishing trip.

Perhaps this is time to mention various miracle glasses that are advertised in a multitude of magazines. The pitch presents a picture of some vague, foreign invention that insures bright vision through the water. Almost always these nonpareils are gimmicked up with form-fitting plastic frames, slitted lenses and eyebrow shades. Prices are not astronomically high, but neither are they low—ranging about twice what you would pay for standard American polarized sunglasses.

There are no miracles. All of these supposedly sensational see-through glasses utilize the polarizing principle. Most of them are fitted with small strips of poorly aligned polarized material for lenses. There is a see-through capability, but it is inferior to that of everyday American glasses, and the space-age frame assembly usually induces perspiration and discomfort.

Binoculars are quite as important to the salt water fisherman as proper sunglasses. Moreover, they serve on the offshore and inshore grounds, on the beach and the high seas. Field glasses can be valuable, although they are seldom as efficient as binoculars, and there is a place—albeit small—for the spotting 'scope.

Too many anglers feel that tremendous power in a glass is both desirable and indicative of status. Actually, the fisherman who displays a binocular of 10-power or more on the beach or the off-shore grounds only displays his ignorance.

For all practical purposes, the 8 x 50 binocular is just about the limit. Beyond 8-power, which magnifies eight times, a glass cannot be hand-held steady enough to examine any segment of sea or sky. The big instruments must be mounted on tripods—and tripods are seldom found on the deck of a bouncing boat, or even on a sand beach.

Powerful binoculars, here defined as anything over the 8 x 50 magnification boundary, together with various spotting 'scopes, can be useful only when they are rigidly mounted and used to examine specific areas. Hand-held, they are abominations.

Binoculars in the 6 x 30 to 8 x 50 power-objective range are ideal for use by sport fishermen, and perhaps the 7 x 35 or 7 x 50 is best of all. Since they provide stereoscopic vision and excellent depth of focus, these instruments are far more versatile than the field glass (paired telescopes) and the various simple telescopes or advanced spotting 'scopes.

In many cases the 6 x 30 glass is entirely adequate. Although it does not possess the magnification or field of a 7 x 35 or 8 x 50, the smaller glass is light, bright and compact. Some versions are manufactured in miniature sizes, and the standard is about half the size of the popular 7 x 50.

It is only fair to note that more powerful binoculars are now produced in very small packages. These are efficient, but never as pleasant to use as the man-sized type. Therefore, if light weight and small size is important, by all means look into a good 6 x 30. If, on the other hand, you plan to operate from a beach buggy or a boat, it may pay to invest in a 7 x 35, a 7 x 50 or 8 x 50. Don't be bamboozled into purchasing more powerful glasses. Beyond 8 x 50, hand-holding is difficult. While magnification is improved, it is impossible to control "jiggle."

One often hears campfire tales about "night glasses" which are supposed to be available at low cost. Actually, there is no such thing as a true night glass—unless you are willing to invest in heavy military optics, complete with buzzing black boxes and infra-red electronic devices.

Binoculars with large objective lenses are more effective in poor light, because they pick up more of the available illumination. Thus, an 8 x 50 glass will be more effective than a 6 x 30 or 7 x 50. This, naturally, is a valid conclusion only if both instruments are of comparable optical quality.

Up until a very few years ago, there was no doubt about the relative quality of American, German, and Japanese binoculars. American and German instruments led the world, and may still hold an edge. However, for the practical purposes of sport fishermen, the new Japanese glasses are so close to perfection that any choice would have to depend on individual preference.

Moreover, Japanese binoculars are bargain-priced, compared to German and American instruments. You can purchase an adequate Nip glass for $35, or an extremely good one for $50 to $100. Naturally, in this age of competition and all-around baloney, the Japanese are also producing some inferior glasses. So are we—and so are the Germans.

Therefore, do not expect to buy practical binoculars from the cut-rate firms advertising "amazing bargains." Instruments selling for $3.50 to $9.98 invariably are toys. Binoculars list-priced at $25 are hardly better, although some of these are quite usable.

When you consider a glass, check it out for certain features. The best should possess scissor frames, so that they can be adjusted to the width of individual eyes. There should be a central focusing knob, or individual focusing of each lens. In fact, if the central system is employed, one of the lenses should also be fitted with a focusing ring—so that you can get sharp focus for each eye. If you ordinarily wear spectacles, determine whether the binoculars provide some measure of adjustment for this.

Before you plunk cash on the barrelhead, focus on a distant object and check for distortion. Vertical and horizontal lines should be perfect, right out to the edge of the field. Color correction is important, and this will be apparent at the edge of the periphery: if there's any blur of irridescence or purple rimming, the lenses are not optically well ground.

Certain American importers have now lent their names to Japanese-made binoculars, and here, as always, it is wise to purchase an established trademark. That's because reputable importers have to maintain reasonable standards or suffer the consequences. Moreover, established firms offer repair or replacement facilities when there's a necessity.

Latest wrinkle in optics is the "zoom binocular," patterned after the Hollywood and TV zoom lens. With this advance one can glass an object at one distance, and then shift to a close-up. Some of the current glasses are push-button controlled, with dry cells used for power take-off, and some are manual. They are spectacular and quite effective—within reason.

If the zoom technique is employed, greater weight and bulk is necessary. Finally, if the glass ranges from reasonably low power to very high—as some do—the top of the spectrum involves the need for a steady platform. Up to 8-power there is no problem. Beyond that, hand-holding is uncomfortable.

Optics for the outdoorsman have progressed—and will progress with each passing year. There are, however, no cure-alls. Practical developments still revolve around optically ground sunglasses, dark enough for the conditions encountered, and utilizing the polarizing principle when there is a need to see through surface glare. Prices, in a generally inflationary economy, are lowered with each passing year.

There are no miraculous inventions and there are no recent break-throughs in the science of optics for anglers. Trade with the established firms. Chuckle at advertisements which promise latter-day magic. Use the best available and you'll find that reputable concerns will serve you well.

38
TACKLE BOX MAINTENANCE

RECENTLY THAT DEAN OF NAUTICAL SCRIBBLERS, BOB WHITTIER, had occasion to remove all of the gear from his boat and take inventory. He discovered a bewildering variety of interesting (often unnecessary) items which he had been transporting over the ocean. Resulting research fueled a masterful article on—how to avoid clutter.

Inspired, but delayed as always by one thing and another—like fishing and talking about fishing—we decided to work over our tackle boxes with the same end in view. Results were even more startling than those reported by Boatman Bob. Among other items unearthed were the following: a dozen or so scales from a blue marlin, carefully wrapped in a stained, dubiously labeled envelope; a shark tooth, species unknown; a fair-sized stone which had nothing whatsoever to recommend it either artistically or practically; a half-empty tube of toothpaste which at some stage in its career had been holed by a rusty hook; and an endless jumble of odds and bits of tackle which have no possible use now or in the future.

The lesson to be learned from our experience is a simple one, and one which we never seem to get through our respective skulls: check a tackle box regularly and dispose of needless items. Not only will this lighten the load, it will prevent damage to tackle of all sorts. For example, one rusted and stained bucktail jig stored with new ones will often rust and stain the new ones also.

As noted, we are not good at practicing what we preach in this whole matter of tackle box clutter, but we have learned various things over the years. First, a resolve to check tackle box contents at least twice a year to keep clutter at a minimum.

Before going further, it should be made clear that no fisherman who regularly tries almost every method of angling known and who travels widely for his sport *ever* has too many tackle boxes, bags, belt carriers, and the like. This is a fact alien to the logic of friend wife, but it is so, and you know it.

Unfortunately for those with neat and tidy minds, each trip calls for a collection of tackle just a little bit different from that used on the last trip, with the result that every container is crammed full. Therefore whatever is taken in a single container is really a sort of compromise geared to the weight, bulk, and necessities of the trip at hand.

Ideally, the solution would appear to be a different tackle container equipped for each possible fishing excursion. This would mean several dozen boxes, half a dozen bags and other assorted holders—a place large enough to stow all of this gear and a bankroll big enough to buy duplicate items by the score. It is obvious that few, if any, people can afford to fish in this manner. Besides, there are times when various types of gear must be combined in the smallest possible space, so that the individual tackle box solution is not ideal at all.

We compromise and, although the compromise is not ideal, it is the best we have been able to figure out. The first step is to acquire several large tackle boxes—and some handsome marine-oriented containers are now on the market. In each of these, store tackle required for a certain *type* of fishing.

For example, our offshore big game box contains, among other items, large hooks, various heavy leader materials, crimping pliers and sleeves to match, big trolling lures and teasers, bait-sewing equipment, and other gear that is used almost exclusively for this type of angling. A couple of reels are also carried in the container, a box spacious enough to handle winches up to the 6/0 size. Larger reels are best carried in separate containers and we have found an ordinary airlines travel bag well suited to this job—although hardly adequate if the reels are slated to go into an airliner's baggage compartment. There you'll need more protection.

If a trip offshore is scheduled, if there is plenty of room aboard the craft to be used and if there are no transportation difficulties, our one large box is taken aboard, along with rods and larger reels if needed. We know that all normally required for such a venture is with us.

At the other end of the angling spectrum, we have a tackle box stuffed with light casting equipment for spinning, marine bait casting and fly fishing. The box is large and you wouldn't want to tote it while hiking the edges of a tide marsh; however, it serves well in a beach buggy, a small or large boat. On the credit side, such a container holds practically everything necessary for that particular type of angling. The gear is in one place and we can make our on-the-spot selections for transfer to a smaller carrier without any undue amount of searching. Similar rough divisions are made for other types of fishing, medium trolling, surf casting and bottom bouncing, for example.

This division of gear into categories simplifies matters when you are in a hurry to get started. Others might divide tackle in a different manner, depending on the types of fishing they most often prefer, but the basic idea is sound. Some arrange tackle in workbench drawers in this same way, thus dispensing with tackle box storage. We prefer the boxes because we can then cut and run at a moment's notice. Besides, our workbench drawers are filled with spares to refill the tackle boxes!

There are enthusiasts who swear by a whole series of tackle boxes, in each of which is stored a certain type of gear: one for plugs only, one for reels and lines, one for hooks, and so on. In our opinion the great disadvantage with this system is that another box must be loaded for every trip, with certain items taken from each "basic" tackle box. Here, again, it is impossible to grab one container with the certain knowledge that everything required for that particular type of fishing is included among its contents.

So much for the basic distribution of tackle by types. Unfortunately, things get complicated when space or weight is at a premium. Then, of course, items must be taken from the large boxes, selected for the particular requirements of the moment and put into a small shoulder bag, belt container or even a couple of pockets. Here proper packaging, for want of a better word, pays off.

In each of our basic tackle boxes we have items packaged in plastic boxes that are small enough to fit in the larger container's compartments. Although the hard plastic employed to manufacture these packages will crack at times, after heavy use, the boxes are far superior to cardboard or wood. There are two reasons for this: first, you can see what is inside without opening the box itself or fussing around with a label; second, moisture neither softens nor rots the material.

Items of one type are in these plastic containers. For example, in our surf-fishing tackle box we have a small container packed with swivels and snaps of the sizes most commonly used for this type of fishing. The package may be transferred readily to a small shoulder or belt carrier as required. The same may be done with hooks, made-up leaders and countless other tackle components. This system avoids the necessity of duplication, saves time when making transfers from one carrier to another and prevents tiny items from becoming hopelessly lost in a mass of larger tackle. Try finding a small swivel among a dozen trolling feathers and you will see what we mean.

Although some small lures may be packaged in this manner for ease of handling, by and large the compartments designed to hold these lures in a good tackle box will serve well. The exception is when a plug sporting many treble hooks is too large for any standard compartment and therefore must be dropped in with reels and various other snag-prone items. Then a box for such a plug will keep it from imbedding its hooks in everything close by, including your own hands.

There are a few basic items we carry in all of our tackle boxes. Some, it is true, are duplicates; others are the same general order of equipment, yet of different sizes. These pieces of gear include the following: a small bottle of nail polish; winding thread of a size suited to the tackle concerned; at least one spare guide and tiptop, again of the proper size; ferrule cement; reel lubricant; a small roll of plastic electrician's tape; a screwdriver and wrench combination for reel tinkering; file, or hook hone; pencil or regular flashlight; basic reel repair parts; a sailmaker's needle to rig eels, mullet or other baits; and matches in separate waterproof containers.

If you do not carry a knife and pair of pliers on your person at all times when fishing (we do), both might well be considered worthy of duplication in all boxes. Pliers should always feature good wire cutters, and these cutters should be hefty enough to sever the shank of a hook in the event that some unlucky member of the party pierces himself, or just to replace used-up barbs.

Also, if you will be using a specific outboard motor during most of your fishing junkets, by all means tote spare spark plugs, shear pins and cotter pins in each tackle box—together with the basic tools to install them. On manual-start outboards it is a good idea to tape at least one shear pin and cotter pin to the operating handle.

As an aside, we have found it profitable to stock two or three plastic Band Aid strips in each tackle box—*and in our wallets.* A superficial cut can be tremendously handicapping if, like us, you bleed copiously upon the slightest hook-prick or contact with sharp gill covers.

Some may consider other items basic to every major type of

tackle box. A ruler, for example, is handy. However, a ruled scale on the box itself or on a rod butt serves as well. One ruler that is never lost is a known measurement of your extended hand. For example, the distance between the spread tips of thumb and little finger of the senior member of this team is exactly eight inches. The junior member boasts eight and one-half inches on one hand, nine on the other. (One of his little fingers is an old battle casualty.)

Scales are useful also, but we manage to get along without them. Records can wait until we reach a tested Toledo, and some of the tiny models are a mite less than completely accurate.

Obviously, the system of transferring from a large box to a smaller carrier fails miserably if these items are not replaced where they belong after a trip is over. We have made it a rule to do this for so many years that the action is now automatic. We can replace material in the basic tackle boxes when half asleep—and often do so!

The owners of beach buggies or offshore sport cruisers do not have to worry about this problem. They have plenty of space for tackle storage and their basic boxes are ready at hand always. Often, however, these operators of mobile tackle shops become so dependent upon their vast storehouse that they are almost helpless when the time comes to travel with a minimum of gear. An angler bearing two huge tackle boxes is not welcomed with glad cries aboard a 14-foot skiff, nor is he very fleet of foot on a remote mud bank.

Cutting down on what is to be carried in any tackle box or bag is often difficult. The lure guaranteed to murder fish can never be predicted. When cramped for space, we compromise again and try to include at least one, and preferably two, of each general type—unless we know for a fact that the fish sought dotes on a particular offering to the near exclusion of all others. Thus, when choosing plugs, our small kit will contain a surface popper, a subsurface swimmer and a deep-running darter or swimmer. Similar choices are made for other types of lures with depth, action and color all taken into consideration.

Sinkers are always a problem. To carry all shapes and sizes for any type of fishing makes a tackle box feel like an anvil salesman's sample case. One way to cut a corner on these particular items, especially when trolling or when using light tackle, is to stock an absolute minimum of the patent shapes and weights, together with a small quantity of sheet or strip lead. From this lead, weights of any desired size may be cut and wrapped around leader, line, or the hook itself. Some manufacturers have realized the advantage of this and now put up strip lead sinker material with easy-breaking joints. Naturally, where specific sinker types, weights and shapes are known to be required, we carry them in sufficient abundance to induce a permanent stoop.

There are certain items which should *not* be included in tackle boxes. One of these, in our opinion, is insect repellent. Although a necessity in certain areas, modern repellents (at least quite a few of them) can turn lure finishes and even synthetic lines into a gummy mess. This happens if the repellent container leaks or breaks, and they are always apt to do one or the other. Keep the bug dope in a pocket or in a separate container and there will be no problem.

It is also a mistake to put fresh bait of any kind in a tackle box unless it can be guaranteed that there is no liquid leakage from the creature concerned. Such a guarantee is next to impossible. Once a box has been seasoned with bait juice, it takes weeks to remove the lingering aroma.

Another warning: do not store any of the new soft plastic lures with standard artificials. Some of these have the power to reduce enamels to liquid: indeed they usually dissolve paint on contact.

As mentioned at the outset, there is one major difficulty we have with all of our tackle boxes, and this difficulty should be included among items *not* to have in the boxes concerned. Whether it is Yankee thrift or just plain stupidity, we do not know, but we are always reluctant to toss any bit of worn tackle away. The result: unnecessary clutter.

If a swivel is corroded and does not turn properly, it is easy to spend fifteen minutes trying to repair and lubricate it. When the work is finished, chances are better than even that the swivel still will not turn. Toss the thing into the nearest trash barrel and save trouble all around. Bits of twisted leader wire, bent or rusted hooks, nicked and cracked rod guides all should join the malfunctioning swivel. Get rid of them.

We make exceptions with certain types of lures—probably too many exceptions. A compartment in each tackle box is left empty and lures that are damaged during a fishing trip are deposited in it. These are items that can be repaired with a minimum of labor. Presumably, this compartment is cleaned out when the box is back in the workshop. In actual practice, we often fail to do this and clutter is thereby increased.

While space and weight problems are considerably solved by a large boat or beach buggy, clutter remains a handicap. In our beach buggy wanderings, we customarily tote several boxes—something that would be impossible on the lone safari down a sand beach or a brackish stream on shank's mare.

Among the boxes is one which may be unique: it is an angler's tool kit. In it, we carry basic items of repair and salvage. The inventory includes heavy cutting pliers, screwdrivers and wrenches; heavy sailmaker's needles; rubber cement and patches; quantities of single, treble and double hooks in various sizes; screw-eyes, hook hangers and wobble plates; stainless steel wire for re-rigging lures; plumber's chain for rigging eels; small cans of penetrating and lubricating oils; hanks of linen, heavy braided nylon and assorted monofilaments; an assortment of guides, tiptops and ferrules, together with the necessary cements; and, of course, strategic outboard motor parts.

Clutter? Of course! The last time we checked our repair kit we found—tucked in among the tools and component parts—an old-fashioned squid snatcher, a Cuban blue snail shell (cracked), two dogfish spines, and a bottle cap marked "Old Sea Dog Rum."

Many may consider our methods of handling tackle box stowage problems inefficient. Perhaps they are, but we have yet to find any better methods. For the large boat and beach buggy set the problem is a comparatively simple one. For those who are limited by space and weight, the solution must be a compromise. Recognize this, proceed accordingly, and you will be well on the way to solving a problem.

39

GAFFS, NETS AND CLUBS

A FRIEND OF OURS, WHO NEVER VENTURES UPON MARINE WATERS, likes to say: "The difference between we-uns and you-uns is that you use gaffs and we use landing nets."

It might simplify matters if this were so. As matters stand, the average inland angler thinks of salt water fishing as "deep sea sport," and he always envisions huge gaffs biting into the flanks of monstrous fish.

Actually, as every modern marine angler knows, there is a place for the net and the hook: each is important, depending upon the tackle employed and the fish to be landed.

Landing nets are used by a considerable number of salt water anglers. They are favored by those who harvest salmon in the Pacific Northwest, by bonefishermen in the tropics—by fly casters and light tackle anglers everywhere!

An adequate West coast salmon net must be a sturdy piece of equipment. While it may ordinarily scoop up fish in the 5 to 20 pound bracket, there may be occasions when a 50-pounder is in the offing. For that reason party boat skippers and knowing small boat anglers carry wide-mouthed nets with deep pouches.

Fly casters who seek game fish on both coasts are quite as thoroughly committed to the wide-mouthed, deep-pouched net. Moreover, a long handle is considered necessary, since it usually is considered necessary to reach far over a boat's gunwale to make that vital connection.

Nets appeal to sportsmen who wish to release their quarry after capture. That's why the tropical bonefisherman employs this tool to the almost total exclusion of any other landing device. A gaff wounds or kills, while the knotted mesh is gentle.

When, for any of various reasons, a fish must be killed, the net is surer than a gaff on those in the small-to-medium range. It is a practical weapon where single barbs are used—yet it poses a distinct handicap when treble-hooked artificials turn the trick. Multiple barbs are troublesome: the angler spends valuable time untangling his lure after each catch.

Landing nets are not very effective on sharp-toothed fishes—or, at least, not after the first two or three are brought aboard. Blues, for example, will destroy a net quicker than you can say "chop-chop," which is precisely what the bluefish chatters at all times.

While any inland angler may fill his needs with a small, short-handled net slung over his shoulder on a length of rubber-cored shock cord, a marine fisherman usually requires something much larger, fitted with a long handle. Fish are bigger on the sea coast, and usually it is necessary to reach for them.

This may be the only major difference between fresh water and salt water landing nets. Generally speaking, the marine version is larger and more rigidly constructed. It is wide-mouthed, deep, and designed to capture big fish.

Seagoing nets, quite obviously, feature corrosion-resistant metal parts and synthetic twine. Nylon cord is excellent, and there are other branches of the synthetic family that serve as well. Cotton and linen rarely last a season in the briny.

For boatmen, particularly, a landing net should be long-handled. One should be able to place the pouch well under water where it will stream with the current. The fish should be played so that it swims head first into the confining meshes. Trying to scoop a gamester tail first often results in failure.

The better nets will float when they are dropped overboard, an accident more frequent than is usually supposed—or admitted. See that yours is buoyant, either due to a wooden handle or capped aluminum tubing.

Gaffs, to a landlubber, conjure up huge hooks such as those employed on giant tuna. Marine anglers know better, but too often they choose the wrong hook for the job in hand. An adequate gaff is a job-rated tool, and the salt water model may range from ultra-light to heavy.

First off, any respectable gaff should be sharp. Keep the point razor-edged and your success ratio in landing fish will zoom in direct proportion. Many game fish carry an armor of scales, and these miniature plates will turn the point of a dull gaff. There is no excuse for a blunted hook, although countless numbers of great game fish owe their freedom to people who eschew hones and files.

Hook sizes and handle lengths vary, depending upon the game sought. For that reason a majority of erudite charter skippers carry several gaffs. These range from tiny fixed hooks, designed to snatch small fish, to the huge, detachable flying gaffs used on giant tuna.

For small game, a bite of two inches or even less may be entirely adequate. Anything over this width is likely to straddle the body of the quarry and allow its painless escape. There is a tendency, coastwide, to choose oversized gaffs.

School stripers, for example, are best taken with a very small gaff. These are available at ridiculously low prices, or you can make your own by grinding the barb off a 14/0 Martu or Sobey big game hook and binding its shank to a suitable handle.

Increase the bite as you go to larger fish. A three inch gap may be ideal for trophy stripers and other gamesters in the 30 to 60 pound bracket. As the size of the quarry increases, so does the practical gaff size.

Handle length depends on strategy employed. We have never favored the short hand gaff, a tool so abbreviated that one must practically shove his hand into the maw or the driving spines of a thrashing gamester to drive it home. Granted, this may be ideal when the quarry is well played out and a point may be driven through the lower lip, and it is fine when a beaten fish is to be released. In this case, the relatively painless lip or jaw-hooking technique is necessary.

Note, however, that the short gaff can be murder if a fish is green and prone to thrash mightily after it has been impaled. Why ask for trouble when a longer handle can provide insurance?

There is, of course, one case for the short-handled gaff. Anglers who wade for their fish cannot tote a bulky hook, hence they settle for one measuring, point to butt, something like 18 inches or less. Wade-fishermen make good use of folding gaffs, which are magnificent inventions—providing that they do not fold at the most embarrassing moment in time and space.

If you wade with a standard one-piece gaff, there is a necessity to cap the point with something like a cork or a rubber ball—so that it will not pierce some tender part of your anatomy in transit. We have used sponge-rubber balls attached to sash cord; corks, and patent caps of various designs. All seem to become disengaged at the worst possible moment, and we have leaky waders to prove it.

There are wade gaffs with a hook at one end and a billy club at the other. These sound like Pulitzer prize winners, but we have yet to find anyone who can gaff a fish with one end of a tool, and then belt it senseless with the other end of the weapon—without resorting to some form of legerdemain alien to an honest angler. When wading, we carry a gaff—and a billy club. They're separate items.

Boat fishermen and jetty jockeys require long-handled gaffs. The minimum handle length is approximately four feet, and the maximum seldom more than six. Party and charter boat skippers, quite obviously, may need longer handles. Length must be determined by the reach necessary to hook a beaten gamester.

Night fishermen, whether they operate from jetty or boat, find it helpful to paint gaff handles white. Some add stripes of blaze orange fluorescent tape or paint to catch the last blue light of day. Visibility is a great help when you arrive at that final lunge which decides success or failure. Aimless probing is an abomination.

Perhaps it should be emphasized that gaffs are not necessary on a sand beach, where game fish can be landed high and dry. Here, unless stingrays or sharks are the quarry, one can make better use of a billy club.

Gaff hooks now on the market range from high carbon steel to stainless, with handles fashioned from tubular fiberglass and hardwood. All are effective as long as certain considerations are taken into effect.

A gaff hook must be sharp. Some of the stainless models are blunt and must be filed or honed to a fine, tapering edge. Carbon steel hooks seem to differ in design from the stainless steel product, being well tapered down to a needle point, a feature which is all-important.

Unfortunately, the well-shaped high carbon steel hook rusts. An angler must provide constant maintenance, with a regular touching-up prior to any fishing trip. On the credit side, they're strong, less likely to blunt than the stainless article, and are inexpensive. Some of the best sell for pennies, say 50¢ for a good three inch hook.

Everyday anglers use inexpensive gaffs, as do commercial fishermen, yet there is much to be said for the stainless steel hook. First off, of course, it does not rust or corrode. While slightly more expensive, it has a greater life expectancy. On the debit side, a stainless steel gaff must be ground down to a needle point—and then touched up more often than the time-honored high carbon steel article.

Any gaff is lost without an adequate handle. Initially, all gaff handles were fashioned of hardwood, and the only criterion was grain which would suffer great stress without splintering. Nowadays the fiberglass handle has become commonplace, and there are new requirements.

Whether wood or glass, a gaff handle should be rigid and tough enough to withstand levering a hefty fish over a solid gunwale, yet light enough to float if the gaff is lost overside. These are doughty requirements, yet modern hooks fill the bill.

Before we are deluged with letters protesting the practice of "levering" a fish over the gunwale, be assured that we do not advocate that technique. Having made contact with gaff or net, the quarry should be lifted straight up, with the net or gaff handle in a vertical position. Unfortunately, in the excitement of landing a big one, fishermen sometimes forget the facts of life.

As far as flotation is concerned, aluminum or heavy tubular fiberglass handles can be capped so that they boast sufficient air space to be buoyant. Those with wooden handles usually float.

While a billy club, sometimes called a "priest" or a "persuader," is hardly a landing device, it certainly figures as a vital tool in the capture of certain fishes. A well-fashioned club will, with a single blow, stun sharp-toothed or sharp-spined fish before they can bring these weapons into play against human flesh.

The best billies are simple hardwood clubs. Some are rendered deadlier by a shot of lead at the business end. Wade-fishermen had best string the persuader on a loop of elasticized cord, or provide a snap fastening with which it can be secured to a waist belt. The boatman's club should be racked with his gaffs, ready for instant use when a still-green heavyweight is thrashing around in the cockpit and threatening to impale all hands on the treble hooks stuck in its jaw.

Among other landing devices, certain patent fish-grippers are good sense. These range all the way from special gloves with steel points riveted into palm and fingers, to the steel tongs used by cooks (to handle sweet corn). All are practical when gamesters are small, sharp-toothed or spiny. Tailers, used by Atlantic salmon fishermen, have never created any ripple of enthusiasm on the seacoast, but they might be effective under some conditions.

A towel or other hank of cloth can prevent difficulty. Years ago, every surfman carried a towel tucked into his belt. This was used for many purposes, not alone that of a shield between hand and fish when it was time to extract a hook from the jaw of a still flopping prize. A towel remains an excellent item of equipment aboard a boat or in the tackle box of a surfman.

Purportedly, the Law of General Cussedness boasts one clause (in fine print of course) which declares that fishing will always be magnificent when an angler forgets to bring his gaff or net. Quite possible, but there's a worse fate.

Get out there someday when the monsters are obliging, and find your gaff or net totally inadequate. That's why some fishermen unaccountably become golfers!

40
WHY THEY STRIKE

ONE PLEASANT BY-PRODUCT OF OUR LABORS IN EDITING AND PUBLISHING *Salt Water Sportsman* is the mass of valuable information received from readers. Properly interpreted and placed in its own niche, each item adds something to our knowledge of sport fishing—even when the basic report seems contradictory.

Such as, for example, a recent communication in which the writer tells of catching flounders *on a chum bag*!

While this is the stuff of which double-takes are manufactured, the explanation opens avenues of thought which have little to do with any new and revolutionary fishing method.

Edward Buist of Clifton, New Jersey, had written to commend a Jersey flounder fishing article by Milt Rosko and, as seems usual with many of our readers, to give us a neighborly account of his own angling activities.

Midway in his letter, almost as if this was a common occurrence, he inquired: "Did you ever catch a flounder on a chum bag? *We* did, and they were good-sized, all three of them."

It seems that Buist and his buddy had prepared a chum bag on the spot, a curiously rigged article, but evidently effective. Let Ed tell about it:

"My friend tore a piece off an old T-shirt, punched some holes in it and put some of my special-made chum inside, along with a 4-ounce sinker. Then we attached a size 10 flounder hook to the bag via a short length of mono, and started fishing. Our rods were kept busy, as we had expected, and—three times—when we raised the chum bag there was a flounder on the attached hook."

Nobody doubts that chumming attracts flounders and many other gamesters. This, however, was the first time we'd heard of anyone attaching a hook to the bag itself. While hardly "sport fishing," Buist's adventure indicated that scent or taste (closely allied) had attracted flounders—which then gobbled a baited hook attached to the bag. Obviously, the chum bag held no terrors for flatties. While a blob of cotton simulates no known marine tidbit, flounders evidently found its seeping contents delicious—and were persistent enough in their attentions to grab an attached single bait.

All of which raises an ancient question: why does any sort of game fish strike a bait or lure? Perhaps there are a variety of reasons. Answers, if they are ever found, will be of inestimable importance to anglers.

Personal experience in sport fishing, together with innumerable reports from friends who have observed both characteristic and unusual strikes delivered by different species, lead us to the multiple-reason theory.

The simplest, and probably most ancient of explanations for the strike of a game fish holds that the creature is hungry and attacks that which it supposes is a natural bait—with no hooks or strings attached. That's logical enough.

Yet, during the past forty years or so biologists and scientific fishermen have had occasion to doubt that this comfortable theory always holds true, or even that it is good reasoning in a majority of cases—without qualification.

It has been said that game fish take lures or baits because they are hungry, angry, curious, defiant, sexually aggressive, or because of instinctive reaction to color, action, sound or scent. Note that each of these triggering emotions has been proved with specific game species, under certain conditions, but that none can be singled out as a constant overriding stimulant. Unless, of course, hunger is selected as a basic fact of life in the sea.

For a sport fisherman, there are additional factors. These include the depth at which a gamester is feeding or cruising, clarity of water and wave action, temperature, amount of light, or lack of it, surf or current, tidal stages, bottom conformation, and weed growth. There are others well known to salt water anglers.

Although marine biology and the science of sport fishing have yet to provide exact answers to all of the problems involved, sufficient knowledge has been amassed to serve as a rough guide. The real secret weapon of a successful angler, in addition to skillful employment of tackle and knowledge of the quarry he seeks, is a basic understanding of the reasons why fish *may* strike, coupled with immediate reaction to whichever single or multiple triggering emotion seems to dominate the game at any given time.

Confusing? Not at all! If you cast a surface commotion plug 40 feet to the right of a cruising barracuda, and that marauder races to attack the lure—it is reasonably logical to assume that sound attracted the fish and that the triggering emotion was anger, curiosity or instinctive reaction. Okay, maybe with a spice of hunger, too! But note that a choice fresh bait, lying on the bottom, some 40 feet away, probably would not have attracted the 'cuda's attention.

Similarly, when striped bass studiously ignore a lure of one color, yet compete with their schoolmates for an identical, but differently hued artificial, only a singularly dense angler will discount the frequent value of a specific color in arousing fishy emotions.

Our reader's hyper-efficient chum bag points up the come-hither virtue of scent or taste, and it is no revelation to state that a great many specialists who swear by cut or live bait find themselves convinced that scent is highly important. Watch a channel bass fisherman replace his chunked mullet or spot head when it has been bleached white by the scouring of sand and water. Real seaworms draw more strikes than exact plastic copies, although the look-alike fares quite as well when sweetened with a short length of bona-fide squirmer. Trollers deduce that fish can smell or taste the difference. Vision is not a determining factor in this case.

Fish, like all living creatures affected by the slow process of evolution, are variously equipped to cope with their environment. Some see better than others. However, marine biologists have concluded that fish are, in a word, nearsighted. Examination of the fish's eye indicates that, while a majority of species employ sight to find food, "it is not unlikely that the fish really notices movement or changes in outline rather than actual objects."

This may well explain a gamester's disregard of a perfectly visible hook stuck through the back of a mullet or protruding from a seaworm. Note, however, that visual ability varies with the species. For example, the eyes of a tuna are in demand by surgeons because such eyes are very similar in construction to those of a human. Anyone who has tossed whole fish to schooling tuna, then placed a hook in one of the offerings—and had it completely ignored—can vouch for their keenness of sight. A catfish, on the other hand, sees very little.

If most fish are nearsighted, their cautious approach would provide time to make a careful appraisal of any bait or lure for best results. This seems to prove out, for most users of natural bait fare better when they move the offering from time to time. Simply lifting the tempter clear of the bottom and then permitting it to settle back may comprise movement. Better still, if casting to any considerable distance, let the bait lie still for a few minutes, and then move it forward to a new resting place. It is very likely that a cruising game fish will spot movement first, and then move in for a closer look.

At that point, scent or taste may become a paramount tempter. It has been amply demonstrated that game fish will gobble fresh baits they have never encountered before, but which evidently appear delectable because of motion or scent. Eels kill gamesters on grounds where eels are unknown. Pacific salmon eggs are gulped by Atlantic species. Where bait is difficult to obtain, fresh morsels are flown in from half a continent away—and they catch fish. We recommend baits common to any given area, yet bow to the fact that exotics often turn the trick.

Next to hunger, anger, curiosity, and defense of home and fireside are usually considered primary reasons when a fish strikes. Often, without a doubt, the reason is a combination of emotions. Defense mechanisms are more complicated.

For example, many species establish definite areas in which they are kingpin and they will drive all other creatures out of that area if they can. A good illustration of this is a species which protects its eggs or young on the spawning grounds. This establishment of areas of influence goes further, however. It may even be a mobile factor, as when one fish takes the lead position in a school of its fellows. A lure, under such circumstances, may be considered something that tends to disturb the status quo and it is therefore attacked.

Attention of a fish may be attracted, whether the fish be hungry, angry, curious or status-seeking, by many means. These—where artificial lures are concerned—can be reduced basically to motion, visibility and sound.

Motion or action is a fundamental requirement in any good lure. Although there are times when a fish will strike at something which has no motion at all, these times are rare. The "dead plug" usually has just completed action, or it is actually working in a tidal current.

Variety in the types of motion keep lure manufacturers in business. The fuss and splutter of a surface plug, the slight wiggle of a weighted bucktail inching along the bottom, or the rhythmic rise and fall of a diamond jig near the ocean's floor are all examples of this motion.

Note that the angler himself may be the one who imparts such motion to the lure. By twitching the rod and by varying the retrieve, many actionless artificials can be converted into killers. In other cases, lures such as trolled spoons wobble and dart all over the place because of their construction and balance.

Motion inherent in the lure itself, as distinct from motion given to it, must also be considered when trying to attract fish. The "breathing" action of feathers, bucktail, nylon or saran dressing on any lure is an example of this. So is the waggle of a jointed plug or the sinuous undulations of a plastic eel.

Well-educated anglers are fully attuned to proper retrieves, yet they know that today's bring-back may be worthless on another occasion. For some curious reason, perhaps just as a person feels all charged up on one day and bone-weary on the next, fish sometimes love rapid movement; again, they get lazy and will take nothing but a slowly moving target.

Speed must vary with the species sought, with water temperatures, (slow it down when the sea is cold), and with the amount of light. It is a rule of thumb to slow retrieves during the hours of darkness, although this also varies with the species and with water temperature. Obviously, speed of retrieve can effect lure action and, often depths.

Simulation of an actual bait species quite naturally provides exception—but not entirely. Shape, color, and action remain very important, perhaps for different reasons. All contribute to the visibility of the lure from a fish-eye viewpoint.

Color cannot be disregarded. It has been proved that certain fishes can distinguish one color from another, even during the night hours—although the degree to which they can make this distinction is still open to question. It seems evident from experiments conducted that some species are more talented in this type of art appreciation than others. Color, whether it be reflected from a shiny surface or a dyed feather, makes a great deal of difference.

The visibility of any color under water varies considerably, and changes with depth. Yellow appears to be seen at the greatest distance in clear water. Reds and blues are quite apparent in the depths. Black is prominent in milky or clouded water. Often in certain areas a specific color will produce more fish than any other hue. Indeed, the fish's taste in color may change from year to year, even from month to month. Occasionally colors which are not commonly found in the underwater world, such as the fluorescents, are excellent fish attractors.

Color does not stop with the hue alone. Reflection, or lack of it, makes a difference in visibility and therefore qualifies as attraction. A spinner or salmon flasher owes most of its appeal to intermittent reflection. Here, as in other lures, colors or flash may appear and disappear, shimmer or waver. A come-hither effect is involved. The lure is attractive because it intrigues curious interest.

Sound must be counted as a basic attraction. Although sonic appeal has been emphasized by various lure makers, without earth-shaking success, this aspect of fish-teasing is as old as lures themselves.

Human beings can hear the noise a popping plug makes as it splashes and gurgles on the surface. So can fish—and they can hear a great deal more besides. Sound travels under water more rapidly and farther than in the air.

Before those scientifically informed begin to howl, let us make clear that there is much disagreement on how and what a fish actually hears. The ear structure does some of the work; so does the sensitive lateral line—and perhaps the whole body reacts to vibrations. No matter what the answer may be to this question, there is no doubt that underwater noises have an effect upon fishes. Some of these noises act as an alarm, while others act as attractors.

Classic example of the attraction phase is the sound made by a fin-clipped pigfish. Seatrout fishermen in Florida often keep such a specimen tied to a short line which is secured to the anglers' boat. The noises of pain and distress made by the unfortunate pigfish attract big seatrout to the area, and the trout are then presumably caught. This is no old wives' tale—it works. Obviously, a lure that made a sound similar to the pigfish's grunts of distress would have an advantage over a silent lure.

Any object drawn through the water makes a sound, sonic or subsonic. The trick is to have the lure make an attractive noise, rather than an alarming one. Unfortunately, no one knows for certain just which noise is most seductive from a fish's point of view. It is reasonable to assume, however, that future lure development will emphasize this line of attraction.

Perhaps one lifetime is too short to learn all of the lessons, but we can help ourselves to better sport by deliberating on the possible emotions, instincts, or needs which cause a fish to take a bait or strike a lure. There's a reason for everything under our sun, and an angler may find calculated experiment worthwhile when standard procedure draws a complete blank.

41
THE PANIC BUTTON

A GROUP OF MODERN AMERICANS WILL INSTINCTIVELY TURN THEIR heads toward the sound of squealing rubber tires on a road surface. The noise means that an accident has either been closely avoided or else is in the making. It is, in brief, an alarm to which the human animal reacts with a surge of adrenaline, an increased pulse rate and an attitude of defense.

Although only the surface has been scratched in the field of fish behavior, similar alarms obviously produce reactions among the creatures of the sea. Let a shark swim within close range of any estuarine area and activity among smaller ocean creatures may suddenly halt, just as song birds are miraculously stilled when a hawk wheels close overhead. Whether such reactions are conditioned—that is, built up as the result of many experiences with the same danger—or whether they are purely instinctive is something no one knows at this time. For the discussion that follows, it makes little difference.

The alternative to "freezing" at the approach of danger among marine species is wild panic—and this is just what any predator desires. Protective coloration is disturbed, noises and perhaps even odors of fear are given off, and the attacker has easy pickings.

However, the predator itself has a handicap. Whether it is sound, sight, odor or a combination of all three is unknown. The fact remains that many marine creatures can detect the approach of an enemy readily and protect themselves by going into their shells, burrowing, hiding or "freezing" until the danger has passed. In the case of some of the more popular sport fishes, this sense of alarm, for want of a better word, is highly developed. Anglers should be aware of this.

Blood is a fairly obvious alarm factor, but there are other odors which are more subtle and more difficult to explain as far as their effects are concerned. If it was not Izaak Walton, it was someone in the same period who warned anglers against fishing for trout below a ford where milkmaids washed or crossed regularly. Apparently there were milkmaids all over the place in those days. (In our many years of fishing, we have never encountered this hazard.)

However, the fact that fresh water trout are "put down" by human scent in the water has been commented upon by anglers for years. Dan Bowers, writing in a mid-60's issue of *Field & Stream*, cites a more modern example. Scientists working on Pacific salmon in British Columbia discovered that odors from the human hand had an immediate and violent action on the fish as they swam up a ladder alongside a dam. A minute trace of such human odor virtually stopped the run and alarmed the salmon considerably.

Why? It is easy to understand why the odor of a shark or a sea lion might trigger such a reaction, because these creatures are natural enemies of the salmon. Man, the greatest predator of all, is not such a natural enemy: there are very few people who go around catching salmon with their bare hands. Engines of destruction, from a salmon's point of view, are nets, spears, and hooks. It seems incredible that the faint trace of human odor on such devices would be connected, in the fishy mind, with danger. Possible, of course, but in our opinion, highly improbable.

What to us seems far more logical is that a human being smells, to a fish, like some other thing that has been connected with danger throughout that fish's life. We will not even hazard a guess as to what it may be that, under water, has the aroma of a human, but the idea opens up a fascinating field for research. If the odor were isolated, solutions of it might be used to drive marine creatures from place to place. More important, from the anglers' viewpoint, a rinse to counteract such an effect could be developed so that everyone would not have to bait a hook with sterilized rubber gloves on his hands. (No one does this, of course, but a few salmon skippers of the Pacific Northwest make a point of scrubbing up prior to preparing baits.)

Odor alone, as mentioned earlier, is not the only alarm factor which must be considered. Visual reactions on the part of fish are equally important. The sight of a shadow across the water may spook certain species because they connect such moving shadows with predators. An angler with the sun low and at his back is working under a handicap, particularly where he works the shallows or where fish are feeding close to the surface. Even the slightest shadow of a whipping rod may be sufficient to cause the quarry to swim for cover until the assumed danger has passed.

Light can do just as much damage as shadow in this area. A highly polished surface, like the side of a boat, may reflect sunlight so that it appears to be a weaving beam underwater. The reflection of bright sun on the shaft of a fishing rod used in casting under certain circumstances will have the same effect. When night fishing, any bright light that is not steady and constant will startle fish both large and small. Just why they are startled is in doubt, for only at great depths are fish illuminated in a manner which might be considered dangerous to species preyed upon. Perhaps it is just the fact that light, under such circumstances, is unnatural and unusual.

If fairly steady and maintained, both shadow and light can act as an attracting stimulus. Many species like to lie in the cool shadow of a bridge or pier. Cobia may even take up station in the shadow of a boat's drifting hull. Similarly, a steady light at night will draw bait creatures and the predators which feed upon them. Note that the key word is "steady." Flashing lights seem to press a panic button. In some areas where surf casters seek gamesters at night, the bottom fisherman with a lantern is tolerated, but he who continually flashes a headlight to choose lures or pick out a backlash lives dangerously.

Even colors can have an unusual effect in triggering the alarm system in fish. Obviously a white shirt worn by a wader during bright sunlight is all too visible to fish on a shallow flat. A color which blends with the sky should be chosen or, if fishing with a background of marsh and bank, hues which blend with that background should be selected.

Lure color may also create panic among fishes, just as—properly chosen—it can add to the bait's attractiveness. For example, when activated fluorescent pigments were first developed, back in the 50's, we conducted experiments with them—and came to the unsound conclusion that lures so painted actually alarmed many sport fish. Wet sharkskin is slightly fluorescent and we theorized that fish were instinctively alarmed by the sight of something that was supposed to be a lure, but which gave every visual indication of a known danger. At that time we failed to counter the argument by noting that lots of forage fishes also boast slight fluorescence.

Our experiments were all very well as far as they went, but they did not go far enough. Run on a single species of fish in a restricted area and confined to surface lures under bright sunlight, the results were spectacular in a negative sort of way. Since that time, however, we and many others have found that fluorescent lures of one sort or another can be highly effective, particularly in deep water, but often right on the surface.

Again why? It seems obvious that circumstances alter cases even among fish. Alarm triggered by visual impulse under a specific condition does not necessarily mean that the same alarm will be present under other conditions. In fact, the reverse seems to be true, and the impulse actually attracts because the fish concerned may associate it with food. All of which makes the task of the angler that much harder: he must realize that what alarms in one case may attract in another. To be able to distinguish among these cases marks the difference between a good fisherman and a poor one.

Noise also can be both an attractor and a repellent. The pop and gurgle of a plug working on the surface will bring predatory species to investigate. However, that same plug making those same noises will panic tiny bait fish. What is an easy meal for one group is considered an alarm signal to the other. It all depends upon which is the alarmer and which the alarmee—if there is such a word.

It is easier for an angler to understand the noise factor than to understand other causes of alarm, perhaps because humans can hear many of the noises themselves. Thus fishermen will curse someone who pounds on the bottom of a boat in shallow water because it is obvious that such pounding will startle every finny creature for hundreds of yards around. Similarly, the noise of an outboard or other motor speeding (or even idling) on the flats will scare all underwater inhabitants half to death.

Some anglers carry silence to rather absurd lengths, cautioning against loud talk in a boat. There is little evidence that the human voice, above water, scares fish. A sonic boom will empty a flat, however, primarily because the sound level is so high that it produces a shock wave of vibrations. Anything that disturbs the even tenor of a habitat must be suspect.

As in the case of light or shadow, reasons for the alarm cannot be defined exactly. Natural enemies do not make a habit of emitting noises like a huge bass drum, nor can even the smartest of fish produce sustained roars like an outboard motor. In part, perhaps, the alarm may be generated because the noise is unusual and not in keeping with conditions which the fish links with normal safety. Bottom conformation and depth are additional factors. Noise is amplified in the shallows: it reverberates from a hard bottom and is partially muffled by deep mud or silt. Finally, one must consider conditioned reflex.

Many years ago, when the internal combustion engine was comparatively new, Pacific coast whalers found that they could run close to whales and harpoon them without difficulty. After a very short time, the noise of a boat's propeller would send the whales to sea at high speeds. Cetaceans, of course, are of a much higher order of intelligence than fish, yet similar reactions have been observed in the case of many sport species.

Commercial tuna-clipper captains, for example, have found that schools which have been chased often and from which some members have been harpooned, netted or hooked tend to be far more wary than schools which have never been molested. Sport fishermen have discovered the same facts, not only among the various tunas, but also among a host of other species. In heavily fished areas, the angler who approaches fish carefully will enjoy better results than the marine hot-rodder who tears through a school in a cloud of spray.

With this in mind, careful trollers skirt the edge of a visible school. Casters try to hook gamesters from the leading edge or the flanks of such schools—and it is an unwritten law to haul the captive out quickly, before his distress signals spook the entire congregation. Some specialists will not release a hooked fish while the school is still undisturbed, because it is felt that the injured specimen might then communicate its fear and cause the entire school to sound. A specimen that happens to escape, after being hooked, is likely to transfer its hurt and fear to fellows in the school.

We are not about to damn motor noise out of hand: it can be an attractor in its own right. This is particularly true in the big game fishing world where large marine species often come up to see what all the ruckus is about. Giant tuna do this, and so do many billfish—although the latter may be spooked by a change in the engine's tempo. Whether these gladiators connect the noise with some forage fish in trouble, or whether they are simply curious, is anyone's guess.

Communication among fish is little understood and it is not our intention at this time to delve into the subject. However, it should be noted that alarm is spread from fish to fish in a school and that this communication often is accomplished instantaneously. The flash of a turning minnow will cause others in the school to turn, so vision evidently is involved. From experiments done with sonar and with underwater sonic devices, definite alarm signals have been recorded among a great many marine species. This indicates that noise is also a factor. To date, no one has developed a method of distinguishing scent emissions underwater, but it seems probable that the sense of smell must also be taken into consideration. Animals of many species (including man) give off a particular scent when scared: fish may do the same.

We realize fully that nothing in this is earth-shaking, and that many will consider the whole discussion purely academic. However, the angler who appreciates, either consciously or subconsciously, reasons for alarm in the quarry he seeks will take more fish than the phlegmatic brother who ignores this extremely sensitive subject.

42

MEMORY IN FISHES

THERE HAVE BEEN A GREAT MANY BAD JOKES ABOUT THE RELATIVE merits of an angler's intelligence as compared to the brain power of a fish. Most of these labored jests concern the fact that fish spend so much of their lifetime in schools. We are not about to increase the supply of such painful playings on words, but the fundamental comparison still has its points. Man, in his supreme conceit, seems to feel that only he can learn or reason, while all lower creatures operate on instinct or on reflex action.

We are not suggesting that a silversides with a pinhead-sized brain can take over the controls of a steam shovel. However, enough experiments on fish reactions, memory, and intelligence—call it superior reflex action if it helps your ego—have been conducted over the years to indicate that brain power among our finny friends cannot be ignored.

Basically, the cerebral hemispheres of the brain in any creature equipped with such a device control conscious action, while the cerebellum controls reflex action—that is, action which might be considered automatic. Removing your hand from a red-hot stove lid is a good example of reflex action. It takes no conscious thought unless there is something the matter with your nervous system. In some fishes, the cerebral hemispheres are tiny, but they are there. In most, they are lumped together as part of the forebrain, but apparently serve much the same functions, though small. As a matter of fact, the cerebellum is no great shakes for size either! No fish that swims can be considered a mental giant if brain size alone is used as a yardstick. But we believe that many scientists and others underestimate just what an angler is up against.

From the fisherman's point of view, two of his quarry's brain functions are important. The first of these is memory; the second, reaction to some stimulus or other. Whether you classify these functions as reflex actions or as reasoning depends upon your upbringing and is immaterial in any case. The combination of both factors may produce what might be called learning in the higher orders of animal life. In all that follows, we may oversimplify things a little to avoid becoming entangled in a maze of psychological terms, but the facts are basic.

Let's look first at memory. There have been many experiments run under controlled conditions in aquaria or in fairly large impoundments of water which seem to indicate conclusively that fish have memory of a sort.

One of the more common of these experiments is presentation of foods of one kind or another with the foods being made up in various primary colors. A blue pellet of pressed shrimp may be delicious; a yellow one of cereals, just passable; a red one of alum, very nasty to fishy tastes.

After a time spent in dropping such pellets where the fish can see and eat them, any member of the school will gobble up the blue offerings, grab the yellow when the blue have disappeared—and ignore the red pellets entirely, no matter how hungry they may become.

This type of experiment has been varied in many ways, such as administering a mild electric shock if the fish touches the red pellet, and awarding a special gustatory reward if the fish swallows the blue. Psychologists call this sort of thing a conditioned reflex and give the fish no credit for memory or learning. We once administered to a psychologist an ice-cream cone filled with lovely, white, warm mashed potato—to illustrate some of his own conditioned reflex reactions. But that is another story.

If the same procedure of feeding colored pellets to fish is continued for several days, the fish evidently remembers its lessons well. However, the most interesting point is the fact that it remembers its lesson even when the experiment is stopped. Different species retain this memory for different periods, as nearly as can be determined, but all definitely retain the memory for an appreciable time.

One of the most fascinating of these experiments was conducted a good many years ago and conditions were not artificial in any way. The three types of food pellets mentioned above were fed regularly to a school of small snappers living under a coastal dock. Feeding was stopped for a week, then resumed. The snappers still avoided the red pellets. Periods of feeding were set further and further apart until the time between them reached more than four weeks. Still the snappers avoided red and gobbled blue. The interesting point was that there undoubtedly had been some change in snapper population during this four-week period, yet the word was passed along in some fishy manner unknown to us.

You can see where this leads. If a fish is hooked on a certain lure and is released or escapes, it may well remember that lure and avoid it in the future. In addition, it may well be able to transmit its memory of unpleasantness to other fish in the vicinity so that they in turn avoid the same lure. Almost every angler who has done much ocean fishing has had the experience of using a lure which is a killer for a time. Suddenly it becomes worthless. Obviously there are many factors involved—bait supply, weather, temperatures and water conditions, to name a few—but a fish's memory and transmission of this learning to its fellows may have a place in the overall picture.

Unfortunately, things are not that simple. There are literally hundreds of examples of a fish hitting a certain lure, being released, and returning almost at once to hit the same lure again. Sometimes the fish will be re-caught on the same tempter days or weeks after its original experience. Whether it does not associate danger and discomfort with memory of the lure in question or whether it is simply a very stupid fish, no one may ever know despite many experiments along these lines. However, there is enough indication of memory among various species to show that sticking to one lure hour after hour and day after day is foolish if you want best results. You may hook the silly fish that has not remembered, but you will miss the smart, old, large one that associated danger with a certain type of gimmick which attracted it in the first place.

Memory, learning and reaction to some outside stimulus are so closely connected that it is impossible to separate them completely. Some time ago, we watched with interest the actions of a small member of the angler family—the fish, not the human variety. This species, which lies on the bottom and attracts its prey by wiggling a fleshy spine in front of its enormous mouth as a sort of lure, had been introduced into an aquarium in which there were several schools of salt water minnows. Whenever the schools passed close, the little angler fish would wave its lure violently and the first three or four minnows which investigated were gobbled up without ceremony. After a short time, however, the minnow schools would swim by the tempting lure without pausing, even though the angler was doing its utmost to attract them. Among the minnows, just how much of this caution was engendered by memory of past dangers? Only those which had been gobbled up were in a real position to show memory of the facts, and for them it was too late. Yet the other minnows had learned that the angler's lure was a deadly one and they reacted to avoid the danger.

This point is one to remember as far as the fisherman is concerned. Assume that a fish has been hooked in a school of its fellows. If the hooked fighter leaves the school, chances are that the line will not scare other fish by striking them. Sometimes, but not always by any means, the hooked fish will express fear through some method unknown to us and others in the school will become alarmed and leave the vicinity. It is therefore wise to take fish from the edge of a school, rather than from the center, whenever possible to minimize the danger of what might be termed total alarm.

Apparently a hooked fish often does not realize what its main source of trouble is and does not associate the hook and line with danger. As a result, it sends out no alarm signals and several of its companions may follow closely, even striking at the lure in the hooked one's mouth. When the quarry is lifted out of the water by the angler, others in the school can be seen searching for their missing friend and for the meal that friend was munching.

In the case of some species—dolphin and the amberjack families are good examples—a hooked fish actually keeps the school in the angler's vicinity. Boat fishermen know this and try to hold one specimen close to the craft while other lures are dropped to its circling schoolmates. With other species—striped bass and tuna can be cited—the school may become alarmed after several fish have been hauled out of the water. Under these circumstances, the fisherman will do well to let the school rest for a short period before going after them again.

Alarm may be triggered by a variety of things. Some old salts decry the release of a fish caught from a school, because they maintain that the freed specimen will sound the alarm immediately and thus spook the entire school.

Memory, reaction to an outside stimulus, learning—or whatever you want to call it—is not limited to lures. If bait pours out of an inlet at a certain stage of tide, predatory species will gather at the inlet mouth to feast on the free meal provided. They will continue to gather daily, all other conditions being equal, at this same stage of tide even when the bait supply vanishes. Only after the bait has been absent for several stages in a row will the predators change their feeding grounds. Usually, of course, change in the time of day, with subsequent change in daylight available when the tide shifts, will alter the picture to a certain degree. Add changes in weather and an exact experiment is difficult to conduct under natural conditions. The smart angler, however, will return to the same spot at the same stage of tide if he has taken fish there on the previous tide.

In the long range view, some of the examples of memory and transmission of experience—for want of a better term—are fascinating. Some of the Pacific salmons follow migratory patterns evidently set centuries ago when the land bridge between Alaska and Siberia was far different from its present form. Anadromous fish time and again will return to a river which has long ceased to flow. In these cases, memory is stronger than experience. (Or call it instinct, a word which is used to describe something quite impossible to define with precision.) At any rate the fish continue to react to this force so long as any of that particular race remains alive. They do not learn short cuts even after repeated failures.

If this seems a contradictory statement, note that in a shorter view fish evidently do learn. Changing of a river bed will not deter anadromous species from seeking the headwaters for spawning and they will learn the new routes after a comparatively short period. This may be because those fish which do not learn do not survive and produce descendants, but the fact remains that some do change their habits to suit the circumstances.

This shorter-range picture may be carried even further to show another example of memory as linked to learning. One of our favorite fishing spots for striped bass used to be in a rocky cove on the end of an island point. For centuries, alewives entered this cove and swam up a small stream to spawn in the pond at its headwaters. Bass gathered at the stream's mouth to feed on the herring hordes of springtime and, later in the season, to gorge on the year's hatch as it returned to the ocean.

In the 1940's, the owner of the property dammed the stream to create a duck and goose pond that was entirely fresh. As might be expected, the alewives returned year after year to their native stream and tried unsuccessfully to reach the old spawning grounds. Also, as might be expected, striped bass gathered in the same area to gobble what they had learned to expect.

After a period of years, the alewives died out or sought other streams, yet the bass continued to gather at their former lunch counter even when there was no bait available! Eventually they discovered that pickings were slim, with the result that this particular cove is no longer one of our favorites. That the game fish returned even after the bait fish had left indicates to us more than a conditioned reflex, for the reactions lasted from year to year over a period of several years.

There is another classic example along slightly different lines which, in our opinion, shows something more than instinct or reflex action. Any angler of experience has seen predators herding bait. Among billfishermen, the action is so well known that a special phrase has been coined to describe it—"balling the bait." Scattered feed is driven together into a frantic, compact school so that the predatory species may dine with a minimum of effort. The game fish may do the job alone or may work together in schools to achieve the same purpose. Watch such an operation and you will be convinced that there has been a preconceived plan of attack—not infallible every time, we grant, but infallible enough to indicate something more than reflex action.

Mark Twain once said that the human appendix was constructed to gather grape seeds and thus make itself known. Modern surgeons, who once tweaked tonsils and adenoids out of unsuspecting youngsters as a matter of course, now feel that these accessories to the human body serve a definite purpose and should be left strictly alone unless they cause serious trouble. We submit that the cerebral hemispheres of the brain of a fish or their equivalents in that nerve organ, even though tiny, are also there for a purpose, and we feel that this purpose has been illustrated in the foregoing.

Angling success is likely to improve when the angler assumes that fish have some powers, however limited, of memory and learning. We respectfully suggest that many fisheries scientists would do better in their chosen field if they would use this hypothesis as a starting point.

43

THE INVALIDS

IT IS UNFORTUNATE THAT A MEDICAL MAN AND A CHEMIST CANNOT spend a year or two under water consulting with the fishes of the sea. Diseases of, and injuries to, fish in the ocean are little understood and the reaction of those specimens afflicted are understood even less. However, these reactions have more than passing interest to the angler.

Off Mount Desert Rock in Maine, there is a codfishing spot known as "The Bull Grounds." For centuries, it has been a good area for commercial fishermen seeking this Atlantic species and it undoubtedly would be just as good for sport fishermen if they wished to travel the necessary mileage. Oddly enough, every fish caught on those grounds will have a sore or scars from a sore on its skin.

Early in the season off Hatteras, North Carolina, bluefish are taken both by sport and commercial men—not the small snapper size, but large adult blues. These early arrivals invariably have some injury, apparently due to attack by some other sea creature or to contact with something which has resulted in a major hurt. Sometimes the wounds are healed, but more often they are in the process of healing. The same phenomenon may be observed in catches of Pacific yellowtail in the early season at various points along the California-Mexico border. These examples are only a few from many similar ones.

Analyzing the causes for such gatherings of the lame, the halt and the blind is a risky business at best, but we plan to pass along a few observations for what they may be worth. First, from all evidence at hand, it appears true that there are certain areas in which diseased or injured fish congregate, even if such gatherings are limited to a certain time of the year. The question then arises:

do they school in these areas for therapeutic treatment or do the areas themselves produce the disease and injury?

Before proceeding further, let us arbitrarily disregard pollution as a cause of disease or death. This is a major item to disregard, but it would complicate the picture unnecessarily as far as this discussion is concerned. Suffice it to say that pollution can and does produce disease and death in the fish world.

Returning to the question, it seems apparent that there is little proof of "healing waters" so far as marine species are concerned. However, it is very difficult, if not impossible, to obtain proof of this sort. Every person who has had a fresh water aquarium knows that, if one of the glassed-in tenants begins to look a little green around the gills, a brief sojourn in a tank filled with brackish water, or water to which medication has been added, may well restore the ailing fish to health. Higher animals, if rats and mice can be considered such, will instinctively dose themselves for various diseases by eating therapeutic foods and, if possible, will make a change in habitat to effect a cure. There is no reason to assume that fish might not do the same thing, but this has to be an assumption at best.

The negative approach to this problem perhaps offers a partial answer. Fish definitely will avoid certain kinds of water even when food or the availability of it has nothing to do with the case. The Atlantic salmon, migrating from the ocean to spawn in North America, rarely enters a stream while there is still melting snow water being carried out in volume to the ocean. Striped bass shun tidal marshes which contain a high percentage of bog iron. The high percentage of iron oxides in the water evidently does not appeal to them. The degree of salinity in tidal or ocean waters is a controlling factor in the migrations of countless species. If fish can distinguish the types of water to avoid, it seems reasonable to assume that they can also determine the types of water which might be beneficial to treatment of the disease that troubles them. This is all conjecture, of course, and the proof has yet to be presented.

On the other hand, there is much evidence that certain waters or conditions in those waters will produce disease. For example, striped bass taken in the early spring in the vicinity of the Thames and Niantic rivers in Connecticut often have cataracts of the eye. Scientists are of the opinion that this is due to a dietary lack because, later in the season, the affliction is rare among bass in the same localities. These same scientists are first to admit that the afflicted fish may well die off. This does not appear probable, because blind stripers apparently can feed perfectly happily.

Overcrowding, which can happen in nature as well as in an aquarium, is a prime producer of fish disease and death. In the case of most fishes, parasites of one sort or another rank high in the list of ailments which can be fatal. Several years ago, bluefish ripe with roe on the northern Atlantic coast were attacked by a wormlike creature that embedded itself in the roe sac. Although the fish were not killed, the eggs themselves apparently were. Examination of a great many bluefish in a single school showed that the parasite was present in every specimen.

Again, we do not know why the common weakfish, very plentiful in the late 40's from New Jersey through southern New England, suddenly all but disappeared in 1949. Those who blame commercial fishing cannot explain the sudden eclipse of the species. Cries against pollution are equally unsupported. Almost certainly an epizootic decimated weakfish at that time. The species is now making a slow but steady comeback and will undoubtedly build to peak in the foreseeable future.

Quite similarly, in the early 60's, an apparent shortage of striped bass along the Atlantic coast triggered demands for no-sale legislation and minimum bag limits "to prevent the species from becoming extinct." The prophets of doom were amazed when, in 1962, a new year class of stripers surged up the coast. Angling was excellent, and old-timers declared that they'd never seen so many bass. They were right. Maybe there were too many!

During that well-remembered year, striped bass fishermen along the north Atlantic coast reported many instances of dead fish in the bays and on the beaches. We personally witnessed school stripers cartwheeling ashore on the waves to die for no apparent reason. The fish—at least some of them—were sent to marine biologists for examination. Biologists, like the mills of the gods, grind slowly. To date, no report on the afflictions of those bass has issued from the halls of science.

From a fisherman's point of view, it is important to note that learned marine biologists, as well as practical anglers, have suggested that good management may consist in the proper harvesting of a plentiful stock. Parasites thrive when a given species is numerous, both because the attackers have more hosts upon which to thrive, and because the hosts themselves tend to weaken because of over-keen competition in feeding. On the sea, as elsewhere, we deal with a renewable harvest, a resource that must be gathered in or lost for all time.

Although it can be argued that fish seek the equivalent of mineral baths sought by aching humans, major evidence indicates that diseased fish do not gather in areas or schools for treatment, but are diseased because of conditions found in these areas. In the case of deep water wanderers, such conditions may well travel right along with the schools—in fact may be spread in this manner to epidemic proportions. Even if there were such a thing as a piscatorial spa, it would be difficult indeed for an angler to locate such an area.

There comes a time when the ailing fish can no longer keep up with the school. In the cases of larger species, like the tunas and the billfishes, these sick individuals are apt to become "loners"—cruising by themselves. They conserve their sapping strength, seek the food most readily available—if they feed at all—and, in a majority of cases, waste away to die or to be killed. Smaller species, however, still appear to be driven by the schooling instinct to a large degree. It is for this reason that, when an angler catches a "racer"—a fish which is all head and eyes with feeble fighting ability—he is apt to catch another in the same vicinity.

It seems highly probable that this same schooling instinct applies to fish that are wounded, rather than diseased. A bite from a sea lion which misjudged its distance, a too-near miss by a shark, or even a torn mouth caused by an angler's hook may incapacitate a fish to a certain degree. Here again the larger species tend to become "loners," but the fact that they survive fairly regularly is illustrated by the many scarred specimens taken on rod and reel. A healthy fish that is wounded has amazing powers of recovery and will even regenerate lost or mutilated fins.

Smaller fish still seek the protection of the school. A group of injured will be alerted to danger more quickly than a single cripple. The very fact that all members of that school are handicapped serves to keep the whole group together. They are all slowed down in speed of travel and in general efficiency. When cured of their wounds, they can step up their activities and, at that time, are ready to rejoin normal, healthy fellows of their own species.

There is an interesting sidelight on this whole concept, mentioned in a previous chapter. When a fish receives an injury from an outside source, that injury may well be only a minor one. However, if blood is drawn, chances are that the wounded fish will not be able to rejoin the school immediately, even if it could physically turn the trick. The school will avoid a bleeding member of its own kind, unless the species concerned is cannibalistic. This is another factor which tends to force injured fish into the company of other cripples. Even in the sea, misery loves company.

Anglers should remember this fact about flowing blood. Time after time, we have seen a whole school of fish spooked for a long period when we have had the misfortune to hook one of its members in such a manner that it bleeds freely. This experience has not been confined to one single species, but includes the tunas, basses, drums, and salmons. We believe that it applies to all species except the most voracious. Blood from a bait fish is one thing; blood from one of the game fish sought is another.

Those who doubt this would do well to think back on the times when a fish has swallowed a bait or lure, has put up a fight in the area where the school is located and then has been brought to beach or boat bleeding freely. Nine out of ten times successful fishing will stop abruptly. It may resume again after the alarm is over, but the alarm is an instantaneous one.

This does not necessarily apply to a fish that bleeds upon being gaffed for the obvious reason that such a catch is close aboard or at the angler's feet in the wash. It is the hooked quarry swimming through the school and streaming gore, however mildly, that does the damage. This is logical, for a wounded member of their own kind indicates danger to most of the game species—except those that will turn on the injured and devour it.

One final comment on this whole matter of bleeding fish: old-timers will throw a half dozen fits if you start to clean your catch while fishing is still going on. In other words, blood and gurry deposited in the area where fishing is good may spook fish for some time to come. Clean the catch on the way home or, if it must be done at once because of heat, dump blood and entrails into a container to be emptied after action.

As far as species which attack their own kind are concerned, the reasons for the injured banding together are good ones. If they escape the attacks of their erstwhile friends, they form a group of their own, swimming along together in a sort of armed neutrality. The injured Hatteras bluefish cited earlier make a case in point, for blues in a feeding frenzy will gladly chop pieces out of their companions. The schools of wounded apparently observe a moratorium on such antisocial behavior.

TACKLE TALK *268*

Rarely will a fisherman go forth deliberately to seek diseased or injured fish. A catch that looks as though it were about to pass over the great divide is hardly a prize. However, observation of such catches can help in determining the general fishing picture in the area where the sick or wounded have been caught. A great number of diseased fish taken on rod and reel is a definite indication that something is wrong. The matter should be reported to coastal wardens or marine biologists who can look into the circumstances. Whether anything can be done about the troubled fishery is something else again.

In the case of injured, scarred or wounded fish, only a tremendous number of these would indicate anything more than bad luck on the part of the fish concerned. The catching of one or two such unfortunates is a good conversation piece, but little more.

44

TOMORROW AND TOMORROW . . .

THOSE OF US WHO SPEAK SO WISTFULLY ABOUT THE GOOD OLD days sometimes forget that the tackle of thirty years ago is largely antique by today's standards. The "great leap forward" in sport fishing gear, if we may be pardoned for borrowing one of Mao Tse-tung's pet phrases, occurred during the two decades immediately following World War II.

Blessed with 20/20 hindsight, it is easy for us to declare that the past twenty years of tackle development have been as productive as the century that went before. What of tomorrow? Will the angler of 1990 enjoy gear so efficiently designed and fabricated that it will eclipse today's excellence?

There is nothing quite like sticking one's neck out with predictions: it's a dangerous business, although in this case the slings and arrows must be delayed until such time as the wheeling years prove us right or wrong.

There'll be change, make no mistake about it. Our American economy is an onward and upward thing. Progress, in this country, means change for the better. We make mistakes and take our lumps, but we scramble right back into the ring with variations and new departures. Tradition and romance will continue to shape our desires, yet never in the inflexible pattern of the old world. Americans demand a working coalition of romance and efficiency. That which boasts no excellence other than outworn tradition is consigned to outer darkness.

We envision no astonishing changes in basic outfits. All of those used today are specialized, and all are necessary to enjoy marine angling to the utmost. Indeed there will be greater use of outfits which now are regarded as tools of the expert. Fly casting, spinning, bait casting, surf casting, and trolling tackle combinations are well established: none will be phased out, but some will become more popular as sportsmen accept new challenges and hone their skills.

It has become stylish to declare that spinning is a tool of the amateur, that the very simplicity of its operation has created a boom in sport fishing—and that multitudes of instant-anglers spawned by the advent of fixed spool regularly progress to more demanding tackle combinations, thereby becoming skillful practitioners. There is truth in the observation, yet it presupposes that spinning is, and must always remain, the province of a beginner. The exact opposite is true.

Fixed spool may be older than revolving spool in the annals of man's assault on the sea. While the reel moderns associate with spinning was developed by an Englishman, Holden Illingworth, in the late 1800's, some very primitive peoples utilized the basic principle in casting lines off a variety of bone and wooden cylinders. These aborigines had their troubles with line tangle (today we delicately refer to "line slough") but they succeeded in two departments—in casting a reasonable distance and in designing a method of retrieve which, if not ideal, was better than anything demonstrated up to that time.

The future will see tremendous developments in spinning, with most of the current problems solved. Indeed greatest advances may be made in this field as line-twist is defeated and better bail assemblies, line-guide rollers and gearing are assured.

Look for no phase-out of bait casting, fly casting and conventional surf casting. Each will be specialized, often becoming the tool of a dedicated minority of perfectionists. Trolling outfits will be unchanged, aside from improvement in all basic items of equipment. There'll be greater stress on light tackle trolling as salt water angling booms and its enthusiasts become veterans.

Scientific research in World War II spawned most of the great developments in salt water fishing tackle. Such research will continue to improve the end product and there is every reason to believe that materials not now envisioned will aid the angler of the future. Certainly metallurgical discoveries linked to the space age, together with a whole host of improved plastics, will be utilized. It is probable that synthetics will largely take the place of hitherto basic metals and natural fibers.

For example, the sea angler of 1990 is unlikely to employ a split bamboo or wooden rod of any kind: he'll use tubular fiberglass rods and these will be lighter, stronger, and more professionally balanced than any stick currently on the market.

Moreover, the immediate future should see a move toward the standardization of fiberglass rod weights and actions, so that basic weapons may be catalogued for purposes of record.

Entirely new rod types are likely. Back in the 60's, one reputable American firm, Fenwick, produced a salt water fly rod together with a stiffening shaft which might be inserted into the rod's hollow butt section after a large fish had been hooked. The tackle proved controversial, yet it offered a practical solution to certain vexing problems. Can the same thing be done with a single, variable-action rod?

Up to now, designers have been satisfied with limber tips which lend themselves to the tossing of light baits or artificials, combined with much heavier central and butt sections calibrated to take the heavy stresses incurred in playing large game fish. The ideal, still unattained, would be a rod featuring the ability to cast a very light lure to appreciable distances, plus the guts to play and control a heavy gamester after the strike. Unfortunately, a true casting rod rarely serves as a great fighting rod.

This is true whether you seek big fish on a fly rod, or much smaller gamesters on a surface-casting combination. A fly rod must be matched to the line it will cast, hence you need something fairly resilient and practical, commensurate with the angler's strength. However, having completed a cast and hooked a fish, the feather merchant immediately needs more power in the shaft. Any robust tarpon or billfish will make this need immediately apparent.

Contrarily, a surf casting rod is a heaver's instrument: its primary task is to place a bait or lure away out beyond the breaking waves, and this takes a tremendous amount of raw power. Consequently, we have surf rods that are quite capable of throwing, but become liabilities during the playing of a game fish. The planky "throwing" action is an invitation to disaster when light to medium lines are employed. Such rods are great heavers and poor fish-fighting tools, hence manufacturers seek compromises which really please no one. The solution is difficult, and only time will tell whether it can be achieved.

Advanced anglers will always demand the very best weapon for a specific task, yet it is inevitable that dual-purpose tools will become more popular. Fly-spin rods are no johnny-come-latelies: they suit the man who wants to switch from miniature spinning lures to flies without a complete change of tackle. Bait casting and spinning rods are similar enough to be interchangeable in some cases. If the bait caster desires a trigger, this can be attached to a reel clamp. In effect, the dual-purpose rod remains static, while reel and line are switched. The future will see much more of this.

Whatever the rod type, look for further improvement in guides. Advanced metallurgy will insure rings tougher and smoother-surfaced than any marketed today: they'll be rust- and corrosion-proof, and they'll be bonded to rods with tough, fiberglass films. Silk thread wrappings, used as decorations as well as fastenings, will soon disappear—if they have not already done so.

Similarly, there'll be advances in ferrules, necessary because the American angler is increasingly a nomad and must have tackle that can be broken down for ease in transportation. The metal ferrule, with the exception of certain big game connections, will soon phase out, victim of several new departures in which close-fitting glass or other synthetic sections do the same job with greater all-around efficiency.

All of the basic reel types will be improved, but little changed. All conventional winches will boast strengthened plastic spools which will be guaranteed to resist the pressure exerted by hard-packed lines. There'll be greater emphasis upon gear ratios tailored to specific tasks, and better drag mechanisms.

With respect to reels in general, look for the development of a practical automatic drag which will slack off when tension on the line approaches a predetermined breaking point. Some attempts to produce such a mechanism have been made, but none has succeeded to date.

While perfectionists may outlaw such drags for record catches, reels so equipped will be ideal for the beginner, or for the charter skipper who desires to save his tackle and still produce game for customers with multitudes of left thumbs.

During the next twenty years it is very likely that we will use monofilament lines for all types of fishing, with the possible exception of fly casting. Even here there is a better than even chance that research will create tapered mono fly lines of desired density to float or sink, and of a flexibility adequate to the demands of casters. American research technicians dote on such problems, and you can bet that scientists are currently working to solve the troubles associated with mono. Among these are: variables of strength, elasticity, and stability.

As of now, very few monofilaments test out exactly as labeled, with wet test a few pounds less than dry. Some manufacturers, dubious heroes, label 15 pound test mono as 10 pound test—hence they boast "the strongest 10 pound test line in the world."

Monofilaments will be improved. Within the next couple of decades technicians will control this synthetic and make it the standard line for all angling, up to and including big game. Memory will be removed; strength, elasticity and stability will be controlled. Braided lines will phase out as inexpensive mono is perfected for all uses.

Similarly, metallurgy will provide single-strand wires that will be impervious to kinking and subsequent breakage. Wires will be important in the future, for no other line material lends itself to deep trolling without the use of cumbersome weights. Wires will be progressively lighter and stronger, well marked with heat-positioned plastic sleeves.

So far as leaders are concerned, monofilament will continue to get the nod where soft-mouthed, wary fishes are concerned, and wire will be the choice of those who seek the sharp-toothed legions. These leaders, like the wire line previously mentioned, will resist kinking. Moreover, specialized tools will fuse wire and swivels or snaps without knots, bends or sleeves.

Modern artificial lures have been broken down into well defined families of basic types, out of which spring multitudes of variations. The future will see more of these variations, plus a minimum of revolutionary new types. Materials used in the manufacture of lures will be more exotic than heretofore, and today's hypothesis on the lure of sound and scent will be translated into fact.

As far as materials are concerned, wooden plugs will become collectors' items. These artificials, with the exception of those made in home workshops, are being phased out now. While the wooden plug is effective, it requires too many steps in manufacture to be profitable in an industrial economy and therefore cannot compete with the synthetic product.

Look for a predominance of hard and soft plastic lures, hardly a frightening prospect, since each tempter will be an exact facsimile of the one that has proved a killer. It is inevitable that the soft plastic lure, often combined with hard plastic or metal, will become very important in the years ahead.

Soft plastic has already dented the lure market and it will progressively capture a greater share of sales. Manufacturers have realized that exact simulation of natural baits is less important than action, so the new artificials are cleverly designed: they'll improve with each passing year.

No phase-out of metal lures is envisioned: indeed metal will play a major role in the artificial baits of the future, with spoons, squids and even plugs fashioned of steel, aluminum, and various alloys.

Sound, scent, and color may well highlight future revolutions in lure manufacture. It has been demonstrated that all three factors are important, yet to date no one has been able to score any notable success with noisy, smelly or scientifically colored artificial baits.

Game fish and forage fish emit sounds. All marine creatures possess a certain amount of body odor, and all flaunt colors which are used to camouflage their owners and which, in certain situations, mark them as targets.

It is even possible that sound may be keyed so that a game fish, taking the lure, will be of a certain species. In brief, both sound and scent may be used selectively by anglers of the future in order to decoy a specific battler.

Color, always controversial, surely ranks among the most important of lure factors. While most of the basic hues have been used, together with a multitude of combinations, the new activated fluorescent paints offer further promise. These larger-than-life pigments will insure bright color at depths which have hitherto screened all shades. Perhaps more important, many forage fish and crustaceans emit certain amounts of fluorescence. By subtle blending of such activated paints, a lure may be made to look alive.

Bucktail, feathers, and other organic dressings will become things of the past as better synthetics are developed. Already tapered nylon fibers and plastics have supplanted many of the natural materials, and this trend will escalate. Within the next decade it is probable that animal fiber dressings, with the exception of those used to tie custom flies, will have vanished from the marine scene.

Whatever the lure or bait, anglers of 1990 will have to employ a hook. We conjure up no basic change in design, but there is good reason to believe that advances in metallurgy will insure better barbs at lower cost.

All hooks, in the foreseeable future, will be fabricated of stainless steel. While manufacturers currently face problems in tempering, which sometimes causes barbs to be brittle or, conversely, to bend too easily, the stainless hook of the near future will be every bit as effective as today's high carbon steel article—with the added advantages of rust and corrosion resistance.

It might be sensational to predict more in the way of electronic fishing tackle. These things are feasible and can be provided now. Indeed today's angler can purchase battery-powered reels that take command and help to winch in stubborn battlers. However, we do not anticipate any trend toward true push-button sport fishing, for the simple reason that anglers desire to give their quarry a sporting chance. Basic tackle will be improved, yet never to the point where failure is impossible. We need the element of chance and the triumph of skill, if only to justify our own mastery over the sport fishes of the sea.

But we will not discard knowledge, and knowledge will be our greatest aid in the future. Behavior studies by marine biologists will improve the angler-success ratio. More information on why fish strike, and why they do not, will help even the amateur to make the best possible selection of lure or bait at the outset. Oceanographers will chart currents and bottom conformation for our benefit. Weather forecasts will be more accurate. Sounding devices and fish locators will be commonplace tools. We will be thoroughgoing hypocrites, using dozens of electronic aids to scan weather, wave action, current, bottom conformation and fish life—but we will insist on giving those fish a sporting chance once we have hooked them on rod and line!

Perhaps most important, we now enter an era of rapid transportation at feasible costs. Air shuttles will soon place all of the oceans within easy reach of fishermen, and salt water angling will boom as a result. The affluence of our civilization, plus the fact that inland waters have been depleted through overexploitation and destroyed by pollution, leave no alternative other than the sea.

Finally, the next couple of decades will be richer in genuine marine fishing authorities. Ours is a relatively infant sport, still lacking its Izaak Waltons, its Theodore Gordons, and Edward Hewitts. Will the greats of today survive a test of time? We'll tell you, twenty years hence.